The New Love-Starved Bitch
Author's Gold Edition

This book is a work of fiction. The characters, incidents, and dialogue are artistic, written creations and are not to be construed as real. Any resemblance to actual events or persons, living or dead, is entirely coincidental.

CAROL MITCHELL BOOKS

©2014 by Carol Denise Mitchell
All rights reserved. No part of this book may be reproduced, stored in a retrieval system or transmitted in any form or by any means without the prior written permission of the Carol Mitchell Books Publishers.

CDMBOOKS: cdmbooks@aol.com

Printed in the United States of America

Visit Carol Denise Mitchell on the World Wide Web at:
http://www.amazon.com/Carol-Denise-Mitchell/e/B002UM9EKW

Rovella Starr

The New Love-Starved Bitch

Author's Gold Edition

Additional Writing credits by Carol Denise Mitchell
African American Literature Book Club, (AALBC) http://authors.aalbc.com/carol.htm, September, 2006 News Letter named Mitchell, one of their "Authors You Should Know," for her comprehensive handbook, *"Your Rights,"* regarding employee employment rights.

Additional Writing Credits:
What Happened to Suzy, Carlton Press, (1994).
Mitchell resides in Concord, California near the San Francisco Bay Area, where she is at work on a wide range of fascinating writing projects

CAROL D. MITCHELL

ROVELLA STARR

The New Love-Starved Bitch

(Author's Gold Edition)

Rovella Starr
The New Love-Starved Bitch
Author's Gold Edition

"An amazing book of secret love…Fun, fantastic, heartfelt, and seasoned with surprises…A fantastic novel."

Oakland, Post

Wow!! A real page turner!! This book was one that kept me guessing and I was thoroughly entertained. Carol Denise Mitchell is a talent! The character Rovella Starr is one who comes full circle over a lifetime. The way she loved was intense! This is a Must read! "

Kamilah Taylor

Carol Denise Mitchell's soaring novel, "Rovella Starr" moved me like no other novel's ever have. Carol, masterfully includes many real-life issues, using her deft narrative which is full of color and character touching every human emotion; making "Rovella Starr" a modern day, must read classic for lovers of great stories--everywhere!

Stuart McCallum

CAROL D. MITCHELL

By

Carol Denise Mitchell

What Happened to Suzy

Your Rights What Employers Do Not Want You to Know

The Mad Sister

The Love He Saved

Rovella Starr

The New Love-Starved Bitch

Author's Gold Edition

♠♠♠

Dedications

My mother, Tasceaie Charles

Sister in Christ, Wanda Bracy

Marie Westbrook, Yvonne

&

to all Rovella Fans

ROVELLA STARR

(A LOVE-STARVED BITCH)

Carol Denise Mitchell

Rovella Starr

The New Love-Starved Bitch

Author's Gold Edition

The Introduction

Rovella Starr is the charming tale of a mad woman's raging fury and her difficulty to bare her inner buried secrets. This is the compelling saga of a strong striking, but mean spirited woman who did not know how to love. This duplicitous triangle transcends the predictable standards of conventional time; is a story that challenges those who love too hard to learn why they pursue humans as possessions and urges them to uncover to what end does love manifest into pure wicked evilness.

As you will discover in this book, I am a writer in love with what many would call the wrong love, for to get to love, I had to first cut through to the core heart of Rovella. I must say though, this task was near impossible to do. Therefore, I dedicate this novel to Joe Bullet for his genuine acceptance of Rovella and for his kindness to all that he touched. Finally, here is a tale that changes the world's most evil woman, Rovella Starr by forcing her to take a second look at her life through clearer eyes. Set in the backdrop of the exquisite town of Oakland, California and Jack London Square, come with me on this expedition of an evil woman's will to dominate and destroy all the people that love her, and see if she can be saved in time to amend her wretched soul. As I take my leave to become Dana Ann Arbor, enjoy the truth about love's strength and all the interesting characters that come across Rovella Starr's evil path. Stay with us as each incredible character, from Joe Bullet, to Dana Ann Arbor, Mattie Mae Starr, Zebbie, Margaret Fisher and more, it's important for you to get to know them all as to see how they're all merged intricately somehow, into Rovella's Starr's torrid life! Enjoy. And, let us go first to the bald, golden flatlands of the scenic setting of Tulsa Oklahoma where it all begins!

CAROL D. MITCHELL

The Tulsans

When Zebbie J.T. Starr married fourteen-year old Rovella Jean Jackson on June 4, 1943, Zebbie knew from day one that it was not love. To Zebbie, Rovella was the prettiest little girl in Tulsa, Oklahoma and she got her womanhood years earlier than other girls her age and despite the fact she was the town whore, Zebbie knew he had to have Rovella Jackson.

Zebbie first saw Rovella at the intersection of Sheridan Road and Frisco over near the tracks in Dawson in the exquisite city of Tulsa, Oklahoma, Zebbie J.T. Starr and his friend Earl had been at work for nine hours loading trains for the white man as they did six days a week, when Zebbie spotted the pretty girl who would one day be his wife, tongue kissing some star football player from the Tulsa High School football team. The minute Zebbie saw her kiss that guy with all that tongue, in Tucker's Alley, he wished it were he. The girl was very young, maybe fourteen or fifteen and Earl told Zebbie that girl already had a reputation, but never paid it no mind. His over pious mother Mattie had told him to mind his own business; not that of others and that's what he was trying to do.

Zebbie saw that pretty girl again three days later at Walter's liquor store on Peoria Avenue near Apache, not too far from where Pretty Boy Floyd got into that shoot out in 1932 with the Tulsa Police Department. This was a Friday, and it was a hot day, what they call Indian summer in January for Tulsa, too hot to lift crates on those high trains, so the white man let Earl and Zebbie off work early today. The "pretty girl," as Zebbie called her, was standing in the doorway of the store wearing a low cut red, white and blue midriff T-shirt with some butt tight, cut-off blue Levi jeans. Seductively, she was biting into the center of a green Tootsie Roll Pop. To Zebbie, Rovella was looking cute. He walked around the store pretending he was looking for something more than the beer he came in to buy. He heard the pretty girl tell the store attendant, Mr. Frank that she was waiting for her cousin, Joe Bullet who had the money to pay for the sucker she was eating. Having left the tracks, Zebbie was tired, he looked bad and he had only come here to get a beer; not pick up women. He didn't smell good, but he wanted to say hi to

–9–

Rovella Starr
The New Love-Starved Bitch
Author's Gold Edition

the pretty girl anyway, so when he got his nerves, he walked up to her and said hi. At first she acted like she didn't hear him, the way women do sometimes when they know a man is trying to hit on em and they want to pretend they don't know. She was flirting with him and rubbing it in. This girl was good at what she did. Zebbie could feel his eyes smile at her as she snapped the rest of her green sucker off the white stick. When she playfully flipped the sucker's white stick onto the floor, Zebbie gave her his best smile. Though she was playing along with his game, to Rovella, Zebbie was another big, ugly, greasy looking nigga from the railroad company who was out looking for some good young pussy, but she had news for him. Rovella, who was still standing at the checkout counter coyly said hi back to Zebbie while staring back at him with her sexy, green, villainous eyes. Next, Zebbie walked up closer to Rovella. He then stared directly into her green eyes and offered to buy her another sucker. Rovella rolled her green tongue at Zebbie in a very grown up womanly manner and said, "No thank you, sir. My Mama said not to take candy from strangers." Minutes later in a surprise move, she stuck her telephone number inside Zebbie's beer sack. She had written it on the back of a Tootsie Roll Pop wrapper. When the cousin she had been waiting for showed up to get her, his face was so scarred, the boy she called Joe Bullet scared Zebbie ten steps back from the girl. Out of the store, the boy with the two-toned face gave Zebbie the "don't even try it with her look." He said, "Come on let's go," to Rovella. She went. Then he said, "Mama will have a fit if we're out too long." Next, he dragged the pretty girl right past Zebbie, who was standing in front of his Plymouth staring at the two of them like he had seen a monster or something. "You too young to be talking to that ugly punk," Joe told his cousin, loud enough for Zebbie to get the message. After seeing this boy's face, Zebbie knew if that boy didn't have looks, he sure had a lot of nerve.

About a month after that meeting, Zebbie found out that Rovella Jackson was so grown up at fourteen that her family had been lying about her age to try and compensate for the womanly things pretty girl was doing around town. Rovella was a high yellow, shot-short, shapely, well-developed young

CAROL D. MITCHELL

woman who at fourteen had the body of a twenty-year old woman. Rovella was the talk of the town already on the bar scene around Tulsa. People said she was a slut who had bedded all of Tulsa's sons and was working on the fathers. From what Zebbie could tell, apparently she either lived alone or had parents that were blind or impervious to her very open ways. Zebbie's longtime friend, John Bertman bet him a hundred dollar bill that he'd never get that gorgeous, high yeller woman, Rovella to say I do to him in a year." Zebbie said back, "Why buy the cow when the milk is free, man?" They both had a drunken laugh behind that one. Zebbie found himself liking the girl, despite her suspicious reputation, and he had done a little research on Rovella. By the time he had taken her out a few times and knew her for six months, he knew one thing for sure. He knew that Rovella would do anything, even marry him to get away from that aunt her mother gave her to. Around town, everybody knew that them Bullets wasn't no joke. And the last one you wanted to mess with was Rovella's Aunt, Teresa Bullet. She had her husband Peter so henpecked, he quit coming to the bar a day after he married Teresa, and that was twenty-five years ago. Teresa knew everybody's business and when her sister Darnetta gave her that bad child, Rovella; the town knew Teresa had met her match. But not even Teresa Bullet could tame this wild child.

Zebbie was a good OLE country boy from Monroe, Louisiana. His mother Mattie and his father Bo moved to Tulsa in 1912 because Mattie had heard about how easy it was for Black people to get voter registration rights and they arrived in time for the largest voter turnout in city officers election. Mattie was at the head of the table when the Socialists demanded a second election. She said that was what freedom was all about, "being heard" and exercising your civil liberties.

Mattie had five boys: Louis, Tim, John, Bo Jr., and the baby, Zebbie, all Starr boys. Bo Sr., died early in life. He had sugar and by the time of his death, the doctors had cut off two of his toes and his right arm. Mattie told her boys he was better off dead. Bo had always been a good provider and his death, at age thirty-nine shook up the Starr household. But as she had been known to do now for over twenty-five years, Mattie held her family together. Being a good mother did not mean Mattie was the best person. She had a tendency to show out at the church. Some regular worshippers had even seen her take a dollar or two out of the collection plate. Her holy witnessing was not all that honorable. And, talk was she held the Holy Ghost a little too long sometimes for most people's comfort. All that said, Mattie was the leader of this town and she had clout since she was not afraid to let people know the truth about them. Now Zebbie would be the last child Mattie had

—11—

Rovella Starr
The New Love-Starved Bitch
Author's Gold Edition

to walk down the wedding aisle. Zebbie Starr, born August 12, 1926, would be only seventeen when he married fourteen-year-old Rovella Jackson on June the 4th, 1943.

One day before their fateful wedding day, Rovella had to weigh the consequences of her actions. Was getting away from Teresa Bullet worth marrying the ugliest boy in town over? Zebbie had been good to Rovella in the past few months. He gave her his ten-year old green Plymouth. It wasn't a new car, but it did run good enough for her and Joe Bullet to go anywhere they wanted to go in town. License or not, Rovella could wheel that piece of steel better than the men workers could on the tracks. Aunt Teresa was always hitting somebody and finding excuses to call the authorities on her each time she tried to defend Joe Bullet's scarred face. Rovella was sick of all the Bullet's except Joe. She hated Peter for being so timid and never standing up to Teresa. She hated Darnetta for being whiter than Teresa is and for giving her away after the town discovered a disturbing family secret regarding Joe Bullet and her. And she hated any man who talked to her breast before saying hi to her face. Moreover, she hated anybody who faked the Holy Ghost like she thought Zebbie's mother Mattie did every Sunday morning at church.

Joe Bullet had it hard for he had on him a bewitching face. Rovella was the only person he knew who looked at him as a whole person, rather than a side show attraction. Joe Bullet needed Rovella more as a friend and confidant, than to fight his battles. Now as she was about to leave-loving her had so much meaning to Joe Bullet he could find no way to express it except to be there tomorrow for her big day. Whereas it looked like Rovella Jackson had something against the world, Joe knew he had secured a rare corner in the heart of a woman most people swore was evil from the heart.

Today Joe felt Rovella staring at him on the back porch of Teresa's charming red and white five-bedroom house. He was right. More than anything she wanted to tell Joe Bullet how much she loved him. She had never told anyone in her life she loved him or her before. Telling Joe she loved him was so painful for Rovella that she began to cry. Before she could

CAROL D. MITCHELL

dry up her tears, Joe turned around to face her. He paced up the nine stairs of the back porch. As usual, he took his shoes off then he jumped into the hammock Peter put out on the porch last Fourth of July. "Are you crying cause' you don't want to marry Starr?" he asked Rovella

"No, I ain't crying about that, boy. I ain't crying about nothing," she said, lying to Joe.

"Zebbie is the only good one in that Starr family. He done everything for his Mama since his Daddy died a time ago," he said swinging side to side in the hammock.

"I don't care what he done Joe. I ain't marrying him for support. I want out of this house and out of Tulsa one day," she said. Joe believed Rovella. After all, she was the only person he knew that shot her words straight from the hip. What you see with Rovella Jackson is what you get.

Zebbie knew from day one that marrying Rovella was going to be the biggest mistake he had ever made in his life. All the woman wanted was his money and any material possessions he could provide her with. With that, she had the nerve to refuse to nap with him before they were married. To Zebbie, now all the woman had going for her was good looks, and to him she was the finest Mulatto woman he had ever seen in his life. Others said she was the finest woman Tulsa, Oklahoma had ever produced. With jet-black, wavy hair all the way down her back that swung like a pendulum across her 17-inch waist nobody could touch the girl and she knew it. All that beauty came with a cocked right eye and some guys argued that her stray eye made Rovella sexier. With her coke-bottle figure, drunken men were wishing and ugly women were hissing. She had a pert, round ass that swayed like it was made solely for sex. Her huge tits were headed straight up north to heaven. Wearing garments purely for tease, around town Rovella was known for her jellybean colored T-shirts that she took home and redesigned with a slit down the middle chest to torment men wherever she went. To Zebbie, he felt lucky to be getting a woman like Rovella Starr. She was dumb, but to Zebbie, that took nothing away from the ease she was to the eyes, for this butter-skinned stallion, was to him: Quite lovely. Those aside, wherever Zebbie took Rovella, she was sure to embarrass him. She cussed like a sailor and fought like a man. Seemed to Zebbie that if things didn't go her way, Rovella either bought, stole or dealt it into being her way and the only sensitivity she had was toward that scary looking first cousin of hers with the hurtful-looking - half black and half brown face. People in town said Rovella would literally kill somebody if they said one sly word about Joe Bullet's messed up face. Zebbie learned that Rovella didn't care who she hurt and she hated Mattie. There simply was no other way to put it, Rovella thought

–13–

Rovella Starr
The New Love-Starved Bitch
Author's Gold Edition

that Zebbie's mother, with her lard eating ass was the most despicable person she knew. She told Zebbie minutes after meeting his mother that Jesus was gonna get Mattie for there was no way that Mattie was as sanctified as she pretended she was. Shortly thereafter, Rovella quit going to church with Zebbie as each Sunday Mattie ran her big fat ass down the aisle hollering and screaming and yelling like she had the Holy Ghost. Preacher Stanley could never finish a sermon without her drama. After church Mattie would get home and cuss everybody out for ten hours. Rovella knew that Zebbie and Mattie had a conference about her days before the wedding day Rovella learned from a family member that Zebbie talked about her to his mother like he had something against her. It was not anything for Zebbie to hang out at the bars telling people bad things about Rovella to his drinking buddies. One day when Zebbie's friend, John Bergman tried to seduce Rovella to go to bed with him, she tricked that fat bastard into telling her about the bet Zebbie made with him and everything. After that night, she wanted nothing more than to marry Zebbie to make him pay for all the horrible things he and Mattie had said about her. When Mattie told the ushers at the church that her son was marrying the town whore, Joe Bullet confronted Mattie about it and Mattie assured Joe it was all a lie. She told Joe Bullet to go home and soak the right side of his face with some alcohol to help it blend in with the other half. When Joe told Rovella about that, she said to Joe, "Don't you worry about it Joe. I am going to marry that ugly bastard on June the 4th, if for nothing else to get that mean ass, Holy Ghost faking bitch of a woman back. You watch me Joe. One day Mattie is going to pay for what she said about me and for telling you to put alcohol on a birthmark. And they call me dumb," she said. At that moment, Teresa Bullet wished her niece a happy wedding day tomorrow. She could tell by the look on Rovella's face that she was up to something.

Teresa Bullet had been a Registered Nurse in Tulsa since before Orcutt park had roller coasters. She was a stellar well-respected skinny fifty-five year old woman who could spit tobacco into a can from five-feet away. Known for making the best white, skillet corn bread in town, Teresa Bullet ran her

CAROL D. MITCHELL

pleasing stucco home with God and a good switch. On her way out the door to work the night shift at Tulsa's County Hospital, one night before June the 4th, Teresa had a few choice words for her niece.

"Rovella, you been getting into trouble all of your life reason why Darnetta handed you over to me. Never you mind the other stories they got going around this town about your Mama. Nobody knows what makes you so angry. You have been in and out of trouble all of your young fourteen years. Now you have met a strong black man who lost his father to a terrible infliction that ate up most of his body, leaving his son Bo Jr., crazy enough to kill a beloved sheriff a few years back. Oh dumb-ass Mattie don't think nobody remembers that shit and how she borrowed money on her house to send Bo to Compton, California. What I'm trying to tell you, Rovella, is Zebbie he is a good boy and I think he might love you. He's ugly, kind of hard on the eyes. He is awkward, with long lanky limbs, true enough, but he works hard on the railroad tracks and he knows how to bring home the bacon. He's husband material Rovella and he the only good boy Mattie ever had. His choice could be to stay at home and take care of that gold digging Mama of his, but he chose to call himself saving you from me, Peter and responsibility. Girl you better know how to recognize a blessing when it come to you. They ain't the best people in Tulsa, no they ain't. In fact, them Starr's is a mess, but I do know one thing," Teresa said, picking up a piece of cornbread out of the pan. "Ugly as that boy is, Rovella, he about the best choice you got out here in Tulsa. This is 1943 honey. I done seen a lot of changes in this town. My family been here since oil was discovered at Red Fork. Your Uncle Peter's father worked on the Sue Bland No. 1 then he retired over at Citizen's Gas Company. I know baby. Be nice," she said. Teresa grabbed a napkin for her cornbread. She finished eating, then she walked over to where Rovella was sitting at the wooden dinette table and she kissed her gently on the left cheek. She balled up her napkin, tossed it in the garbage, and then she picked up her bag, walked out the door and went to work.

This eve of her wedding, Rovella knew Teresa must have been trying to advise her in a motherly fashion. It didn't work. She hated Teresa for the dispassionate way she treated her. Tonight she watched Teresa get into her new sky blue Buick that she got for herself last Christmas. That was the first time in a year Teresa took some time out to tell her more than she was gonna get a whipping. It was either her or Joe that was always getting a whipping and now Teresa was giving her advice like she was a grown woman or something and it almost felt like she cared. But to Rovella, she was only

−15−

Rovella Starr
The New Love-Starved Bitch
Author's Gold Edition

doing this for the reason being - this was her way of saying take what you got coming to you and good riddance.

CAROL D. MITCHELL

The Wedding Day

On June 4, 1943 Rovella stood out on Mattie's front lawn and told her that she was doing the Starr family a favor by marrying ugly Zebbie Starr today. Mattie looked at the wench and went to calling on the Lord. Rovella was about to march herself down to the courthouse in a dingy white no-name wedding dress that she paid two dollars for at Tulsa's Mo-Dee's thrift store. This train wreck of a wedding dress was not fit for Halloween; much less a wedding. The formerly white monstrosity had a fist sized hole in the lower back hem where the trailing train should have been. When he first saw the dress on June 3, when Rovella first showed it to him, Zebbie told his future wife she couldn't wear the dress. Rovella told him if he said one more word about her dress the wedding was off. Zebbie left the front yard in disgust. There were two red wine stains on both back sides of Rovella's wedding dress the cleaners said they couldn't get out. Rovella told the proprietor at "Tulsa's One Stop Cleaners" that she didn't care about the stains. The most important thing was that the dress be clean. After the cleaning, Rovella put the dress on anyway. After all, this wedding was not about love; it was about escape. When she went into Mo-Dee's for a wedding dress, this was the only one on the rack. The woman was nice enough to mark it down from three to two dollars, and to Rovella, who was young and unworldly, this was a deal. Rovella was a fine woman that made a nightmare of a wedding dress look like she was the Queen of England. With a perfect size two figure, Rovella knew nobody would notice the dress for her perfect body. She had on white shoes that were in far worse shape than the dress she had on. The shoes were scuffed and when she tried to polish them, black marks seeped through the white polish on both sides of the left shoe, the right shoe had a broken heel. Leaning down to tape the left strap of the right shoe, caused her dress to rip on the right side. She asked Mattie for a safety pin and put that back together fine. With the wedding party of Mattie, Zebbie, Rovella and Joe Bullet assembled; it was now off for the six block march to the church. Teresa and Peter Bullet hadn't liked Mattie since Bo shot the best sheriff Tulsa ever had. Like most of the community, the

Rovella Starr
The New Love-Starved Bitch
Author's Gold Edition

Bullets turned their nose up at people like Mattie Starr, who according to the Bullets (*were a disgrace to the race*). They hadn't liked her before their niece met Zebbie and they weren't going to no wedding of Mattie's son; not even to show support for their only niece.

On this hot day the Pinkham kids on Lambert Street came out to play stickball in the street like they always did on Saturdays. The nine boys and two girls from the Pinkham household watched the pitiful wedding entourage march down the dusty streets towards the church called, "God's House" where all of Mattie's boys had got married. The gossips said: "there go Mattie again, marching to the courthouse church, marrying off the last of her ugly Starr boys."

There were lemon-aide stands set up along the road leading to the church. As Rovella, Zebbie, Mattie and Joe headed towards the railroad tracks where Zebbie worked, Rovella checked herself out in car windows along the way. Today she was pleased that her pancake makeup, red rouge and sinful red lipstick had all gone on perfectly. At one stop Rovella looked into the mirror, pursed her lips against a piece of toilet paper to make sure it was even like her white Mama - Darnetta had taught her to do when she was a little girl. Nobody who saw her believed she was only fourteen-years old and that's what all the whispering was about today as the ladies of the church gathered along the steps of the row homes in the neighborhood, this June the 4th, to wish Zebbie Starr a happy wedding day. Miss Scott, Miss Thomas and Ms. Willis, all women of God watched the wedding march on Ms. Pepper's front lawn. Their gossip was louder than a whisper.

"I cain't believe Peter and Teresa done turned that poor troubled girl over to that ugly Starr boy like that. She might as well be cattle. Poor Child," Miss Scott said.

"Chile, Darnetta, that's her daughter. You know that story. Poor Chile," said Miss Thomas.

"Ya'll shut up. God don't like no gossip. It's a blessing that boy will put

CAROL D. MITCHELL

a stop to that girl messing with our men," Ms. Willis said.

"Chile, look at Mattie," said Ms. Thomas. "She couldn't even press her hair for the last son's wedding and she got that white turban on backwards. "What a shame," Ms. Scott lamented. When Mattie walked past the Pepper yard, the chorus of women said,

"You have a good day Mattie!!"

"Thanks!" Mattie said back, as she wiped raining sweat from her thick brows. Mattie waved to her friends from the church, who then bade her, another good day, while she looked at this hussy walking in front of her. The first thing come to her mind was Darnetta, that white trash that gave her daughter to her sister Teresa as she was ashamed to have a black child. Mattie knew everything about that OLE uppity Jackson clan. She knew Teresa came out more black than Darnetta and she didn't mind taking in what Mattie thought was a possessed child. As Mattie watched Rovella today, she knew the child was confused for more reasons than that her Mama and Daddy made her that way. Rovella was cursed, and to Mattie that child had grown up much too fast. Mattie was sure that the core of Rovella's wretched soul would enter light one day. Darnetta and Teresa both had that white Mama and that black Daddy and thought they were better than other Negroes in Tulsa. Nobody loved Rovella. And for this and these reasons Rovella didn't love nobody. This girl didn't know what love felt like and from what Mattie could see today, she never would. She couldn't even march her scandalous ass to her own wedding without causing problems. The whole town knew through the gossip at the church that Rovella had been sexually active since she was eleven-years old and it started with her Mama's own husband. Mattie knew about the football team and the town drunks that Rovella had been with and she was only letting Zebbie marry the girl to save her. Mattie knew that Zebbie would be the perfect tamer for a girl like Rovella. Mattie knew too that her benevolence towards this girl was that, benevolence. Mattie was nobody's fool and if this girl rubbed her too far the wrong way, before they made it to the church, she'd have to show Rovella who really is he boss.

Joe Bullet marched with his cousin Rovella and her wedding party. He would be sorry to see Rovella leave the house. He knew she had a bad mouth and didn't care how she talked to people. Joe knew she stole things and drank at night when Teresa and Peter were not looking and there was a

—19—

Rovella Starr
The New Love-Starved Bitch
Author's Gold Edition

whole lot of mess that Rovella had going on that poor Joe Bullet could not tell the truth about. Together he cut class with his cousin and as he walked with this so-called wedding party, he couldn't believe that Rovella was marrying the ugliest boy in town. For years, it had been his job to worry about Rovella and to protect her. He was the doorkeeper for his favorite cousin. Her being a bitch never stopped him from screening the men in town whom had to have a piece of this juicy peach. It went for Zebbie. Joe had spent some time with Zebbie over the last few months at the house on the many nights he stopped by to court his cousin. He told Zebbie about his birthmark that had been given hi trouble all of his life. He told Zebbie he loved Rovella and that deep down inside her treacherousness, she really could be a nice person and that one day she might even find her way into being a good wife to him. Joe liked Zebbie seeing as he was too goddamn ugly to be a problem for Rovella. Joe had watched his mother discipline his cousin. Sometimes when Teresa beat Rovella with that switch, not one tear fell from her emerald green eyes. Teresa had fought Rovella like she was a man trying to instill some values into her. Teresa always told Joe: "Don't matter what I do to that girl, what I say to that girl, don't nothing work. She's as hard headed as they come," she'd say. Joe Bullet watched his cousin go in and out of juvenile hall and every night she was gone he prayed that God would do something to rescue Rovella and today he believed that God had given him the answer to his prayers in the form of Zebbie J.T. Starr. This June 4, 1943 Joe watched Rovella looking pretty and all in that mess of a filthy wedding dress. Before he knew it tears of happiness flowed down his two-tone face. He remembered some of the nice things she had done for him to get her own self in trouble. One day she beat up two of the town's toughest dudes to defend his ugly face. When she ended up back in juvenile hall for that, Joe cried everyday like a baby until they let his fine-looking cousin out. The future would prove Rovella's loyalty to him in ways only someone who loved him could do.

Today, if they could only make it to the church without her causing any problems, Joe would be ever so pleased with God.

Joe remembered a time, back in 1941; Rovella trapped a wild field mouse in a Smucker's jelly jar. She used a steak knife to punch holes into the cap of that jar for the mouse to breathe. When Teresa left for work one night and Peter had gone to work on the railroad tracks, Rovella went out to the garage and brought that jar in the house, then she took it to school that next Monday. When Rovella got to her eighth grade science class, she took that weak, tired, rabid mouse out of that jar. With some glue, she pasted that mouse onto the teacher's chair. Later, when Ms. Donna Clark, the teacher, sat on that mouse, that hungry rascal bit a hole right through that teachers' white cotton dress. By then, Joe Bullet and the other students had arrived at class in time to see the red and white ambulance take the teacher away. That woman was screaming to the top of her lungs. The bold Rovella cased slowly up to the stretcher the scared teacher was strapped onto and she told that lady, 'That's what you get for letting people laugh at my cousin, Joe Bullet. I done told your ass a million times his face is like that cause' it's a birthmark. You supposed to be a teacher," she said, putting her finger in that woman's face. "You think I didn't see your smirk when Mike Walters called my cousin Neapolitan face? I sat there and watched you do nothing and I knew on that day I was gonna get you for messing with my cousin. Now that sick, hungry mouse done bit a hole in your ass. I hope that sick rat bit your ass right off!' she shouted.

Two days later, the teacher, who was rabid, remained in Tulsa's County hospital fighting for her life. The teacher did survive and was teaching at another school out of the Tulsa Unified School District.

Fond thoughts of Rovella from Joe Bullet never lasted longer than a flash in a pan, before the girl was in trouble again. Joe watched now as right outside of the church, when the wedding party was about to go in, Rovella started telling Mattie she should be glad Zebbie got something like her to marry. Mattie was a fat, tootsie roll colored church going woman who knew mental illness when she seen it. To her Rovella was a classic example of what it's like for somebody to be seriously disturbed. To Mattie Rovella was a high yellow bitch, who had been used and spoiled by the men of Tulsa. Rovella commenced to tell Mattie in a haughty manner that Zebbie could never give her the life that she so wanted and deserved. When Zebbie heard what Rovella said to his mother, he took the worried Joe Bullet aside and told him they were going to fight, but don't worry this is the only way for Rovella and Mattie to seal their own marriage to each other.

Mattie had heard enough. Zebbie's mother stopped walking and those citizens of Tulsa who would report the forthcoming actions tomorrow around the community pretended like they didn't see the fight that was coming. And those that should have been concerned about the fire brewing between Mattie and Rovella tried to ignore it.

Rovella Starr
The New Love-Starved Bitch
Author's Gold Edition

It was a sizzling day in Tulsa. And on days like this Mattie always worried she was going to have a stroke, especially if her high-blood pressure got too far up. Mattie's only wish today was that this little yellow hussy was not going to start trouble and embarrass the family on this, her last son's wedding day. Tired, Mattie stopped walking. She looked over at the church under the elm tree where Zebbie and Rovella's cousin seemed to be in their own little world, flirting with young girls that passed by the church. Mattie turned her attention back to Rovella, she then dug her heels in the landscape outside the church, and then she put her hands on her hips and looked at Rovella like she was this morning's garbage. Next, the big tootsie roll colored black woman who was wearing the stark white turban, sized up her future daughter-in-law. With her large eyes bubbled, she took a real good look at Rovella, who was gearing up to start trouble. With her puffed hands tucked inside the pillow crevices of her wide hips, Mattie began to tread slowly around Rovella, who was checking her fine reflection from the glass mirror of a gold powder compact she had stolen from the dime store on the way to the church this morning. Mattie dug her feet into the sand and to Rovella she looked like a bull out of Spain. Rovella stood inches away from Mattie, with her waist length, jet black hair shining and her green eyes staring madly into the middle of Mattie's sweaty forehead. Rovella then rolled her eyes at Mattie. She then flipped the sweat from her own forehead, and she leaned forward, tossing her long hair straight into Mattie's face. Unable to take it anymore, Mattie shouted at Rovella…

Mattie screamed, "Rovella!" Before Rovella could lift her finger, Mattie grabbed her by the veil and ripped it completely off. Rovella looked like somebody's rag doll flying through the hot air with all of them mosquitoes and summer fruit flies dancing around her head. Each time that Mattie tore into that young ass, the big woman took in more air and beat her future daughter-in-law again. You could hear faint laughter of the Pinkham boys hollering, "Get her Old Miss Mattie Mae. Show that town slut who is the boss! They hollered.

Mattie couldn't walk that fast so when she tossed a blow, it had to mean

CAROL D. MITCHELL

something. She was a fat woman, whose thighs rubbed together, making it hard for her to move freely with Rovella, who was flying all over the place. What Mattie lacked in speed she made up for in strength. She was such a strong woman that each time she laid into Rovella, Rovella lay on that dirt road like she was dead. Rovella's defeated stance gave Mattie enough time to catch her breath and dry her seat enough for her to go at that ass repeatedly. It was a crying shame, said the onlookers, but all of them had wished for years that somebody handled the Jackson girl. She was fast in her tracks, and the town knew if anybody could lay a whipping on that girl – it had to have been a woman who successfully reared five boys. For a half-hour Rovella and Mattie were outside the church acting like niggas and to Zebbie and Joe Bullet both, it was downright embarrassing. The temperatures had soared to 100 degrees and the preacher had already been ushered into the church wearing a wet cold towel over his head. When he pulled up in the driveway of the church and saw Mattie and Rovella having at it, he told Zebbie, when Ms. Willis and them had called him and told him that Mattie was out here fighting her daughter-in-law to be he couldn't believe it. He said he didn't want anyone to see him going into the house of God with fat Mattie and the town tramp out here acting like ignorant fools. "But as you know," he said to Zebbie, "we would not have this new church if it wasn't for the generosity of Ms. Starr," he said humbly.

Zebbie thanked the preacher for coming. Next, he nervously went back outside to make sure his mother didn't kill that poor girl. Now Zebbie used his white handkerchief to wipe a continual flow of sweat from his brow as he watched Mattie write the final chapter to the ass kicking Rovella should have gotten years ago. Zebbie turned towards the quiet Joe Bullet:

"I was a little worried," he said, taking a deep breath. "But you see young blood," he said, pointing to his mother and his future wife, "that whipping your cousin is getting today is gonna make a real woman out of her," he told the bewildered scarred face boy. Joe Bullet shook his head in assent and wished that this wedding would hurry up and take place and be over.

Zebbie had not dressed up for the wedding since he had given all of his money to Rovella Starr for the last six months and he didn't have a dime to his name. He wore his red class sweater shirt with the white background and the black diamonds with a faded pair of overalls that he didn't even bother to iron to his wedding. By now the only relative Rovella had that gave a hoot about her enough to be at her wedding, had been shocked into total submission by all that was happening to Rovella. Quietly, Joe felt Rovella deserved Mattie's ass kicking. It was the first time he saw Rovella lose a fight. Her

–23–

Rovella Starr

The New Love-Starved Bitch

Author's Gold Edition

losing against the pitiful Mattie didn't mean he didn't love her. Rovella had done fine handling Mattie, despite the fact she picked herself up off of that ground looking more like she had been through a shredder than a pretty girl who was about to get married. When the gossip spread later on that day, the church women said: "Mattie, the overweight diabetic, blind in one eye and hypertensive mother-in-law to be gave that child a righteous beating with one hand wrapped around her back."

CAROL D. MITCHELL

Life Goes On

After the fight out on the church steps, Mattie stood up with her son. When the preacher asked her: "Who gives this man to be married to this woman?" Mattie proudly stepped forward with her white turban tilted to one side of her head. In her loud, earth shaking alto tone, she said, "I do." After the ten-minutes of service, Rovella walked away from the church with Zebbie with blood dripping from every pore in her body. Her white wedding dress was torn into shreds enough where the red stains on the dress could not be seen. The heel had come off of her right shoe, the left one had turned from white to black. Her gorgeous black hair looked like a wild hornet's nest, as the wedding party walked quietly into the future.

On March 12, 1944, Mattie Mae Starr was the mid-wife who delivered Rovella's first son, Eric Bo Starr. On January 16, 1945, Mattie brought into this world Rovella's second born, Shane Edward Starr. By January 1948, when Rovella was six months pregnant with her third and last child, she had enough of Tulsa, Oklahoma and Mattie Starr. The War Department had ordered Douglas Aircraft to stop manufacturing army planes; putting 2,500 Tulsans out of work, one of them Zebbie. When Mattie told Zebbie, he had better try to get his job back on the railroad tracks with John Bergman, that was one interference too many for Rovella, When Mattie insisted on delivering her grand kids, Rovella let her. Mattie financed their house across the street from her, Zebbie agreed with that move too. In fact, Mattie got Zebbie the job at Douglas Aircraft in 1946. Now Rovella wanted out. Beginning of the New Year, 1948, nine-teen year old Rovella told Zebbie if he didn't move her out of Tulsa before her last baby was born she would divorce his ugly ass and leave him and the kids. Always eager to please his wife, whom people hated more with each passing year, Zebbie contacted his friend on the West Coast that told him Oakland, California was a decent place for him and his wife to live. Therefore, by February 1948, Zebbie visited Oakland, California for a week. He applied for and got a job at a shipyard in San Francisco, California that was only ten miles from Oakland. With the help of a generous broker and a resistant, but benevolent Mattie, Zebbie did on July 15, 1948

−25−

Rovella Starr
The New Love-Starved Bitch
Author's Gold Edition

move his family to a modest four bedroom home on Market Street, in West Oakland, California. The house was old and rat infested, but to Rovella, it was a nice respite, if it meant not seeing fat Mattie anymore. On the other hand, without Mattie there to perform the proper birthing procedures for Rovella, she had trouble delivering her last child.

On August 11, Zebbie begged Mattie to get on the next flight to Oakland to help Rovella deliver the baby. Mattie told Zebbie she was tired. She said she was afraid of planes and that she didn't want to be bothered with Rovella. On the morning of his last child's birth, Zebbie was on the water of the San Francisco Bay. Rovella told Zebbie she had another week before her delivery due date, but on August 12, 1948, Ray J.T. Starr died at childbirth due to lack of oxygen. Rovella's water broke at 8:00 A.M., that morning. She had called emergency services. Later, the Paramedics who arrived minutes after the birth, cut the umbilical cord, then they wrapped the cold, stiff baby boy inside warm sheets. Rovella and her two young sons were crying to the top of their lungs when Rovella had been told by the EMT technicians that her baby, Ray J.T. Starr was dead. Paramedics then prepped Rovella for the ride to the hospital, ten minutes later to everyone's surprise, the tiny body in the bundle started moving. The paramedics did CPR on the baby. Next, the cute baby boy with the large black curls and the dark moon-sized eyes let out a weak cry of life. Surprised to learn that her son was alive, but may have suffered brain damage because of what Paramedics called, *"Lack of oxygen,"* Rovella Starr privately vowed from her hospital bed at Oakland's Providence Hospital, to block out Zebbie, Shane and Eric in deference toward this child whom she presumed would never lead a normal life. While her four and five-year old had been shipped to Mattie, she held her miracle baby to her breast, Rovella was glad Mattie was not around to bond with her baby before she did. This baby was a gift from God. She had lost him once, but she would never lose him again, so help her God. Five days later, from the moment Ray J.T. Starr was carried back into the doors of the home on Market Street in Oakland, California, Rovella Starr

CAROL D. MITCHELL

waged a battle for her son's happiness that would make him a prisoner to her, perhaps for the rest of his natural born life.

Zebbie J.T. Starr had been in the church all of his life. His childhood preacher and Mattie both had enlightened him to what the devil was about. However, by 1963, twenty-years into his marriage, Zebbie had three teenage sons. Two had thrown themselves into activities that left him unable to enjoy their lives. His fifteen-year old handsome, but slow son strictly belonged to his wife. Zebbie was convinced that Rovella was the devil incarnate. She beat Shane and Eric into submission. The only good thing she did for them was put both boys through Catholic school, letting the nuns instill their good values. Eric, at 19 married a rich white girl, Paula Till. Together they had a baby boy they named Zebbie. His wife, after being called all kinds of white bitches by Rovella refused to bring her child around Rovella. Eric's wife was a beautiful, nurturing woman, who detected early that Rovella was no child's role model. Neither Zebbie nor Rovella saw the child much unless Eric was willing enough to bring the baby around during the holidays without Paula. When Rovella learned that Mattie had flown out to the west coast to deliver the child, she was inconsolable. To Zebbie, who loved his grandchild dearly, he knew Eric and Paula were doing what was best for the child. Rovella had willingly steered Eric into law, intuitively knowing she would need free prejudicial services.

Shane, on the other hand was a Mama's boy who constantly vied for his mother's attention. Rovella had attended all of his AAU track meets. If Shane did not take first place, Rovella threatened to shoot runners and judges alike. An award winning sprinter, high jumper and all-around athlete, Shane uprooted from the Starr home the summer of 1963 to attend *The University of Southern, California*, on a full athletic scholarship. He promised his mother he would be back to teach locally after receiving his graduate degree. Shane confided in his father, to whom he was dearly close to, that Rovella was hard to defend to others who thought she was mad. He told his father it was Ray who took up most of her time. According to his grandmother Mattie, she was the best mother a lunatic could be. When Eric and Shane were little, Rovella filled their bedroom with toys and media entertainment; and during each summer, she shipped her boys to Mattie in Tulsa, Oklahoma, but never Ray. Ray was too good for anybody except for Rovella. Rovella attended a few special events if Ray was involved in them. She only attended *Parent Teacher's Meetings, (PTA);* to check on Ray, making sure his teachers was qualified to school Ray. Shane has such a tough time in Catholic school, she was adamant not to put Ray, *"Through a system of a bunch of nuns who needed more than anything to be fucked."* Instead, she reminded the older boys

Rovella Starr
The New Love-Starved Bitch
Author's Gold Edition

that Ray needed her more since he was slow, leaving Eric and Shane to rely on tenderness through Zebbie and Mattie. Zebbie agreed with his sons, that Ray was the only thing in Rovella's life that she loved more than her ugly first cousin, the ever suffering, scar-faced, Joe Malcolm Bullet.

In her thirties now, Rovella was a crass woman who had no respect for human feelings. She was wretched, she was ratchet, and she was always at it with the neighbors over Ray. If anybody looked at the boy the wrong way, Rovella threatened him or her with her shotgun. Whereas Zebbie only wished that the woman could love him half as much as she loved Ray, Zebbie was suffering miserably inside a lonely marriage that introduced him to signs that Rovella might actually be sexually abusing their youngest son.

One night in May 1966, Zebbie came in late from San Francisco to find eighteen-year old Ray in bed with Rovella. Ray was sound asleep when Zebbie entered his bedroom to see Rovella lying naked aside from his son. Unaware that Rovella customarily put Ray in the bed with her – Zebbie backed into the living room. There he called his son Eric in Berkeley, California to ask him if he knew anything about his mother napping with Ray. Both of his sons told their father at night that their mother had been mothering Ray since he was born and that Ray rarely slept in his own room. They assured their shocked father that Rovella was not abusing their brother or Ray surely would have told them everything as he always had. Livid over his findings, Zebbie could not be consoled. All he knew was that his wife had not had sex with him for ten-years. She didn't cook for him and when she did cook, she cooked only enough for her boys. Before going to bed at night, she washed the pots, then she put them back on the shelf, leaving Zebbie a note (*often-times*) telling him there were TV dinners in the freezer.

This warm spring night, Zebbie sat in the living room turning over the words of his older sons in his head. He was tired physically, but he was even more tired mentally and all of it was because of Rovella. Ever since they married, he had not been happy. The highlight of his life was his children and he was sorry he was not there for them. Luckily, he did see both of his sons' graduate from High School and he saw Eric graduate from community

CAROL D. MITCHELL

college, and later go to law school; but, he had wanted to be more involved in his kid's life. Unable to reconcile what he had seen with his own eyes, Zebbie eased up out of his brown rocker. He paced to his bedroom again and he watched an undisturbed Ray sleep comfortably next to his mother. Unable still to believe his eyes, Zebbie walked over to his bed shaking, as he aroused Ray up out of a deep sleep. Right then, a shocked Rovella lifted up out of her sleep. Immediately she pulled, the bed covers up over her nude body. It was dark in the room and Rovella reached over to turn on the nightstand light to make sure it was Zebbie and not an intruder who was standing over her son. With the visitation of light, a shocked Ray rolled over next to his mother and attempted to wipe the glare from his eyes. Upon waking, Ray saw his father standing over him with terror on his face. This night Zebbie's mood was far worse than anyone could ever have anticipated. Zebbie was madder than Ray had ever seen his father. When Zebbie yelled at his mother, who was to Ray "The only good woman alive," *(according to what Rovella had always said to him)*, all Ray could do was watch his father in horror. The big, scruffy man with the large hands, the big feet and the long arms – charged toward the bed, scaring them both.

"How long have you been doing this to your child, Rovella?" he shouted. The shocked Rovella watched her crazy husband, with the thought in mind that if "this nigga" laid a hand on Ray, she would straight up shoot his ass. No matter how crazy he looked, or what he said, protecting Ray was all she was worried about now. She didn't answer Zebbie. Soon, he raged at her again.

"What the hell is wrong with you, Rovella?" he asked. "I'm standing here watching you nude and in bed with your son and I'm asking you to explain it and you say nothing?" he asked. "Answer me you dirty whore!" he shouted. Rovella continued to stare at Zebbie, while Ray, in his typical manner withdrew into a silent quietness. Zebbie knocked over the bedside lamp. He continued to seek answers from Rovella.

"How could you do this to your son, Rovella? For years you have claimed you are tired and that you cannot have sex with me; yet, here you are laying up here disrespecting your child and me," he shouted. Zebbie then raced to the dresser bureau for one of Rovella's gowns. When he found something, he snatched it out of the drawer, threw it to her and shouted at her to: "Put it on now!" Rovella snatched the gown from him and she stepped into it as she kept a watchful eye on Zebbie's enraged actions. To her he was ridiculous to accuse her of such foolishness and she was not ready to answer his crazy charges about her son. Tonight Zebbie accused of her being a terrible mother, forgetting that she had raised her sons well, as

Rovella Starr
The New Love-Starved Bitch
Author's Gold Edition

one was on his way to being a lawyer; and, the other a track coach. "Fuck everybody," is what she thought. "Let him go on and get mad," for what he was saying to her now, she thought then and there that she would never forgive him anyway, so he might as well clear his conscience, for all she cared. Later, Zebbie began drooling and acting more of a fool than he had ever before. As Rovella sat on her bed with Ray waiting for Zebbie to settle down, she was fed up with him and had been so for almost twenty-years now. As she finished buttoning up her yellow, lace gown, Zebbie made Rovella think.

"The nerve of Zebbie to barge in here; breaking her good lamp, and was accusing her of doing something bad, with Ray. She would never even think of doing anything that sick to her kids. All she wanted for Ray was to protect him. Nightly, she educated her son on the pitfalls of dating money hungry women and how the bad women would get pregnant by a man to trap him. She rubbed his head, because since he was a small child, Ray endured terrible headaches. Her touching Ray was merely motherly love. She gave him much education about life and that was all. She knew perhaps better than anyone; how one mistake, could ruin a person's entire life. She was his mother and it was wrong for this jealous, confused, idiot, to be standing in front of her amid the brightest light in the house talking shit and saying all of these horrible things in front of her son. Horrified now at his increasing rage, Rovella jumped out of bed, and then she pushed Zebbie out of her bedroom. Zebbie forcefully pushed his wife back until she fell over the broken lamp. Rovella was not hurt; but, delirium over this ghastly accusation made her madder.

"Look what you made me do," she shouted, examining her arms. "Be glad there's no blood you ugly ass bastard," she shouted, lifting her thin body up off the cold floor. Her eyes filled with contempt, Rovella hated Zebbie more now than he could ever have imagined. Whereas before she was going to be quiet and let this blow over, now she attacked Zebbie.

"Don't you know I will go in there and get my gun and blow your ass away, Zebbie?" she asked. "Get the hell out of here, you sick son-of-a-bitch!

CAROL D. MITCHELL

You wonder why I won't sleep with your sorry, ugly, ass. Hell, I don't give a good god-damn where you go Zebbie. Accusing me of those awful things with my son? You got a problem! How dare you! All the things I have done over the years to support your ass. Get out of my house now, bastard!" she shouted. She said it again, "Get the fuck out!" Zebbie pushed Rovella aside. He then walked to the bedroom door. Shocked, Ray had never left the bedroom, but he got scared when he saw his father yelling at his mother and knocking her to the floor. Unable to figure out what to do, Ray stood silently in the middle of the bedroom floor. There, he watched the two of them with tears rolling steadily down his handsome cheeks. The mere essence of Ray's innocence left little for him to draw on in defense of his mother. He was confused and unwilling to articulate the fundamental teachings his mother was giving to him – but this perceived man-child, a figment of his mother and father's self-served, overworked imaginations; quiet as it is kept, was not retarded. Ray sure as hell, was nobody's invalid or fool.

To Ray, Rovella was the good woman, his protector, and his teacher. He believed from her teachings that she believed she was emphatically, the only good woman left on this earth. Now, to him, he hoped that would be a good enough defense to offer to his enraged father to protect his hurt mother. Slowly, Ray approached his father. It was the only time tonight that Zebbie stopped yelling. He had always cared about his children. He dim-wittily felt in his heart that Ray was a sad disappointment. As a man, he blamed himself for not being there when his last child was born. Now he listened to his son with a heavy heart.

Ray asked him: "Papa? Mama told me the women in Oakland are all bad and they're not good like Tulsa women are and she wants me to not get any of them pregnant," he said. Ray was timid and docile to appease. To Zebbie, it was evident that Ray truly had not understood the jest of what all of this was about. Nevertheless, as a perceived man-child, he was doing his best to defend his mother's action. After speaking to his father, the scared man walked with his head to his chest, down the hallway to his brother's room. He then stuck his head out of the bedroom door to bid both of his parents' a goodnight. Then he slammed the door shut.

Zebbie looked on in dismay, remembering how his beautiful son stood in one spot throwing around childlike mannerisms, and speaking in the tone of a child to defend his awful mother. Zebbie thought by the vacant look in his son's eyes – which he clearly did not understand that it was wrong for a man his age to be sleeping in the same bed with his mother for whatever reasons. With Ray out of the way, Rovella raced to the bathroom where she locked the door, and then she sat on the toilet and cried.

–31–

Rovella Starr
The New Love-Starved Bitch
Author's Gold Edition

Zebbie sat on his bed blaming himself for not being home for his kids. He was trying to make a living and he was doing all that is required of a good husband. Tonight Zebbie was sitting on his bed for possibly the last time ever wondering what he could have done differently to save his marriage. Zebbie held his head inside his large hands. He closed his eyes to look for the reality of his actions. He was sorry that he accused Rovella of child abuse. He knew that there was no way that Ray could know the extent of what his mother had done to him mentally, but, deep inside his heart – he knew that Rovella would never take advantage of Ray. Despite that, he felt she had crossed the line by letting the boy sleep with her for so long. As if these were the last moments of his life, Zebbie knew that he had given Rovella everything. She had indeed raised his boys good; but, the marriage was and always had been purely a loveless union on Rovella's part. However, over the years, he had hoped that Rovella would fall in love with him, but she never had. With recognition of that, Zebbie really had stayed with Rovella for the kids. He didn't want to be one of those hapless fathers that cheated on his wife and didn't care about his children's welfare; or be one that shunned his responsibility towards his kids. For those reasons, Zebbie never messed around on Rovella. Working from sun up to sun down, he was rarely home at nights to share a bed with his wife. Whenever there was a break in his job, he came home. As much as his beloved mother hated Rovella, she always told Zebbie to stay in the marriage and pray for change. A veteran member of Evergreen Baptist Church, in Oakland, California, Zebbie was a well-liked Deacon who had mentored children of the church. He had been a positive role model to young men. Right now Zebbie regretted that he could simply not have the love of a wife he had grown to love very deeply.

Rovella was more evil than Zebbie could have imagined. Love blistered his eyes to the real terror that Rovella was. Some of her most heinous actions had taken place beneath his eyes. However, Zebbie could

CAROL D. MITCHELL

not see what he didn't want to see in Rovella. When he asked Rovella about Ray and how he was doing in school, she told him the boy was okay, and for him not to worry about Ray's education. Tonight, with the true impact of Rovella's undermining actions clear before his eyes, Zebbie resolved that he could not look at Rovella's face another day. Zebbie was devastated. He simply could not reconcile all of the years of agony, lies and deception that Rovella had put him through and he didn't know how the equation ended up turning into love on his part and more deviousness on hers. The idea that something was wrong with Ray Starr left Zebbie malignant that Rovella had not let Mattie deliver the baby. Grief turned into gripping pain, leaving all of this much for this kind-hearted man to bear. As he reflected on the past, Rovella's actions became more morose to him by the minute. It was Rovella, who led the authorities to where Bo Jr., had been hiding in Compton, California. She did that a year after they were married to get back at Mattie, Now Bo Jr., was on death row at San Quentin, for killing that Sheriff in Tulsa, back in the early forties. Rovella's immutable battles with Mattie over the years had literally torn the Starr family apart. None of the Starr boys showed up for the holidays, because they told Mattie they didn't want to have to hear Rovella talk to their mother or their wives so bad. Later, in 65' Rovella secretly went to Tulsa, Oklahoma, to visit her Auntie and cousin, Joe Bullet. While she was there, Mattie had a crippling stroke. Rovella had told Zebbie that Mattie was being cared for by Ms. Willis and Ms. Thomas of the church and that her stroke was mild and the doctors were predicting a speedy recovery for his mother. Rovella never told her husband that she had Mattie Mae flown from Tulsa the next day to a nursing home on High Street, in Oakland, California. One day the nursing staff called Rovella to come say good-bye to dying Mattie. On that last day, Rovella baked a sweet potato pie. She made sure Zebbie was out on the ships. She called to the south to tell everybody that Mattie was doing fine.

"Don't worry about Mattie Mae. Zebbie and I have put her in a nice home in Oakland, California and she has the best care possible!" she told the family. When they asked Rovella for the number to the home on High Street, Rovella told them to stop the nonsense, pray for Mattie and ready the place for her return. Zebbie had tried hard to get the time off to go back to Tulsa, but his supervisor would not have it. *Tonight, Zebbie was bereaved as he relived his wife's own words. Her truth was callus. It was arresting and it played out in his mind this way:*

When Rovella arrived at the nursing home with Mattie's pie, she thanked the aide taking care of her mother-in-law tipping her with a crisp twenty-dollar bill.

Rovella Starr
The New Love-Starved Bitch
Author's Gold Edition

"Well," said the nurse, "no doubt Mattie got peeps with real deep pockets. I guess I can leave you and Ms. Mattie alone," she said, stuffing the bill into her white coat pocket. Rovella smiled at the aide, simply nodding her head in assent as she watched her sprint down the long hospital hallway. Rovella has sensed this would be a special visit to remember. In respect of those sentiments she wore a knee length, black double-breasted Susan Winton suit and she sprinkled herself with the best French perfume money could buy. With her flowing black hair sweeping across her back, and her perfect nails painted crimson red, Rovella looked like the sweetest daughter-in-law in the world when she gently closed the door. Then she walked over to the north corner of the clean room and closed the white mini blinds. When Rovella had Mattie all to herself, she was dazed to see how Mattie had retired both physically and mentally. The once vibrant big woman with the fire in her eyes, who beat the shit out of her on her wedding day, and talked about her like a dog to Joe Bullet - was bone thin and dying, but old Mattie was not going to let anyone steal her white night cap. It was the same brand she wore to her wedding so long ago. Nothing wrong having stock in a reliable product, Rovella thought. Mattie, who was slightly blind, had blue, thick puss stuck in the corner of her eyes. Her lips were white like winter snow and her skin was so dark it was blue. The black Holy Bible on the plain blue nightstand though ripped and badly torn, was the same Bible Mattie had used for over fifty-years.

With the faint life she had left in her Mattie knew Rovella was here out of evil. When she saw her come into the room without Zebbie, Eric, Shane or Ray and their wives and kids, she knew quietly, in her dying heart that she had to be brave, if she was going to die this way. Too tired to fight, Mattie quietly prayed and waited for the worst. This was Rovella's big payback.

Her tone though tranquil, was precise. The smooth way she sat in the chair next to Mattie had been rehearsed. Her low voice was dramatic, not higher than a whisper when Rovella said goodbye to Mattie using a script written for bitches.

CAROL D. MITCHELL

"You done a lot to me Mattie Mae," Rovella reminded her as she adjusted into the scratched silver fold chair next to Mattie's hospital bed. "You did things to me out of hate and evil," she said quietly, as she looked at her red nails, as strands of her glistening hair fell onto the sides of her face.

"Calling me the town whore and showing everybody how big and bad you were was alright. But bitch!" she said, the word bitch had Mattie's face twitching. Trapped inside a vegetated body, she summonsed for movement that was not there.

"Go on and get mad, bitch. You had all those years to turn Shane and Eric against me, and thank God I kept you from my Ray. Guess what? It worked. I'll be damned if I sent Ray down south for some of your evil poison. Ain't a thing you can do in a dying bed, swaddled in the death sheets. You should have given me a gold medal for marrying that ugly bastard, Zebbie. When you told Joe Bullet to wash his face, you crossed the line. I couldn't believe it when my cousin told me you and Zebbie talked about "us" to that damn church in Tulsa. Yeah bitch. You crossed the line," she offered. Poor Mattie could not wipe Rovella's spit off her nose. For the grace of God, she closed her tired eyes, forcing thick puss to drain down onto the sides of her face. Soon a tear fell out of her left eye and swam slowly around the puss, onto her stark white sheets. The stroke had paralyzed both sides of Mattie's body. She could not speak. Even in this dying state, Rovella thought about kicking old Mattie's ass. And, if she thought it would have made Joe Bullet feel better she would have. However, the divinity that Mattie had faked for so many years took a hold on Rovella's heart. She could feel old Mattie asking God to let her die in peace; and, Rovella was right. With that, Rovella took the pie out of her yellow, green and orange shopping bag.

"I brought you a pie Mattie. You said I made a better pie than you did. That is the only thing you never lied about. My white mother took advantage of me, and the men in Tulsa did too; then here your ass comes. You thought bad was something I wanted to be or that I was born evil. Have you ever wished you could change one thing in your life Mattie? I bet not. You are a judgmental woman who claims that you are a woman of God who never thought about looking beneath the surface to find out who I was. I could choke your tongue out Mattie for being mean to me and for making fun of my cousin's scarred face; and, for not taking one damn minute to get to know me, the real Rovella. But, I don't have to. Too late now, you are dying and when you are gone, I am gonna flush your good-for-nothing ashes down my toilet back to Tulsa. Right now, I want to give you something sweet to put into that sour puss you are."

Rovella Starr
The New Love-Starved Bitch
Author's Gold Edition

Soon as Rovella laid the pie on the nightstand, Mattie began to groan miserably.

She struggled in her deathbed to lash out at Rovella. Her eyes tightened. The call bell was at her fingertips and she could not move one inch. In her dying heart she wanted to go out punching on this mean ass bitch; but, God would not have it. While Rovella was sitting there looking Mattie-Mae Starr dead in her blind eye, Mattie died. Her bubble eyes popped out of her head like springs. Horrific as this scene was, Rovella Starr did not flinch. Instead, Rovella calmly said a prayer from Psalms to Mattie. She then rose to pull the crisp white sheet over Mattie's head. Rovella picked up her potato pie and the telephone. She dialed zero for the head nurse.

Out of pure evil, when the nursing home called a day later to ask Rovella where they should send the body, Rovella didn't tell Zebbie his mother was in Oakland, California, much less did she tell him that Mattie had died until two weeks after her lonely death. It was a horrible thing for Rovella to have done behind her husband's back. When he asked her about that, Rovella simply told Zebbie she wanted Mattie in Oakland, where she could be near Zebbie in case she got worse. She challenged Zebbie to tell her what was wrong with her placing Mattie where they could keep a closer eye on her health if she got worse. She convinced Zebbie that she forgot to tell him his mother was dead, like Mattie was not even a member of the family, much less his mother. Like his mother's death meant nothing to her, Rovella traveled to the nursing home where she signed Mattie's death certificate. Rovella called the *Neptune Society* and she paid them to cremate Mattie's body. After the cremation, Rovella brought the urn with Mattie's ashes in it home and placed the urn over the toilet that Zebbie used. When Zebbie asked what was in the brass urn in the bathroom, Rovella told him it was ashes. The next day Rovella took great pleasure when she flushed Mattie's remains down the family toilet in two flushes.

She had told her husband an insidious story, knowing his hands were tied; and wanting him to act out. Violence was not in the good man's nature, or he would have killed her.

CAROL D. MITCHELL

The salty tears streamed through Zebbie's hands as he thought about his mother's awful passing; and her horrendous burial. He blamed himself for not being with his mother in her time of need. He could hear Mattie begging him not to let Rovella have her body burned in that hot incinerator. Zebbie knew Mattie had always been afraid of the dark and of fire. When Rovella admitted all of this to him, Zebbie wanted to righteously kill the bitch. However, he had talked to the pastor of his church who told him God said vengeance is mine, Zebbie. Not knowing how he could live with Rovella after something like this, Zebbie forgave Rovella by putting it in God's hands. He cleaned his mother's death up with his brothers by lying to them, telling them that Mama's ashes were next to Bo Sr.'s in Tulsa. Now, he only wished that he had never married Rovella on June the 4th, 1943. Zebbie wanted his mother so bad he cried every day. Tonight Zebbie had to prevail on himself still that his mother's death had been painless. With work on the water enduring long hours of physical labor, he had not thought about all of this much until now. Suddenly it hit him how Mattie had been left partially blind, and crippled after her stroke. That had to have been why Ms. Thomas had been calling the ship so much last year, almost every other day – trying to reach him. He wished he had returned her calls to Tulsa, to see what she had wanted. Zebbie believed in his grieving heart that his mother's death, with all of his wife's evilness had to have been painless. He hoped and prayed this night that Mattie had not suffered. And, she didn't.

When it came to Eric and Shane Starr, Zebbie had everything to be proud of. Eric was sharp enough to have graduated from Oakland High, in 1960 when he was only sixteen-years old. Married now, he is well-spoken and articulate and he was the spitting image of his beautiful mother. Shane, also married was smart, handsome, athletic and quiet. This young man was very capable of caring for himself. Zebbie had collected all of Shane's track successes, though Rovella had been the one who attended most of his track meets. Shane had a few problems keeping girl-friends, partly because of his mother's dominant behavior, but he was married now and at least he and Eric both had great futures. Tonight Zebbie prayed that Ray would one day find the kind of happiness Eric and Shane had. He wanted this man-child to grow into his manhood, and get away from Rovella before she ruined his life as she had his and his mother's and God knows who else. This evening with all of his thoughts leading him to only one destination, Zebbie walked down the hallway to his son's room. Ray had locked the door. Zebbie wanted to say goodbye to his youngest son. Instead, Zebbie placed his head against the postern, unable to believe that so many years had left him a stranger to what was really going on in his life. Turning his head from side to side in sheer

Rovella Starr

The New Love-Starved Bitch

Author's Gold Edition

anguish, the bereaved Zebbie asked God to have mercy on him, his sons, and his wife and he cried uncontrollably.

What Rovella did to his mother and the way Mattie was buried would go to the grave with him. It could not be reconciled. In Zebbie's wounded soul, he was through with this life. Killing Rovella would leave his sons without a mother and his grandkids without a grandmother and leave him in greater pain, for it was sadly true that he could not live with or without Rovella. And, he would not know how to rid of her if he wanted to **KILL** her. With Mattie gone in such a horrible way, Zebbie had no recourse. Life was not worth living anymore. The penalty for his sins was death. Next, a caring and respected father, a good husband and a loving son, got in his car and headed towards the Golden Gate Bridge in San Francisco, California, where he leaped head first to his long, cold death.

CAROL D. MITCHELL

Ray J.T. Starr

You could tell how much Zebbie J. T. Starr was loved by the hundreds of people that turned out for his funeral. Even in his last days, Zebbie took care of his family. He provided air-tight insurance policies and benefits that would sustain his family, comfortably without Rovella ever having to work. Eager to leave Tulsa, Oklahoma behind her forever, Rovella had Zebbie's funeral at St. John Missionary Baptist Church in Oakland, California and the internment was at Rose Lawn Cemetery in Livermore, California. Rovella refused to shed a tear over Zebbie and she was pleased that the merchants had never recovered his body. She had promised Joe Bullet a day before her wedding that she would make both Mattie and Zebbie pay for what they said about her loose beginnings and Joe Bullet's scarred face. Today, she considered her job done. Shane read ever so eloquently, Psalms 23 and Ms. Willis and Ms. Thomas who had flown all the way from Tulsa to be at Zebbie's funeral both stared at Rovella Starr like they could kill her:

"The Lord is my shepherd; I shall not want. He maketh me to lie down in green pastures; he leadeth me beside he still waters. He restoreth my soul; he leadeth me in the paths of righteousness for his name's sake. Yeah though I walk through the valley of the shadow of death, I will fear no evil; for thou are with me; they rod and thy staff they comfort me. Thou preparest a table before me in the presence of mine enemies; thou anointest my head with oil; my cup runneth over. Surely goodness and mercy shall follow me all the days of my life; and I will dwell in the house of the Lord forever.

"Psalms" 23b

Rovella Starr
The New Love-Starved Bitch
Author's Gold Edition

Today, Rovella was losing her children. Eric and Shane clung to their wives. Shane in particular had few words for his mother. At the service, Ray stood over his father's casket shocked and unable to believe that the father he loved so dearly was never going to get out of the black casket. Later, Rovella rushed up to the front of the church. She ran her hand along the brass rail of the black casket, and waited for mourners to clear the path. It was a hot day in Oakland, California, too hot for sure to be wearing black. With Shane out of the way, the ever stunning black clad Rovella pulled her favorite son aside.

"Don't you shed a tear over this coward!" she warned. Ray shocked told her: "He's dead mother. Get your nails out of my arm. Couldn't you wait until we were out of here to call him names?"

"No," she interrupted, throwing his arm down. "This man, his black ass Mama, and all these country ass people of his are pathetic! They are all a disgrace before God!" she warned. She continued, "Don't you stand there crying over that fool and don't you ever think for one minute to take your own life!" she snickered. "Further," she stated, "he didn't care too much for his family, otherwise he would not have been stupid enough to jump off of the Golden Gate Bridge because of family problems," she challenged. To Rovella, Zebbie deserved to be dead and she would make sure that Shane, Eric and Ray never learned the truth about Mattie's horrible death and burial.

After the funeral, which took place on May 12, 1966, Eric and Shane told their mother they would never speak to her again in life. They didn't mean it. Both boys were trying to hurt their mother like they felt she had hurt their grandmother and father. In time, Rovella would forgive both Eric and Shane – for their harshness towards her because she knew why they hated her.

Eric sadly remembered the last time he saw his father. His anxiety could have been spared had he listened more seriously to his son. On a cold, windy night on the Bay of San Francisco, Zebbie lit up a cigar. He had but only a few minutes to talk to his son who expressed concern over Mattie's ailing condition. He forewarned his father not to let his grandmother come to Oakland. Zebbie always had an easy relationship with Shane and Eric. He was so proud of their maturity, their caring nature and how handsome Shane and Eric were. Sadly, he knew that nothing he could tell them about their mother Rovella would suffice.

During this meeting on the San Francisco boat docks, Zebbie told Eric that Rovella would never hurt Mattie. Eric and Shane had visited Mattie each year for Christmas, and it was assumed that Rovella was alright with their grandmother Mattie Mae. At that time Zebbie had 100% confidence in his beautiful wife.

Looking at Ray who was mingling with his uncles from Tulsa, Rovella was proud that he was such a handsome man and that he was coming into his own. She feared however, that Ray would never be ready for the worldly tricks and games of the women of the world, especially if he met a bitch like her. Let the games begin!

Rovella told Ray that the black women of the world were all evil like his grandmother Mattie and his Aunt Teresa had been. She said the white women were all like her mother, Darnetta and had memberships in the Klu Klux Klan, and that these were the types of women that he should stay away from and stay away from Mexicans and Asians too, especially those whores from the Philippines because they ain't shit either, she stated. As the sick woman told her sons all of these things, she did so because she never had a positive female role model her entire life to reference. Rovella based her biases of all women solely on what happened to her growing up. Uneducated and misinformed, Rovella believed what she fed to Ray. For the grace of Ray, what Rovella didn't see was that Shane and Eric knew nothing was wrong with Ray other than he was quiet and extremely loyal to a dominant mother, who had treated him like a baby, forcing him to withdraw and keep to himself. They painted another picture of women for Ray based on their own personal and professional experiences. Shane told his brother Ray:

"Ray true love will hit you so hard, you won't have time to evaluate from where it was born and color won't make a difference. But brother I guarantee you will know it," he promised his brother. Ray, in his typical quiet, meek way smiled at his brother, as he nodded his head in assent.

About a year after Mattie and Zebbie's death, Ray, under the influence of his worldly and hugely successful brothers, brought home a good-looking girl he met at Oakland High School named Carla Jeanette Scott. Rovella would play the kind of mind games with Carla that would eventually spread throughout the neighborhood and keep women away from Ray for almost twenty-five years. Everything about dark beauty Carla Scott was appealing to Ray. The woman was so earthly stunning, that her mere essence

Rovella Starr
The New Love-Starved Bitch
Author's Gold Edition

threatened to melt away every tale Rovella had ever told Ray about the "No-good-black-woman." Ray had been talking to Carla for two-years before he finally convinced the statuesque beauty from Watts, California to come to his home. At 5'11," with an afro hairdo to rival Angela Davis and a curvy, lean body pretty enough to stand up to a Jayne Kennedy, the bronze skinned Carla Jeanette Scott was the Brenda Sykes of Oakland, California. Despite the complete brainwashing job and the sixteen medications Rovella had Ray on, when Ray brought Carla home to meet Rovella, the mad mom set out to get rid of this hot Mama. Plan (A): Rovella sent young Ray to the corner store for some grits with the clear thought in mind that she was going to have a little talk with this Carla girl and run her away from Ray immediately. No sooner had Ray left the house and turned the corner on Market and Jefferson, the mind games of Rovella Starr began. The scared girl didn't know whether to sit or stand to wait for Ray. Rovella stood at the front door where Ray left Carla with her arms crossed at the chest. Her green eyes looked ferocious as she stared down Carla Scott.

"Well, I guess I am supposed to say it's nice to meet you Miss Carla?" she smirked. Rovella made Carla nervous. The girl surmised that she could put up with Ms. Starr for five-minutes. With that, Carla nodded at Rovella, but the young girl did not intend to say anything verbal to the woman.

Ray don't do nothing but talk about how fine you is and how smart you is. He said you was his teacher's aide at school. That makes you about eighteen or nineteen if you flunked last year?" Rovella said dryly. The shy Carla turned her brown eyes away from Ray's mother as she was immediately afraid of Rovella and she knew right away that something sinister was wrong with this green-eyed woman with the long, black, witch hair. Rovella's large cocked eye rolled fiercely in the socket and then when it got back in focus, that wild green eye landed straight into Carla's dark brown eyes. Rovella then paced around Carla like she was a lion who was sizing up her prey. Every now and then Rovella took a handful of her long black hair and tossed it over her shoulders. When Carla sat down in a brown bean chair near the

CAROL D. MITCHELL

front door, Rovella then circled around the chair that Carla was sitting in and she kept staring at Carla with the most evil look Carla had ever seen. To Carla, she was trying to be cool, but to her this bitch was trying to start some shit she didn't want any part of. As Rovella continued to pace back and forth and around her chair, Carla hoped that Ray would hurry back through that front door. With the dubious ways that Rovella was acting today; Carla had surmised that Zebbie Starr had not killed himself for nothing. The whole school had heard about the suicide that made the front pages of the Oakland Tribune, last year. When Carla saw that scratchy, brown shot gun sloping in the crease of the living room wall behind the creaky front door, she prayed that Ray would hurry up with his slow ass and come back. She tried not show signs of fright or stress, but Carla suddenly felt her body begin to tremor. She was scared as hell of this woman, but she had to play it cool and try not to let Rovella see her fear. After all in August of 1965 she had survived the three-day riots in Los Angeles, California, that obliterated her house in Watts, CA and prompted her family to move to the Bay Area. Surely, she could oblige the evil Rovella Starr for ten-minutes. Carla then noticed how the house smelled of Pine Sol. As she looked around the pacing Rovella, she noticed how clean the house was too. The green long carpet was old, but clean. Noted on Market Street for being a reclusive family, Carla jumped at the sight of the slab of shade in the front window that effectively hid the afternoon sun. Rovella had reasonably pulled off her attempts to shut out the world from her dark home and the pie crust colored blind had the appearance of never having been lifted. In fact the water-stained price tag, though faded had never been cut from the pull string. Carla noticed pictures of Ray, Eric and Shane in silver frames that peeked out from every corner of the mantle over the living room fireplace. There was too on the mantle, a frightening photo of a man with a face that was split in two colors of brown straight down the middle. The left side of his face was dark brown and the right side of his face was crusty, crater beige. The old 5x7 photo in the silver lame' frame was the most grotesque face Carla had ever seen; yet, his picture was displayed most prominently on the meticulous mantle. In an effort to forget how scared she was, Carla had picked out what to her had to be Ray's baby picture. He was handsome, with his wide toothless smile, his large dark brown eyes and his forest of black curly hair. He was adorable in his baby red, white and blue navy outfit. At sixteen, to Carla Ray was of course an even finer man. To Carla his brothers were nice looking, only Eric had their mother's searing green eyes; however, to Carla Ray had won hands down in the good looks department. She knew he was somewhat slow and on the quiet side, but he was a gentleman, and he was the most popular guy at

Rovella Starr
The New Love-Starved Bitch
Author's Gold Edition

school for his cool clothes and for the gentlemanly way that he carried himself. As she did everything she could to avoid the continual examination by Rovella Starr, Carla tried to focus now on other things, like the shotgun. Suddenly, Carla felt more uncomfortable and unwelcome in Ray's house. Picking up on the girl's fright, Rovella honed in on playing more mind games with the girl.

"Oh, so you may be as tall as a giant; but, you the quiet type huh?" she asked. She continued. "You gone sit there at the window pretending like you ain't scanning over all my shit, huh?" Rovella asked. Carla didn't answer her back. There was nothing in Rovella's house she wanted. Raised in Watts, California, her mother had taught her to respect her elders and she wasn't thinking about her. This was Ray's mother and she would tolerate her ill behavior for a minute!

"Didn't you hear me ask you a question?" she asked Carla. When Carla didn't answer her – Rovella resorted to her low blows, aimed at running the girl out of her house. Intimidation had kept Ray's other little girlfriends away; but, this little bitch was not an easy nut to crack, Rovella thought.

"I have been looking at you. You are too dark for my Ray. Look-a-here girl," she said, pointing to her face, "I don't think you light enough to fit into this family. You ain't good enough for my baby. You ain't never gonna be good enough for my son. Let me tell you something right now, you little whore. If you think you are gonna come into Ray's life opening up your nasty, long ass legs and talking that nasty trash about having babies, love and marriage, to trap my baby – you got another thing coming. He is mine," she said, thrusting her finger into her bony chest. Carla took deep breaths. She didn't know what to do now. She had never expected to come here to fight. Ray was one of the most sought after men at school. There was talk that Rovella was a murderer who kept a gun at the house to keep girls away from Ray – but she had never believed those stories until now. Then again, who was she trying to fool with this Ray is my baby and he needs my protection shit. Hell, she thought, I grew up rough. Carla certainly was nobody's push

CAROL D. MITCHELL

over and it wasn't even like what Rovella was thinking. To her, Ray was simply her running buddy, her friend. Carla eased slowly out of the chair she had been sitting in. Having lost her patience with Rovella, Carla surprised herself when she tore into this old crazy woman.

Carla walked slowly up to Rovella, like she was another bitch who wanted to test her on the school grounds. The stare down did hang time before Carla cut loose.

"Let me tell you something now, you old bitch," she said. Carla's head got to rolling to match the street fighting motions that Rovella was tossing her way. "You better learn who the fuck you talking to before you come at a person like that, Mama. I know you ain't talking to me like that. You see, we ain't never even talked about doing nothing crazy like what you was thinking, like sex, babies and love. You sick bitch. Everybody at school knows you one sick bitch too. You standing here talking like your own son is yo' man or something," she said, throwing an extra oomph into her words. "And, let me tell you something else, even if I was interested in your son, I ain't gone let an old dried up bitch like you stop me from getting it on if I want it, okay?" she asked, locking her neck to the right side of her head. Nobody had ever challenged Rovella this way. She wanted to slap Carla's neck straight, but she had to respect the bitch for having heart. Soon she saw Ray charge through the door with her grits. Rovella stepped back from Carla. When Ray charged through the front door, Rovella took the bag from her son and walked into the kitchen, never taking an eye off the pretty girl with the large round Afro and the firecracker attitude, and it kind of made the old woman smile. When Ray asked Carla if she was ready to go for a ride on his new Harley Davidson motorcycle, Carla looked him dead in the eyes like he was crazy and said,

"Ask yo' Mama." Outside of the house that evening, Carla became unnerved and Ray had no choice but to take the girl home. Later, when Ray returned home to get advice from his mother, she told him that Carla was one of them street girls from the "Hood" and that her intentions with him were bad.

"Ray, the girl is a whore who dresses like a prostitute, and talks like a thug, but she got the heart to have a career one day and leave you. Recognize son that all of those other women out there are like her or worse," she said.

Broken hearted, Ray walked to his room feeling dejected. On his way he stopped to tell Rovella he hated her and that his father had been right about her all along. After that evening, he never slept in his mother's bed again. When the lovely Carla Scott refused to talk to him again or call him; for many years later, Ray decided to live a lonely life of working and catering

Rovella Starr
The New Love-Starved Bitch
Author's Gold Edition

to his mother's every need out of fear that he could never accept being rejected by another woman again after Carla Jeanette Scott.

In August 1972, Eric and Shane pooled their resources to help their twenty-four year old brother get his first apartment around the exquisite, sunny Lake Merritt in Oakland, California. Two weeks after leaving his mother's home, Ray had to give up his apartment and go back home to be with his grieving mother. His mother's first cousin, Joe Bullet was being tried for the rape and murder of a white woman in Tulsa, Oklahoma that happened in August, 1972. Teresa Bullet was not taking it all well. When Rovella found out about it from her Uncle Pete, she flew to Tulsa Oklahoma to be at Joe Bullet's side. Six days after the trial Teresa Bullet died of a heart attack, at the same time Joe Bullet was being hauled to prison to serve a life term. Teresa's last words to her son were: "You did it you're lying and the truth ain't in you."

Convinced that her cousin was innocent of all the charges, Rovella testified as a character witness for Joe Bullet, and was therefore hysterical when the jury found Joe Bullet guilty on all counts —on the prosecution's strong circumstantial evidence that placed Joe Bullet at the scene of the crime. Rovella and Ray both watched bewildered as they dragged the stunned Joe Bullet away to prison to serve his time. It was a hot day in Tulsa that nobody would ever forget and the court room was packed with media and a nosey crowd, many of them neighbors that Rovella had grown up with. The only question after this confrontation would be where was the sheriff? Rovella, dumbfounded by the conviction of Joe Bullet appeared in front of Judge David S. Brossard. The woman was still so attractive nobody expected what came next. Rovella, with glowing tresses, raining down her back, and dressed in a skin tightening orange and white low cut jump suit jumped over the judge's steel rail. Next, the tiny woman had her diamond filled hand in his face. By the time the sheriff's arrived; the judge waved them off: "My cousin didn't do this!" Rovella shouted. "I have protected him all of his life. The only reason why anybody ever messes with him is cause he is ugly! Every person has messed with my cousin has paid a price. That fat ass white woman who died was lucky he took her to the goddamn hospital. In this racist town they took a man's good will and satisfied the needs of these here white folks to put a nigga in jail and all of you including my Mama Darnetta, should be ashamed of what you are doing to Joe Bullet!" The judge wished like hell he could fuck this stunning, Mulatto, Rovella. He'd let this nigga out for some pussy, but he couldn't tell her that. Instead, he watched Rovella impassively, while the sheriff checked out the nicely packed position of Rovella's fine body and wished attacks like this on the judge took place more often. Rovella finished by promising the judge that if it was the last thing she did in this life that one day she would prove that Joe Bullet never touched that white woman. The judge was calm, peaceful even. He told Rovella Bullet-Starr that Zebbie had not jumped off of the Golden Gate Bridge because she was wife of the year. He said, that her moving out to the West Coast had never killed her own tarnished past and reputation in Tulsa and that if she said another word about this or anything he would hold her in contempt of court and, he'd throw her cacophonous ass in jail in the same cell and on top of her murderous, frightening looking cousin. The judge then slammed the mallet on his desk and closed his court forever.

From the age of twenty-four to the age of forty-eight, through medication and mind games, Rovella had carefully woven a protective shield around her son that was virtually impenetrable. She had forced a husband to his death, assaulted a judge, and flushed her mother-in-law's remains down the family toilet and essentially neglected Eric and Shane. She made a spectacle of herself at her cousin's trial that made the front pages of newspapers throughout the country and added more stress to Joe Bullet's life than he could handle.

The outside world had not been kind to Joe Bullet. What they did to him in prison, the rapes, the beatings, and the games is what horror movies are made of. When she received Joe's letters from prison, what he didn't say haunted Rovella; and, what he did say, it literally ran the woman crazier!

Dear Bad Ass Rovella:

Don't want you to worry about me. Prison life ain't that good, but it ain't your fault and this is something that I have to go through. You know how a black man's life is gonna be in the south. They think a black man did it when it come to a white woman and that ain't the truth. I heard somebody say a lawmaker involved in my case had a relative involved in all of this, but this ain't the place to believe in fairy tales. You can't take care of me anymore Rovella and I can't take care of you either no more, so quit wanting to hit on people that say bad things about Joe Bullet. We both is grown now. You always being concerned

Rovella Starr
The New Love-Starved Bitch
Author's Gold Edition

about me, huh? Many times I said to myself; if you wasn't my cousin, I would have married you and protected you from the bad of the earth. You know, all the bullshit, that kind of thing.

When I said that you smiled and said, "Stop it boy!" Rovella, you used to call me boy all the time. Remember? I loved it. Somebody else call me boy and, ooh, girl, those would be fighting words. I am glad I can make you smile. You have been more family to me than Teresa and Peter. Teresa hated the bond you and me have and Mattie hated it too. I will never break that bond. I watched Zebbie, the whole time y'all was getting married and I thought he would be the one to make you happy and it seed he made you madder than anyone. Nobody understands you pretty Rovella, but me. But I sear on my heart, Zebbie loved you fully. Nobody knows you like me. If they saw you through these eyes, they will see the pretty girl that just needs a little love to put out all those fires. Don't blame yourself for what happened to me, Rovella. Go on and raise them kids and find a man to make you happy. I will write again. Please send me a few dollars for the commissary and some pictures of how everybody looks and tell Ray, Shane and Eric to keep in touch.

Love always,
Joe Bullet

CAROL D. MITCHELL

The Most Famous of Them All

By 1983 one of the world's most famous writers, twenty-nine year old Dana-Ann Arbor thought she'd try marriage again when her longtime assistant, Dillon introduced the star writer to Zim Danube, a handsome six-eleven world famous star center for a world famous basketball team on the Wes Coast. The author and the basketball genius courted for three months. The happy couple then married at the end of the year in 1983. Thirty-four year old Zim was a good, doting husband who was proud of his wife's dark beauty and immense fame – until his own fame and fortune took a turn for the worse when his team found out he was addicted to crack cocaine. His ultimate trade to the Golden State Warriors, a losing team on the West Coast was devastating to Zim. With word of the trade, Zim tried to kill himself. Unable to break his increasing drug dependency, Dana-Ann, the former orphan turned millionaire financed one drug rehabilitation program after another for Zim, until she came home from a book tour one night in March, 1984 and found Zim dead in his favorite white leather lounge chair. The unexpected death of her husband Zim spun the author into a virtual depression that lasted for at least five years. From there on, the delightful, pint-sized writer turned down dozens of marriage proposals; she cranked out her best writing and flourished as a star writer – who was more famous in Europe than she was in the United States. With all off her success as a writer, Dana Ann Arbor was a failure in love. Therefore, the great author made a vow to herself that she would never marry again to simply accommodate the ideal of marriage for somebody else's self-seeking needs. The next time she married, she told John and Carol, her adopted parents that it was going to be for love and for love only, no matter how God bequeathed that parcel of love to her.

By fall of 1999 the completion in the Dana Ann arbors writing circles grew and prompted Dana Ann to forever seek original concepts for her writing. Tired of writing about the no good black man and his woes, Dana Ann churned out three Russian period novels, all taking place in Moscow and the Soviet Union. With good people behind her like her promoter Dillon and her assistant Brenda, Dana Ann was working on her twentieth novel.

–49–

Rovella Starr
The New Love-Starved Bitch
Author's Gold Edition

With little time on her hands to play the dating game, and less time to be concerned about finding a husband, Dana Ann had thrown herself head first into writing novels.

One day during December, of 1999 Dana Ann was sorry that she had let Brenda leave her home office so early in the day. Working now on a novel about physical abuse in nursing homes in the U.S. private sector, Dana needed Brenda to get research statistical information for her from the Department of Records at 1221 Oak Street, in downtown Oakland, California. Unable to reach Brenda at home or on her cell – Dana Ann decided to take the trip to the Government office with Dillon. No sooner had she called her most tried and true employee, she heard her long time promoter Dillon's car hit her driveway. She smiled as she thought of Dillon. She said to herself that if she could find a man like Dillon that she would be okay. Dillon was one of those good, dependable brothers people's Mama says would make any woman a good husband. He was not a handsome man. His thinning brown hair was knotted up in greasy spit knots. Dillon described himself as being the last man on earth with a Jherri Curl. To Dana Ann that nest of brown hair on top his head was plain greased nappy hair. He even teased Dillon that his hair was nappy – but almost good enough that if you wet it right and put a little grease on it, it looked okay. Dillon loved Dana Ann. He was frustrated that she had not met a good man who could appreciate her for the gem she was. He was a nice, soft-spoken guy who had won loads of respect universally with writers. Tall, with yellow skin, people called Dillon red. He had brown, blotched freckles, nine on each side of his cheeks that to Dana Ann made his skin look like day old corn bread. His oval eyes were a light, tight booger green and his thin lips were the color of *Bazooka Bubble Gum*. His signature smile revealed a set of big white teeth that were perfectly lined. A loyal employee – and an even better friend, Dillon had been with the author for twenty-years. He had too been a good rootstock for the good guy characters in the *Arbor "Love Story" book collections*. A caring and loving husband, who had been married to his high-school sweetheart, Pat for twenty-one years, Dillon quit playing matchmaker for his good friend Dana-

—50—

CAROL D. MITCHELL

Ann Arbor after Zim. To him…The last guy he introduced her to was a stalemate and he was still blaming himself for what happened to Dana Ann in that marriage.

At the door before he rang the buzzard, Dana Ann was glad to see Dillon.

"Hey, what's up dude?" she asked, doing her cowboy impression. Dillon stood on the doormat. He teased Dana by running his hand through his hair. Then he pretended that his hand was stuck. She laughed.

"Boy, you have lost your mind, I swear. Better go get one of them perm kits. Get a good one next time," she warned. They both laughed.

"I asked you what's up," she reminded him as he stepped into her home.

"Not a thing but you," he said, as he rolled down to kiss her on the cheek.
"My girl is looking happy today," he said, putting an emphasis on the word, "today." "Guess what?" he asked her. "Pat took the girls camping at Lake Merritt today. You could not have called at a better time. When you told me you couldn't reach hot Mama Brenda, I dropped by her pad. Her Mama said she drove down to Los Angeles with her brother Richard.

"Well, that explains why I couldn't reach her on her cell. They're probably driving through that grapevine as we speak. Well, Dil' you know I got that deadline to meet. We need to go down to Oak Street right away. I think 99' and 00' are going to be great for us," she said. Dillon smiled. He watched Dana closely as she put on her coat. He'd be damned if she was not the most lovely dark-skinned woman on the planet. He thought whoever named her Dana had been right on the money. That name described her perfectly. For modern times sake though, she looked to him like a shorter version of his model and friend Naomi Campbell. With skin a deep, rich chocolate, her exquisite taste in clothes was impeccable. Dana, as Dillon called her, always wore limes, peaches and cream colors that gave a striking contrast to her ebon skin. Beauty and generosity were the adjectives that described her best. Dillon was forever grateful that Dana had bought for he and Pat a 1.2 million dollar seven bedroom red brick house in the prestigious Oakland Hills. Her generosity had not stopped there. Telling people that she would not be where she was without Dillon and Brenda, she paid them both handsome salaries that topped six-figures. To Dillon, Dana Ann was the sweetest woman he knew and he believed she was admirable that way because the Morgan's had told him from where she came and Dillon believed that Dana Ann knew how to value life. To Dillon, Dana Ann deserved the best and he wished every day that her prince charming would one day

Rovella Starr
The New Love-Starved Bitch
Author's Gold Edition

come along. Today, she paced over to the red marble bar area in her home where Dillon waited for her. Leaving her left arm dangling behind her backside, Dana picked up a crystal glass containing her usual afternoon shot of sparkling imported brandy.

"Here's to you, Dillon. Let's celebrate the last month of 1999," she smiled. When her glass met his, she said:

"I am glad you could come here on such short notice, Dillon."

"Nope, I am the lucky one," he offered. "Thank you for asking," he said gleefully. Next, like the gentleman he was, Dillon walked around the bar as he then helped Dana Ann put her dangling arm inside her coat. She thanked him with a great big smile for being the gentleman.

"Your car or mine?" he asked.

"I'll let you do the honors, Dillon," she answered.

CAROL D. MITCHELL

Love at First Sight

On Friday, December 10, 1999, Ray J.T. Starr was in a familiar frame of mind with his Government boss, Sam Eugene Pittman. Ray, the lead janitor for the Records Department at 1221 Oak Street, in Oakland, California believed that Sam picked on him all the time because others that he worked with claimed that his peaceable demeanor and his solitary lifestyle indicated that he was slow and perhaps borderline retarded. The guys Ray worked with had been making fun of him for the entire two years he had been working for the Government Records Department and Sam Eugene Pittman was quietly the leader of the discriminating pack. In the Government office, to Sam Pittman, it was always good to find somebody less advantaged than himself to pick on to make himself feel better. This year, Oakland, California's most notable recovering alcoholic picked Ray to make fun of. For two years, Ray had been telling Rovella about how Sam and his coworkers put voodoo dolls with stakes in their hearts in his work closet, because he had not married. They spray painted the inside of his work locker hot pink and they called him gay. He told his mother that they teased him about everything from his expensive clothes to the mounds of curly chest hair that spilled out of his blue janitor overalls. This day Sam brought a blue bottle to work. He pulled Ray aside to the janitor's office area to tell him that the potion in that bottle could bring him a love like the one he lost in Carla Scott several years back. To Ray, this was merely another one of Sam's usual voodoo pranks. He listened to Sam knowing that once he got his rocks off for teasing him yet another day that he would soon be gone. Then Ray felt he could centralize his efforts on ending his workday across the street over at the Department of Records, and then prepare for his second of three jobs that he went to every day. Sam told ray that he had purchased the blue potion from a chemist in East Oakland named Margaret Fisher. Sam took the black top off the potion. Next, he put the bottle up to Ray's nose, and then he told Ray to go ahead and drink it. Ray sniffed the potion. He then told Sam it smelled like herbal food coloring and he would never drink anything that smelled that awful. When Ray asked Sam why he was doing this to him, Sam told Ray it was time for him to leave his mother's house and get married. In a bold move, Ray took the potion from Sam over to the

−53−

Rovella Starr
The New Love-Starved Bitch
Author's Gold Edition

janitor's sink and he poured it down the drain. Sam got a good laugh out of Ray today. Now all he had to do was gear up to go tell everybody in the janitor's rank how this day's prank had transpired so he would get another good laugh at the expense of Ray. Embarrassed about the increasing number of pranks being played on him by Sam and some of his coworkers, Ray decided he was not going to tell Rovella about the potion prank. Instead, fifty-one year old Ray stayed at work until Sam gave him the permission to go finish his day at the Government Records Department.

Glad that Sam had given him a reprieve from his daily jokes; Ray headed across the street from the Law Library to the Records Department at 1221 Oak Street, thanking God for having given him another charming day. The sun was not out today. In fact, it was a bit cold, but Ray felt a warm rush race through his body, like God had something special in the works for him. Oddly enough, he stopped on the corner at 14th Avenue near oak Street to look around his surroundings, as he took note of the fact, that he had never felt anything like that before!

The long lines at the Records Department left Dana Ann wishing that she had put off this research task for Brenda on Monday.
"Whew Dillon, what do you think of this line?"
"Well, you know this is the Government. It is Friday, Dana. The lines are gonna be long my dear, even for a bonafied star like you!" He joked. In her sisterly way, the Dana retorted:
"Well, if I had known that, I would have brought a book to read," she stated. They both laughed. As the two of them stood in line for what appeared to have been eternity, Dillon told Dana Ann he was going to leave the long line for a minute to say hello to an old friend who had come into the glass door. When Dillon left the line, Dana Ann forced her stretch around the old lady in front of her to see who had caused Dillon to barge out of the line. Seeing from a distance, that it was the janitor that Dillon was talking to, Dana Ann diverted her attention back to her place in line.

CAROL D. MITCHELL

"Why Ray J.T. Starr, Dillon said gleefully, "is that really you boy?" Dillon asked, running up to greet his old friend. Ray responded gleefully,

"Hey Dillon," he called out, "well, long time no see, man. What's going on?" He asked, with a friendly smile on his face. They traded hugs, then Dillon answered Ray's question excitedly.

"Oh, I'm here with the boss lady," he said, pointing to the line. Dana Ann Arbor, she's a writer. She's writing another book and needed to come here to get some statistical information. We were over there in line, I thought that was you coming in the door, I saw the big broom. I looked again and sure enough, man, it's you."

"How's your brother Jerry? Ray asked Dillon.

"Oh man, you remembered. Thanks for asking man," he said, dropping his head. "Jerry had a rough time, but he survived prostate cancer, man. At first, it was touch and go there for a minute." Shaking away the tears in his eyes, Dillon struggled to change the subject.

"With the grace of God… Yeah, with the grace of God he survived mainly because of people like you man, who was there. Hey, that was fifteen years ago, man. Jerry and Linda remodeled a few Victorians in West Oakland, man. Don't think he'll be back out on the ships anytime soon. He and Linda struck gold rebuilding those old homes in West Oakland man," Dillon said. "So what you been doing man? You are looking great. I bet the ladies still love that long hair you got man. I remember in High School, back in the day the women were crazy bout' them some Ray J.T. Starr. Hey man what ever happened to that tall, fine Brenda Sykes looking chick named Carla Scott? Man, that fine chick was crazy about you," Dillon said. Everybody at school had bets you guys were gonna get married, man. Dillon quickly answered his own question. "Oh yeah, I remember now. That chick told, everybody at Oakland High, she was in the Watts riots and one day she was going back to Los Angeles to practice law. Back in 75', I heard she became District Attorney in Los Angeles, man. I forget who told me that, but I remember somebody telling me that is what she'd be doing now!" Dillon said.

Ray had tucked Carla away in his memory many years ago. He had seen a few women over the years, but he never felt anything for them like he had for Carla Scott. Today, listening to Dillon, he was glad for her. Carla had always been smart and Ray knew that she was gonna be something big one day. He never saw her again after Rovella challenged her and ran her away. Rovella had since run so many women out of his life that Ray had virtually given up on ever finding love. With Ray closing up on him, Dillon patted him on the back and then he changed the subject. Feeling sorry for his old

Rovella Starr
The New Love-Starved Bitch
Author's Gold Edition

friend, Dillon did the right thing when he brought up the football season that was headed for the Super Bowl in January. It was a subject that Ray did not mind handling.

While Dillon glorified the Oakland Raiders, Ray found himself meditative on the ills of his life. He had desired to be like other men have a wife, kids, and a nice home, it had not happened. As he pondered years passed, Ray revisited the idea of having a woman who would love him for himself. Dillon could tell how bad things were for his old friend by the sadness that had seeped from Ray's deep voice. Frankly, Dillon thought it was never too late for a decent man like Ray to find happiness. Ray had as much going for him as did his respected lawyer brother Eric, and his world famous track star brother, Shane. To Dillon he was in good shape, had maintained the handsome physique and looks that drove women crazy at Oakland High School. No doubt, Dillon knew that Ray would be an excellent catch for Dana Ann Arbor. Dressed in a black denim jean outfit, wearing his Oakland Raiders, silver and black cap, Dillon could not wait to give Ray his business card.

"Well," Dillon said, shaking Ray's hand, "here's my card! "Call me sometimes oaky?"

"Ray placed the card in the top left pocket of his blue jump suit, under the white thread that spelled out his name. "Thank you, man. I will call," Ray answered. He flashed his brilliant smile and then he walked in the opposite direction from Dillon.

Back at the line, Dana Ann assisted an elderly woman who had dropped Seven-up on the gray concrete floor. The cute janitor that Dillon had been talking to showed up with his mop to clean up the spill. When he stood face to face with Dana Ann, their love-starved eyes locked into one another. Love was instantaneously launched. Dillon, who saw what happened, was stunned. Observers in the line backed away from Dana Ann and Ray as if they had seen an alien. Suddenly, an aura formed a ring around the janitor and the author that affirmed this mutual trade of matched feelings of

CAROL D. MITCHELL

love. An untapped source of destiny sealed two strangers without words, with strength, power and promises that neither of them was yet aware of. They knew it was love. Ray, wearing a black fur cap with a white puma emblazoned center of his head smiled at Dana Ann. Dana Ann marveled at his perfect teeth, the shininess of his vast ring of curls, and at how smooth his chestnut brown blemish free skin was. His flawless face rich as brown gravy made her want to kiss him. Feeling his shyness, Dana noticed how unused a man he appeared to be. From the moment they met, neither could take their eyes off the other. To him, she was the ray of sunlight in the haze of this bitter cold winter afternoon. She was to him, absolutely dazzling. Her freshly coifed nut brown hair was shaped altogether around her dark chiseled chin. Soft brown curls framed a virtuous round face, and dropped in soft tendrils, nigh of touching her shoulders. Her caliginous skin was the picturesque, canvas for her evenly slanted, sexy, sparkling, brown eyes. Her sensually naked lips were natural, full, and were teasingly inviting. Although the petite Dana Ann was smug in her black London Fog overcoat, Ray noticed her knotted belt secured a healthy, but perfect figure. The janitor, who had taken himself out of the game of love, felt love at once for the stunning author. An expert at covering up his feelings, Ray moved his mop in soft, caring sweeping motions, as he allowed his innermost feelings to waken from the dead of his heart and stream into hers. He cleaned up the spill, secretly admiring her from every angle and she did the same with him. Fully aware of what was happening to his boss and his friend, Dillon excused himself, telling Dana Ann he had business to take care of across the hall. Unable to figure out what do about what was happening before his eyes, Dillon re-entered the picture knowing he simply could not introduce Dana Ann to another deadbeat man. However, to him, Ray was not a deadbeat, he decided then to introduce the two before he and Dana Ann left.

"Before I go and get Pat and the kids, Dana Ann, I thought maybe you would like to meet Ray," he said, pulling the two closer together. Ray was not used to meeting women this way. As the silence of their introduction came into fruition, Ray's shyness left him feeling stiff and bashful. Dana Ann could not take her eyes off the good-looking tall man with the exceptional body. She recognized his shyness immediately. She liked Ray. He had a cute way of smiling at her as if she was the only ray of sunlight that had ever lit up his eyes before. Ray felt his knees buckling. Not since the days of Carla Jeanette Scott, had he felt this way. He tucked his head into his chest, as he recognized these feelings towards this incredible woman were feelings he had been told by his mother to avoid and he had. With the belief that his natural feelings could lead him into trouble, Ray politely excused himself.

Rovella Starr

The New Love-Starved Bitch

Author's Gold Edition

"Thanks for the introduction Ms. Ann," he said, bowing slightly. "It sho' was nice to meet you today ma'am," he stated, with a country drawl and a magnificent smile. "Sam, I believe is waiting for me to get back to sign my work tally sheets," he said. The kind man then tipped his black fur hat to the author, letting free mounds of black hair that was rich with texture and beautified with corals of natural dark ringlets rest freely on his blushed cheeks. Positioning his cap back on his head, Ray said goodbye to Dana Ann and Dillon again. Before Dana Ann could say anything back to the shy man, he was swiftly on his way out of the door, headed back to the Law Library and the Medical Records Department.

Feeling that something special had happened to her today, on her way home from downtown Oakland, California, Dana Ann said little to Dillon. She made it a point not to refer to or speak about the janitor. However, December 10, 1999 was a special day to Dana Ann and to Ray J.T. Starr, for this was the day marking a new beginning for the two most unlikely love pairings that this world would ever see.

CAROL D. MITCHELL

In This Corner

When Ray made it back to Medical Records, Sam told him to go to the third floor and set up the East conference room for a meeting Monday morning. He did that. Next, the happy Ray took the elevator up to the sixth floor where he sat at the table to fill out his daily tally worksheet. With nothing before him but a dusty window, that revealed to him the coming rain; Ray scanned his watch to see that he still had a half-hour remaining on the job before his workday was over. He had filled out the tally sheet before him hundreds of times, and had never even thought about it before. Today, thoughts of the exquisite author he met on Oak Street brought tears of joy to his brown eyes. Thinking about her, with her ebon skin and her sexy brown eyes – Ray had great difficulty filling out his worksheet today. No woman had stayed with him like this woman was staying with him now. She was so well mannered and polite and the way she looked at him had penetrated his heart to the bone. Not only had he seen her staring at him as he mopped up the spill; he could feel her eyes scanning his body. With each stroke of the mop, Ray felt her eyes reaching beneath his exterior. Like no woman had done before, not even Carla Jeanette Scott, this woman had found the key to his heart. For no reason that he could explain to himself, God let him see that Dana Ann Arbor had all the signs of being a woman that Ray J.T. Starr felt he could keep.

As he contemplated the ideal of his special lady, ray knew that she was rich, so she dispelled Rovella's warning about women needing his money. Therefore, he knew that she would not play the games with him that women sometimes play. She was smart enough to understand what medication could do to a man's manhood and she would be patient about that. He knew she would not rush him for sex and that she would wait and let God dictate nature's course for their love. He was sure that she could have any man she wanted and if all he ever got out of her was a date, what they shared today at the Department of Records would be a fine enough memory for him.

As he sat at the janitor's table shuffling the papers he had to fill out, Ray took off his hat, then he combed his large hands through his hair. Unable to do his work, he fantasized what it would be like to kiss her on the

Rovella Starr
The New Love-Starved Bitch
Author's Gold Edition

mouth? Could he learn how to go all the way with her gently and carefully, the way Eric told him a good man was supposed to do to a woman? Shane said that a woman was like a fine piece of crystal that he should handle gently and not break. Ray frowned, as reality was a sobering awakening to him. What had he been thinking? A fine beautiful black woman like her with her reputation and class and alley cat eyes would have nothing to do with him. He was only a janitor for the Alameda Government Records Department. Ray knew that she had her own money. He knew that he did not make the kind of money that would impress a woman like her. Putting his hat back on he thought, the best he could do for the author; would be to take her to Applebee's in Alameda. "Oh my God," he thought. "I can't think of her this way anymore!"

    In an attempt to forget about her, Ray resorted to filling out his work tally sheets until the thought of her crept back into his mind again suddenly, he was concerned about things about himself that he presumed were not worthy of thought. An hour had gone by and he still had not finished the sheets he normally would have finished and had filled out in minutes. What he was doing was silly. Reality revealed to him that at age fifty-one he was technically, still a virgin. He had never had sex all the way with a woman before. A few years back a lady he knew let him stick it in one time, but when her husband put the key in the door, Ray leaped out of the woman's bedroom window before anything happened. He had never kissed a woman fully on the lips before. A woman like Dana Ann would never want him because she was probably dating men in two piece suits whose office he had cleaned. Ray was sure that the men she dated were most certainly the kind of men who could take her to San Francisco's finest restaurants, where the food started at $150.00 a plate. With that, Rovella would kill him if she found out he spent more than $20.00 on a woman. Because of the true reality of the impossibilities of being with Dana Ann, Ray stopped thinking about her again and completed his paperwork. Later, he vowed never to think about Dana Ann Arbor again. Being with her was nothing more than a fantasy. If he was never sure anything, Ray was sure he could not have the only woman

CAROL D. MITCHELL

he ever met who beat off all that his mother said about black women. Dana Ann gave him that funny feeling in his heart that his brother Eric, once told him was love.

Rovella Starr had been watching her son crawl out of a shell he had been in for over thirty-years. Ray's sudden mutation left her wondering where she had gone wrong. For a couple of weeks now, Ray walked around the house with spring in his step. He was happier than Rovella had seen him in years. The world's quintessential Mama's boy was acting like he had met somebody. Now the aged Rovella Starr was activated with suspicion as she worried about her son's behavior. For over half of her life, Ray had been her main investment. The dividends he had rendered for her efforts belonged to her. Zebbie left her well off financially; but, Ray gave her the paychecks from three of his jobs. He took care of the grocery shopping. Ray took such great care of Rovella that she didn't have to worry about the property she stole from Joe Bullet. With Joe the only heir to Teresa's estate, after Peter remarried and moved to Los Angeles, Rovella returned to Tulsa Oklahoma courts. The only stipulation in her win was that she split the proceeds of the sale of Teresa Bullet's estate with Joe Bullet. With no interest in leaving Joe penniless, Rovella decided she would give Joe his share of the estate when he asked for it.

Right now Ray was threatening her emotional security. The aging Rovella Starr was as treacherous as she had been back in Tulsa. If anybody knew that it was the neighbors on Market Street, for half the block had either seen or been threatened by Rovella's brown, sawed-off shotgun. Sitting by the front window waiting for Ray with her rifle in tow, Rovella had ugly thoughts.

"If that bitch Maxine don't get that ugly white French poodle off of my front law, I am going to kill it one day, so help me God."

Rovella watched Maxine yank the dog's collar to get him off her lawn and swore she was feeding that dog crack. Last year Maxine braved the steps of Rovella's lawn to tell her not to aim her rifle at her dog again. Rovella scanned that old drugged out Maxine like she was crazy. Maxine did not like anything better than she did her crack pipe. She didn't give a damn about that dog, other than to make people think she had some culture. She could not afford to give the little skinny thing a chicken bone. One day Rovella shot at the poodle in front of the nagging bitch. When she missed, (intentionally), Maxine ran down Market Street with her dog in tow threatening to call the police. It took Maxine a year to walk that skinny ass dog past her house again. Rovella smiled and waved to Maxine from where she was sitting at the front window. Maxine, a thin bitch nervously smiled back politely

Rovella Starr
The New Love-Starved Bitch
Author's Gold Edition

because she knew Rovella Starr was the craziest bitch alive. For a while now everybody had heard about what she did to poor Mattie Mae. The French Mafia had nothing on Rovella Starr.

With Maxine and her dog out of sight, Rovella diverted her attention to the matter at hand. She had been so successful in killing her son's living spirit that seeing him come alive again, was a threat to her security and happiness. When Ray began buying new clothes, Rovella waited for him to go to work. She searched his room finding books on *"How to Please a Woman."* And she found another book entitled: *"Dating out of Your Class."* Most notably, Rovella found six books by a local author named, Dana Ann Arbor. Puzzled, she could not figure out why Ray would be interested in Arbor's books when he had always read about science of anthropology. Surprisingly, Rovella found an Arbor book entitled: *"Forever in this Life Time."* Turning the book over, she looked at her picture and had to admit even to self, that Dana Ann Arbor was gorgeous. She laughed. To her there was no way in the world that a woman like her would have anything to do with her Ray. Rovella knew she had done her job well on her son. To her she had protected him from the evil doings of women, as she had planned to do fifty-one years ago when her son was born dead. As she sat by the window this cold winter morn, she would wait for Ray to come home for lunch to have a talk with her son about her new discoveries.

While a deranged mother camped in the living room of her West Oakland home waiting for her son to come home with a shotgun on her lap, her son's love interest, a very wealthy writer had fallen in love. Following a long day of social lunches, bullshit talking and two book signings, one with *Stanley Crouch* and the other with *Terry McMillan*, Dana Ann Arbor soothed her tired skin with a bubble bath and re-kindled her meeting with Ray, care of a good *Danielle Steele* novel. When the telephone rang, she held a dispassionate talk with Dillon. She didn't want to talk to him. Three weeks was long enough to forget about the janitor, but she had not forgotten about him. In his usual business fashion, Dillon shot off the good news about

CAROL D. MITCHELL

MGM Studios wanting to offer her a movie deal for her first novel, *"Forever in this Life Time."* The whole time he talked about the deal, Dana Ann wished that he would mention Ray. He didn't. Instead, Dillon told her that the movie deal with worth six-figures and that the studio was already talking to Halle Berry and Angela Bassett for starring roles. She was already rich and she had enough money to last her two lifetimes. With love at the front of her mind, she didn't care about much else. She had built one charity after another for abused children in West Oakland and was now working on an organization for unwed teen mothers. These accomplishments have been her lifelong dreams. Now her dream was to see the janitor, named Ray Starr again. With one effort after another, she failed to forget about him for his love had hit her like a boulder and there was no way on god's earth for her to hide those feelings. Knowing her well enough to detect that she was distracted, Dillon talked about books and movie deals more as he attempted to justify his suspicions that perhaps Dana Ann had a major distraction on her mind. He asked her three questions. She had not responded to one of them because though she was on the telephone with him, her mind was elsewhere. Dana Ann's constant thoughts of Ray made her miss what Dillon said about her upcoming three-month international tour to Chicago, and, Singapore. Privately, she prayed that Dillon would mention Ray. Frustrated, this was not going to happen she wondered if Dillon even knew what the important question of the day really was. It was unusual for him not to get her and be intuitive. As Dillon rambled on about business, to Dana Ann he might as well have been talking Chinese. Surely, he had seen what happened to her and Ray at the Records Department. To date, Dillon had not mentioned the subject of the meeting to Dana Ann. Now, the author, the genius, who had won the Pulitzer prize for her journalism genius; the one who had dinner with *President, Bill Clinton*; and, the one who had met the *British Prime Minister Blair*, three times, could not come up with a sentence to ask Dillon one simple question.

"How is your friend, Ray?" (*She thought*).

Tonight, as she held the telephone to her ear; her thoughts of Ray swept her away. Suddenly, she heard Dillon calling her. She answered back quickly,

"Yes, I am here." She then stuttered through breaths as she hurried to jump back to the reality of her business with her employee. On the other end of the telephone, Dillon knew that Dana Ann liked his friend, Ray. This time however, he was going to let her sweat it out and be sure this was what she wanted before he threw his horse into the race. He listened to her okay

Rovella Starr
The New Love-Starved Bitch
Author's Gold Edition

the movie deal, the tour dates and he had eagerly waited to end this conversation with his boss.

Frustrated, Dana spoke: "Do whatever Dillon!" she yelled. Catching herself, she amended, "You know what I mean. Make the deals and bring me the papers to sign," she ordered. For all he knew Dana Ann would sign over her life and all she owned to see Ray again. On the other end of the line, Dillon and his wife Pat both laughed at the "in love" Dana Ann, the author who was so in love it was cute to the both of them. Dillon had been there for her for so long, the truth was that he only called to make sure that his instincts about her feelings for Ray were on the mark. She already knew about the book deals and movie deals. With business all in order Dillon had the truth he had been seeking from her. Now that he had his answer, he was going to surprise her next Saturday and bring Ray to her book signing at Nordstrom's. The date was already set.

With Pat standing nearby playing the tease game with her husband, Dana Ann picked up on the amusement; but, she was not ready to show her hand yet either.

"Oh, I see now. Well, Dillon, you tell Pat I said hello," Dana Ann smiled. "She's giggling back there. I don't know what you two are up to, but you had better watch out," she teased. They all laughed joyfully.

"Kiss the kids for me. Handle your business and I will see you on Saturday at Nordstrom's," she ended.

"You got it! Later," Dillon chimed, before hanging up the telephone.

When the loud bang rang out from Rovella Starr's house on Market Street, the neighbors barely paid attention to it. The sounds of loud bangs were a regular fixture in this neighborhood as was the sounds of sirens that roared through the streets each night. Nobody gave a shit about a dead nigga or one who got shot and that was not a new reaction from the locals regarding the steady stream of crime in West Oakland, California. Who shot who was not the question and the reasonable defense to loud boom noises was to

CAROL D. MITCHELL

lay low in case the bullet would ricochet and accidentally landed on you; however, this winter eve, one Thursday, in 1999 the gunshots started earlier than usual. Maxine, Wilma and Barbara snatched up their dogs and cats, and then they raced into their homes on Market Street with only one question in mind. Who did Ms. Rovella Starr shoot at this time?

Minutes after the blast, the Oakland Police had not come yet, however, two familiar faces raced up the steps of Rovella Starr's house. With recognition that it was Eric and Shane, the neighborhood, in usual fashion went inside their homes and commenced to minding their own business. Whatever happened in that Starr house tonight, the Oakland Police Department would mark it as a low priority. Therefore, for the resident's on Market Street, there was no use risking what little security they had in this town waiting and looking out the window for protection where there was none. One more dead nigga was just, a dead nigga. Dead niggas in West Oakland meant one less problem for the white man to deal with and that is on the real.

While Shane called the *Oakland Police Department*, Eric advised his mother not to implicate herself in the shooting and sit her ass down. He told his mother to stop crying about it, and be the fuck quiet when the cops did come. Shane asked Rovella what happened, Rovella told Eric she was sitting down by the window with the gun in her lap waiting for Ray to come home. She said she had found some books in Ray's room to indicate he was getting involved with some author and that all she wanted to do was talk to Ray about it. She said that Ray normally comes in from his second job at about 7:00 P.M., but, when he didn't show up at that time she sat and sat until the next thing she knew she had dozed off to sleep. She said later, at about 8:00 P.M., she heard footsteps coming up the stairs. Ray, she said normally does not come in that way; instead, he comes in at the side entrance. She said she got scared, she aimed the rifle at what she thought was an intruder; but, before she knew it the gun had gone off accidentally and she shot Ray by mistake. The bewildered woman was frantically crying, as the shocked Ray lay still in one spot on the living room floor under the fireplace. He was more startled about what his mother had done to him, than he was hurt or injured. Fortunately, upon examination of the leg wound, Shane concluded the shot to Ray's left leg was superficial and had barely scrapped his skin.

"Is he gonna be alright baby?" Rovella asked Shane. As Ray pleaded for his brothers not to do anything that would put Rovella in jail. Shane lifted up the blind to see if the police or the ambulance had come yet as Ray tried to defend his mother.

Rovella Starr
The New Love-Starved Bitch
Author's Gold Edition

"Man, she didn't mean to shoot me! Mama ain't used to nobody coming in through the front door. At work Sam took my keys out of my locker man and this was the only key I had to that side door, so I had to use my key to the front door," he explained.

"Man, be cool until the ambulance comes. You still have to go the hospital to get this bleeding wound checked out," Eric said.

"And Mama, when you called me, I thought you had killed Ray, the way you were hollering," Eric stated.

"You need to think about getting rid of that gun, Mama. I am surprised the Oakland Police haven't put you in jail for all of the times you have blasted that thing," he said. Upset that Ray was still living at home and that he had not branched away from the house since the 70's it was hard for Shane to hold his grief inside anymore. Unlike Eric, Shane had not appreciated being shipped to Mattie every year, while Rovella always let Ray stay home. She didn't miss his track meets, but he'd never forget how his mother terrorized people if he didn't get first place. She embarrassed him as she had embarrassed their father and others. Unlike Eric, Shane hated Rovella for a lot, least of those being the hold she had on his brother, Ray. Shane had made dozens of efforts to help his brother break away from the controls of his mother, since Rovella would not even let him go to Tulsa to see their grandmother Mattie Mae, when they were children. Somehow, Rovella won Ray over to Shane by making him feel that no woman was good enough for him; not even his own grandmother, and that it was Ray's birthright to replace Zebbie because Rovella thought he had been born dead. Over the years, Shane had detected that his mother's fear of being alone was real. Though Ray had long since distanced himself from his mother, Rovella had yet to let go. Eric, on the other hand preferred to stay on the dial of denial about all things concerning his attractive mother, Rovella Starr. But, with what happened tonight, it was difficult for Shane to hide his feelings about his mother and Ray anymore. With Rovella getting older and perhaps senile, Shane was scared for his brother, Ray. With Ray safe after he tied a rag around his bleeding wound, Shane focused more on Rovella, who was beside herself with grief over what she had done to her baby.

"Mother, you cry over this now huh? Dad is dead because this was the day he regretted seeing, mother!" Shane hollered. "You never regret what you do, mother. You are an evil woman. You controlled the funeral, and pulled Ray aside then and told him not to mourn his own father! You tortured people at my track meets and threatened judges. You hated the nuns, running one completely out of the ministry. I couldn't believe you!" Shane shouted. Eric, who kept looking out of the window for the police, covered his mouth to think, and to hold back his anger at Shane for talking to his mother this way. Shane was shouting loud enough for everybody to hear and he continued to vent. Shane was walking around his brother Ray. He cased up to Rovella, looking directly into her sad face. The fine man was dressed handsomely in a new white Nike jogging suit with matching sneakers. He shook with anger, as he continued to spill his guts. Only the dim night light on the neat living room side table remained on, leaving Shane only enough light to lean down and speak right into Rovella's mean, green eyes.

"When I got into the AAU and track, I was running from you!" Shane screamed, pointing his finger in her face. "You have been doing bad things to people all of your life! When is it going to end mother? Nadine and Paula won't even let…" Eric turned away from the window to shut his brother down…

"Come on man," Eric shouted, through clinched teeth. The lawyer, the conservative one in the family had heard enough from Shane.

"Paula's my wife. Little Zebbie's my son! Come on man," Eric said. He continued, "my families my business," he defended. Shane stepped over Ray to confront Eric:

"No man. When Mama starts shooting to kill it's all of our business. Running people away, hurting others, possessiveness, cruelty to others! You're a lawyer. You take people to court for less. Madness is the theme of Mom's life. She shot her own son!"

With tension building inside this house, Eric seized the reins of control. He did not like Rovella anymore than Shane did, but he was a matured man who knew this was not the time to challenge or to itemize his mother's lifetime of wrong doings.

"Shut up!" Eric ordered to Shane. Dressed professionally in a smart, dark blue suit, wearing a white shirt and red tie, the handsome first son of Rovella, had settled a multi-million dollar discrimination case. He was used to being calm under pressure. Tonight Eric was calm and in control.

Rovella Starr
The New Love-Starved Bitch
Author's Gold Edition

"If you feel that bad man, leave. I can handle this. You might say the wrong thing to the cops, and then what?" Eric pleaded to Shane. Disgusted, Shane relinquished and backed away from his brother to have a seat on the couch. Rovella quietly told Shane the shooting was an accident. Still gorgeous and dressed in a tight, red silk nightgown, with her glowing black hair flowing down her back; Rovella was activated by the action going on tonight.

"I ain't saying it again Shane. I was sleep. I didn't see Ray come through the door goddamn-it you fool!" Rovella shouted.

"I'm not Dad or Joe Bullet!' Shane hollered.
Eric said "Both of you stop it!' coming between the mother and son.

"Shane, this ain't the time for all of this. Ray has been shot, man. When the authorities arrive we have to be rational. And, you and Mama don't need to say a damn word. You can't say these kinds of things around cops." Eric warned the two of them. Shane leaped off the couch to attack Eric. Eric stuck his arm out firmly defending his reach, as Ray feared the worse and closed his eyes. Eric clenched his teeth:

"I wish you would man," he threatened. The brothers faced one another in a mad stare down, with Rovella shrinking in her chair. In and out of consciousness, Ray, still lay on the floor pretending what happened to him was not that bad. Eric then took a deep breath to keep from slamming his brother Shane to the floor. He checked on Ray, who signaled he was okay.

"Shane. I am gonna need you to calm your ass down. Mama ain't in any condition man to be hearing all of this drama right now. And, I ain't gonna fight you," Eric stated. Shane jumped into Eric's face anyway. He and Eric had never been close. Given the opportunity, Shane was stronger and he could ring Eric's neck; but, he knew this was not the time for it.

"She could have killed Ray man," Shane cried, expressing concern for his younger brother. With tears streaming down his face, Ray rolled over on the floor, doing everything to hide his pain. He didn't want his brothers to hurt his mother. He had to be strong. "And, this is all you gonna do is defend Mother? Well you handle it man. She paid a lot of money for you to clean up her life's mess. You're Rovella's flunky too like everybody else. Go

CAROL D. MITCHELL

for it bro.' I don't want to ever see her again," Shane cried, before storming out of the house. Shane's struggle with his upbringing had remained quiet for many years. Close to both Mattie and Zebbie, he had good reason to despise his mother. His outburst surprised the whole family because Shane had been the quiet one in the family, but this grand stand came at the wrong time for him to command this stage.

With Shane gone, as Rovella cried, she was not crying for Shane. While Eric and Shane fought, Rovella prayed that Ray would be okay. She saw him drifting in and out of consciousness and she was worried. Tonight, her youngest son lay on this cold wood floor near the front door where she shot him, holding on tightly to his wounded leg wishing that the noise would stop. Fifteen-minutes later, the Paramedics arrived. They treated the bloody superficial wound. Later they told Ray he'd be alright; but, to stay off of the leg for a few days and be careful. After they left, Ray forgave Rovella, regardless of the fact that Officer Jenkins, of the Oakland, Police Department told Eric that had Rovella been holding the gun up one inch higher she would have killed Ray.

Glad that Shane was not here to witness anything; Ray told the officer he was not interested in pressing charges or going to the hospital. With Eric standing nearby shaking his head no to everything, the officer that showed up to take report knew Eric. They were good friends and Eric pretty much dictated what happened next. A few minutes later, the SWAT team and the police were gone. Eric waited for Rovella to go to sleep. He took hours counseling his brother Ray to take the pressure off of his mother and get a life, preferably away from Rovella. Eric left.

The shooting experiences made Ray think of Dana Ann. The mere thought of not seeing Dana Ann again raced through his heart like a wildfire. Shaking off the residual effects of his injury, the strong man visibly shook. In a hurry to put this night behind him, Ray privately took the blame for the accident. He loved his mother with all of his heart, but Eric and Shane were both right. He had to get away from Rovella.

Rovella Starr

The New Love-Starved Bitch

Author's Gold Edition

Love in Full Bloom

In college, Beatrice Griffith told best friend, Dana Ann that after grad school she was going to be the next ambassador to Africa. Instead, the USC class valedictorian moved from Los Angeles to Oakland, California and married a garbage man. Now, some twenty-years later, the mother of five boys had yet to go out and use her most coveted degree for anything. Hers was the enviable, *"stay at home mother lifestyle"* that Dana Ann Arbor had wished for. Beatrice was a strong black woman who had her feet planted solidly on the ground. Happy in a marriage that was now twenty-years old, Beatrice Griffith was a true inspiration to Dana Ann Arbor and she was a great best friend.

When all professional writers wanted to do was talk mainly about this the business, Dana Ann called Beatrice for truth and candor in their many personal telephone conversations. Dana Ann was lucky to have Beatrice as a friend. However, she knew Beatrice well enough to know that she would never see eye to eye with her on the subject of Ray J.T. Starr. Knowing this, Dana took her time to tell Beatrice about Ray. For weeks, the blooming love in her heart was her truest secret. To make sure that what she was feeling for this handsome man was not simply a fluke, Dana Ann dated other men with failed efforts that hastened her feelings to know Ray better. By now she was aware that Ray was challenged and that he was not the man anyone expected her to be with. Fearful that there was no one else to talk about him to, Dana Ann Arbor was going to put her anxious advice to Beatrice, who she knew would if nothing else clarify and find pragmatism to a situation that had clearly blinded her. Nothing she ever told Beatrice or Dillon ended up in the tabloids.

CAROL D. MITCHELL

Beatrice was perspicacious enough to have warned her that her previous marriages to Doctor Frank Michaels and then later to Zim Danube were choice mistakes. She summed those bad choices up by telling her that sometimes worms can hide in an apple and you will not see it until the last bite! The tone of her conversation with her friend this cold Friday evening was surprisingly supportive.

"So what's going on and to what do I owe the pleasure of this call?" Beatrice asked Dana.

"Not much. Just need to talk to you for a minute. How are Eddie and the kids?"

"Fine! Fine, and let's get over the bullshit!" she answered.

"Okay!"

"Okay?" Beatrice asked, "sounds important to me. I think girlfriend I is best to sit down. Sounds like man trouble to me," she chided.

"To sum it up, I met him at the Alameda Record's Department in downtown Oakland, about three weeks ago. Shoot girl. The TV's too loud and I can't hear myself talking to you. I will tell you the rest when I turn that thing down," she apologized. Dana Ann laid the phone down for a minute, while Beatrice waited for this good story to start; she heard the news caster's voice on the other end suddenly go silent. Soon she heard Dana Ann's feet tapping closer to the phone. "You there?"

"Yes. I am here," Beatrice answered, eagerly.

"Brenda was gone somewhere with her brother Richard, so Dillon and me we went down there to stand in a long line for research materials," she said, getting comfortable on her Cort furniture. "A lady spilled a soda. He came with the mop. I saw him, he saw me and I have not thought about anything else since that day. Bee, for me to feel this way about somebody after Frank and Zim…He was standing there with this mop, wearing this cute black fur hat and everything about him was it! I could see him; I could feel him from ten feet away. Our eyes met and it felt so special, so good, and so real. And then Dillon pulled us together and it took him forever to do that. He was so shy, yes; I remember how shy he was. He's a janitor for the Government of Alameda County. So, go ahead and criticize me and get it over with Bee."

"Dana Ann ain't nothing wrong with that. Now, the drama in your tone is what worries me. Girl, you must really like this man a lot. A janitor?" she asked. "Don't let that be the reason. Nowadays with the scarcity of men out there the pickings are slim and ain't nothing wrong with being with a janitor, girlfriend. I mean, at least the brother got a job. This is some hot stuff, Dana. So what you gonna do now about getting with him or have you already?"

Rovella Starr
The New Love-Starved Bitch
Author's Gold Edition

"Bee, already what?"

"Had sex," Beatrice said.

"It's been so long since I've been with anybody, Bee. I don't know what to say to a man anymore. I'm in my forties. I'd look like a fool going down to the Government to talk to this man. I can't just go down to Oak Street and get the man. People know me too well in Oakland. The problem is he's Dillon's friend, but Dillon is acting like nothing happened. Do you think I should do it myself? Get with him? Or, do you think I ought to ask Dillon to hook us up?"

"Dana, Dana, Dana. Maybe this janitor already asked Dillon about you. Maybe Dillon hasn't told you anything because he was the one who hooked you up with the drug addict basketball star. No. I don't think you need to tell Dillon how you feel about this guy. Knowing that nigga like I do, he done probably already told Ray what time it is. Call Dillon and have him bring the guy to your book signing tomorrow. He should really be impressed that a star like you has an interest in him," Beatrice said, curtly.

"Bee?"

"Huh?"

"I hear sarcasm in your tone. You don't think I'd intimidate him do you? What do you mean somebody like me? And, Dillon, oh, I talked to Dillon with Pat giggling in the background today. Girl, do you really think if he knew that Ray liked me that he would hold something like that back from me?

"You said he and Pat called laughing on the phone. They know. To answer your question, yes. It was sarcasm. Secondly, Dillon would be hiding the truth if he and his wife are calling you laughing and they have something planned. You know how sneaky brothers are girl. Wait a minute, Dana. You sho' is asking a lot of questions. This really ain't like you. Girl, I don't know if you know this or not, but you would be a hell of a catch for any man. Be real. This man has got to know by now that you are wealthy. Over all of that, the important thing is that you follow your heart, girl. You're due for love. Don't worry about Dillon. He's the same he was back in the day, sly, sneaky and up to no good, girl, he and his fine brother Jerry. He digs the hell out of you. And if the brother is on his P's and Q's, he will righteously have your back. The OLE crusty fool! He's probably calling Ray now telling him how he caught the big fish and asking him, 'Now man, what you gone do bout' that?" she said. They both laughed.

"Bee, I have got to go. You're the greatest!"

"Just one more thing, Dana," she stated.

"What's that?" Dana asked.

" I hope this ain't that janitor that lives with his mother in West Oakland whose father jumped off of the San Francisco Golden Gate Bridge; the one with those fine ass brothers, one a track star and the other one a fine ass lawyer, up there on "Pill Hill." If it is, I would leave that one alone," Bee advised her friend.

"Oh Bee…And, what would all of this have to do with Ray? Don't be foolish. Girl, I'll talk to you later," she said.

Thirty-years after he started working for the Government, Clay E was telling everybody he was leaving the place in two more years and that seemed to put the seal on setting him up for eternal retirement heaven. It used to be that talking about his wild girlfriend, Lozetta Ann's drinking and wrong doings and how bad the Government treated him was all that he and Ray J.T. Starr talked about. For the last three weeks, Clay E spent his entire 9:00 break time talking to a different Ray. Whereas Ray used to talk about riding his Harley or what fish were biting at the Delta or his visits to various science museums in San Francisco, now all he talked about was a berry colored beauty he met in the Government Records Department. He said on Saturday, that Dillon was going to introduce him to this girl again and Ray was so happy about that, he barely would talk about the gunshot wound his mother gave him on Thursday that had twenty-floors buzzing before the lunch hour.

Clay E enjoyed his talks with Ray. Ray was the only person in the Government that believed his old trite, tired pimp daddy stories. With nothing else to base his manhood on, Ray loved to hear how Clay E had fathered fifteen kids and that all the women he had been with loved him, and wanted him back, even though most of his tales were lies. Clay knew that Ray was slow. Having worked with the Government for a number of years, he knew the clicks were hard to get into, so he opened a door for Ray becoming his friend. In the two-years, they had known each other, Clay E was bothered whenever he heard a woman had dumped or used Ray. As the Monday morning story goes, Ray was dropped like a hot potato when a chick

Rovella Starr

The New Love-Starved Bitch

Author's Gold Edition

learned he was on medication for high blood pressure, diabetes and that he was slow. When Ray fell, Clay E was always there to pick him up and he had Ray's psyche as good as gold by Tuesday. Ray told Clay E that all of the medication his mother had him on had virtually took away his manhood, therefore word around the Government had it that Ray was a complete failure bedding down the hot women of Oakland, California. Clay E knew Ray did not trust women and had resigned his life to caring for his mother and working three jobs. When Ray started talking about Dana Ann, Clay E felt sorry for his friend. He knew after he told him about her that this was a woman that Ray would never be able to net, and if he had not been Ray's friend, he would have laughed him out of the Government. But, he was Ray's friend, and as good friends do, Clay E listened, and then he co-signed on Ray's desires, hoping that somewhere in the mix of Ray's meeting this woman again that God had a miracle waiting for his buddy. So every day at 9:00 A.M., Clay E had to mentally prepare himself to listen to how glad Ray said he would be when he met this dream girl. When all was said and done, This Dana Ann was closer to being more like the impossible dream to Clay E.

    Thelma, Clay E's ex-wife worked at the Oakland Police Department. She called Clay E at two in the morning, to tell him that Rovella had shot Ray and he was okay. Today as Ray tripped across 12th Street to Oak Street holding onto his familiar white Styrofoam coffee cup, his limp was slight, but the smile on his face could not have been bigger.

    "Hey man, good to see you today," Clay E said, pointing to Ray's leg. "Shit happens man," he said, tossing his hands in the air. Ray's curt response to Clay E let him know that Ray was not open to talking about the shooting.

    "Nice weather for winter too huh?" asked Clay E.
"Man, Dillon called last night. He said tomorrow that he's gonna set up a date for me to spend some time with Dana Ann. It's supposed to be a surprise for her man!" Ray said.

    Feeling sorry that his friend had such high expectations for his love conquest, Clay E did not want to be the one to feed into Ray's latest day-

CAROL D. MITCHELL

dream, especially after what happened to him last night. In fact, he was hoping that this long dream of Ray's would be over by now. However, the hurt Ray told Clay E about became a lost reality to this man who seemingly wore hurt without feeling the sting of the pain. As Ray talked about Dana Ann, Clay was lost in remembrance of two-years of suffering that he had seen Ray go through, not to mention the pain Rovella put him through constantly. He was afraid that as soon as this writer realized what she had in Ray the pain of her rejection of his friend would be too much for him to bear. Clay feared soon as the author found out Ray couldn't have sex with her and how lame he was, she'd be gone in a flash. The mere thought of his friend having this kind of pain before him made fifty-six year old Clay E run his fingers through his thinning hair, thinking maybe he could offer his friend a challenge that would make him face reality better and forget about Dana Ann.

"Ray, a woman with that much talent, I mean like what that author has, would be a real hot potato for a man like you to keep up with. I'm letting you know that in case you get hurt, man!"

"Clay, you are a real friend. I think she likes me though. She would never hurt me like any of the others, man," Ray offered.

"She probably does man. I mean, like you, that is. But, you have got to remember, blood. You are a janitor. Even women that you have dated in the ghetto have put you down for that, Ray. Do you really think a high class rich woman like Dana Ann Arbor would really be the right match for you?" Ray frowned. He placed his coffee cup down and rubbed his injured leg. Clay wanted to mention the shooting again, he didn't.

"Clay E, you don't think Dana Ann likes me do you man? You really think that a woman like that wouldn't have anything to do with me?" he asked.

"Oh man. I ain't saying that. Look-a-here, we work for the Government man. That woman is a multi-millionaire. She dates doctors, lawyers and professional sports stars and shit like that man. These men drive fancy cars. They have money to take her places that you can't take her on a janitor's salary, man. "Look," he said, turning around on the bench to face Ray. "You drive an old Green Jeep Cherokee. You own a nice motorcycle and you live with your crazy ass mother who shot you last night and almost killed you. She dictates your life to you man and ain't no woman in her right mind gonna stay around a man who lives with their mother, especially a black one!' he stated.

"Clay E, Rovella lives with me. That's my home, man. She didn't shoot me," he defended in frustration. "She told my brothers' that the gun

Rovella Starr
The New Love-Starved Bitch
Author's Gold Edition

went off accidentally, man," he stated. "I do what I want to do," Ray declared.

"Ray you can tell all of this to women you meet, but I know the real deal man. I'm telling you all of this so you don't get hurt, man. Remember, I am the one who has been married four times. I have been on the job for thirty-years. I know women both ghetto and successful. One thing I can tell you about a woman Ray is that class does not mean a thing when it comes to a woman's romantic expectations. And, a woman ain't gone want no man who lives with his Mama and who is resistant to change, bottom line," Clay E stated. When Ray bowed his head to his chest, Clay E knew he had been too hard on his slow buddy. He searched the silence they sat in for something more optimistic to put down to his friend, but all he could come up with was the truth.

"Maybe it will work man. I'm sorry. I don't want to see you get hurt. Women won't see you as a viable mate living like you living man. The truth hurts man, but if I didn't care about you Ray, I wouldn't be telling you these things ten-minutes after our break time is over. And, look," Clay said, pointing to a man across the street. "There goes that prankster mutha-fucka, Sam, he's probably the one that called and told everybody that Rovella shot you last night. Just look at that nigga, that drunk. He don't even come to the AA meetings anymore," laughed Clay E. Clay E was so funny to Ray, when he talked about Sam. Ray laughed from his belly. Clay looked back at his friend and was happy to see that Ray was laughing.

"I guess you are right, Clay E," he stated. "You have a lot more experience with women than I do. I am listening man," he said, as he poured the last of his coffee down his throat. Ray crushed the Styrofoam cup. Next, his laughter turned into a smile as Clay E., changed the subject to his latest drama on Lozetta Ann. Clay talked about his wild woman from Sacramento, while Ray smiled warmly at his friend. He nodded his assent to make Clay think that he was listening to every word he said. Clay E's mouth moved, Ray traveled to the memorable words of Dillon.

CAROL D. MITCHELL

"Man, she can't wait to see you. Plan something nice for her on Saturday, man and don't tell Rovella anything. Handle your business, man," Dillon said. And Ray was about to do just that!

Rovella Starr

The New Love-Starved Bitch

Author's Gold Edition

A Time to Remember

    The people that were in line to meet Dana Ann Arbor today agreed with book reviewers around the world who said that *"Never Let Go of The Rainbow,"* which had climbed its' way up the New York Time's Best Seller's list to number five in just two weeks, was the star writer's best novel yet. The exquisite love story about a blind Russian girl, who miraculously gets her eyesight for the first time on the morning of her wedding, left the question on everybody's mind, *"Where did Dana Ann get her inspiration?"* With the speedy rise of her twenty-seventh novel, natives stated lining up at Nordstrom's in San Francisco, California at 3:00 in the morning to see the prolific author. Today, Dillon, who ordinarily arrived at Arbor's signings early to set up the table posters, books and handouts and to greet the early birds, was absent. Brenda had done Dillon's set up nicely; but, when Brenda offered no defense to her boss concerning Dillon's absence, Dana Ann worried that something had happened to her most tried and true employee. Unfortunately, ABC, CBS and Fox News had sat up cameras to the signing and the distraction of San Francisco's holiday visitors kept Dana Ann much too busy to be thinking about Dillon's non-appearance for too long. San Francisco was having a lovely day. The bright sun picturesque against a perfect blue sky, brought with it birds that were in chorus and the clunky sound of cable cars from which bells sounded loudly, as traffic glided up and down Market Street, making people excited to be walking about the most magnificent city in the world today. People were laughing and the chatter bloomed into tumultuous excitement when the crowd saw Dana Ann take seat in front of Nordstrom's at her signing table, dressed in a lovely ivory-yellow Christian Dior pantsuit. The media had a love affair with Dana-Ann. The story of her Spartan beginnings as an orphan from John and Carol

CAROL D. MITCHELL

Morgan's Chino, California Orphanage had always been news flair with the media and Dana Ann believed that it was the constant media attention on her that propelled her into instant stardom with her writing. Both Oakland and San Francisco had been good to her and local natives from both towns had for seven-years now looked forward to all of her local signings. Many of her readers even traveled with her abroad. As big as this signing was, the only thing on Dana Ann's mind, *(even in Dillon's suspicious absence)* was Ray J.T. Starr. As she thanked readers and issued personal autographs to them, she wondered if she would ever see Ray's fantastic smile again. With a worldwide tour coming up in June of 2000, she knew that if she and Ray were to get anything started, in the way of romance that it would have to begin now. With only six months before her departure, she wanted to have something to come back home to after her tour this time.

Three-hours into the book signing, with Dillon still nowhere in sight, a flustered Brenda informed the author that the book had sold out and that they would have to turn hundreds of fans way. After she signed the last ten copies of the book for the store, Dana Ann lifted her head in time to see that Dillon had finally showed up. Before she could greet him or see whom it was he was with, an older woman broke through the crowd. The attractive woman begged Dana Ann for a signature. She had never seen a human with such striking, deep green eyes.

"Just one more please?" she asked the fine-looking author. Since the woman had her own book, Dana Ann accepted her book and she signed it to serve the old woman's request.

"To whom shall I address it?" She asked the woman with the emer-ald green eyes. The cheerful woman said, *"I'm so happy to see you. I came all the way from Oakland by Bay Area Rapid Transit, (BART) just to see you. I can't believe it's really you!"* the fan stated. She continued…*"Oh, I'm so nervous to be looking at you in person. It's unreal! Just put to Rovella Starr,"* she said excitedly, *"S-t-a-r-r and Rovella is spelled: R-o-v-e-l-l-a,"* she gloated. After the signing, the skinny woman thanked Dana Ann again, and then she happily disappeared.

After apologizing to the rest of her fans for running out of books, the author found herself blinking several times to make sure that she was not dreaming when she saw Dillon and Ray J.T. Starr approaching her. Her initial puzzled face gleamed. Then, Dillon led Ray to where Dana Ann was stand-ing. Dillon apologized to her for being late and Ray had no idea that the woman who was almost hit by a car right behind him, was his raging mother, Rovella. He told her not to worry about the crowd, that he would handle the close. Then in his typical businesslike fashion, Dillon took off to resume clearing up the table where the signing had taken place. Dressed nicely in a

Rovella Starr
The New Love-Starved Bitch
Author's Gold Edition

crisp white Italian Armani designer shirt that was tucked neatly inside a pair of new blue hip-hop style bell-bottom jeans, Ray Starr's limp was barely noticeable as the tall, impressive-looking man was stupendously happy to see the lovely author again.

Unable to say a word to this gorgeous man, the author looked directly into Ray's glistening eyes. She knew that the long wait to see him had been indeed worth it though it had been far too long. While autograph seekers pushed to get closer to the author and flashbulbs shot her directly in the eyes, Dana Ann barely noticed the distractions. As the author and the janitor concentrated solely on each other, the superb background of San Francisco, California dimmed into darkness as Dana Ann thanked God that Ray's most wanted presence was this time more than a figment of her imagination. She had been thinking of him for weeks now. Today, her dream had come true. Within minutes of his arrival, the happy couple made way to the Green Jeep Cherokee that was parked on Kearny Street. Inside the Green Jeep Cherokee he gave her a hug and showered her with praise. When he offered her a getaway to San Francisco's North Beach, she eyed the quiet man who was wearing a smile that never disappeared. Wishing that the Green Jeep Cherokee had closer seats, the happy woman leaned over to touch Ray's right leg to let him know how happy she was to be riding in the Green Jeep Cherokee with him.

"I think I might be lost," he said. She looked at him with bright eyes that were filled with love.

"That's okay. I like riding with you," she stated, in a soft, sweet voice. He adored her already. For as big a star as she was, she had the decorum of a well-bred Debutante. She represented all the things Ray had only dreamed of in a woman. He looked at her now,

"I think you are the sweetest lady that I have ever met," he said. Next, he winked at her in a sexy way. "Have you ever been to North Beach before?" he asked her.

"I probably have. I don't remember a recent trip there," she answered, meeting his happy gaze. When the author realized he was not joking

CAROL D. MITCHELL

she decided to be quiet about it. Knowing how sensitive a man's ego could be over directions. She decided that she was going to be a lady about it and let this wonderful man navigate his own way. She knew exactly how to get to the beach, but she did not want to spoil the day by being a smart ass. As they circled the same streets in San Francisco repeatedly, she was happy to be with her man. There was no impatience here, only happiness and Dana Ann could not dream of spoiling that happiness for him by being a know-it-all.

Later, by the direction of luck and with help from God, soon the happy couple met the scenic rushing shores of North Beach that was trimmed with night-lights and reminded Dana Ann of Oakland' Lake Merritt. Next, the quiet man who many at work called slow, did not want to talk to the smart, lovely woman who with all of her intelligence was smiling at him and not saying a word. Ray was not experienced enough with the opposite sex to start up a conversation. As he remembered some of the slick tactics, he learned from Clay E., on how to please a member of the opposite sex, he dismissed those games. Tonight he was going by his feelings; that was all that he knew. He could tell by the way she kept smiling up to his face that Dana Ann was happy to be in his company. He was not an executive with a big office to take her to; he did not speak eloquently enough to impress her. He was merely a janitor during the day, a janitor during the eves and he loaded the ships in San Francisco all during the night. Over time, he thought he had been doing all of this work because he was the man of the house and this was his role in life according to his mother. Now, when he looked at Dana Ann, to say that he loved her somehow diminished the way he felt about her.

Feeling that Ray was probably intimidated by who she was, Dana Ann, who was the genius with words, struggled to come up with the right words to say to Ray, who had evoked so many good feelings in her. Ray parked the old Green Jeep Cherokee and then he began smiling at her. He then gently took her manicured hand and raised it to his happy face. Next, he kissed her hand in a soft gesture that was the most caring thing any man had ever done for her before. He looked at her chocolate skin into a set of rich almond shaped sparkling brown eyes that made him feel love instantaneously. He could tell this was the woman that he wanted to spend the rest of his life with. However, he knew too that getting to the point of telling her that was going to take some time. As she gently placed her head against his chest; Ray wanted to protect her and it was the first time in his life that he really felt like a man. Tonight as he touched her and looked into her wanting eyes, his body physically began to respond to her warm touch. Then a warm rush

−81−

Rovella Starr

The New Love-Starved Bitch

Author's Gold Edition

raced through his heart and the pills that the doctor had told him would deaden his manhood lay dormant against the power of love that he felt for this woman. And she felt the same. Dana Ann lifted Ray's signature cap off his head having no clue what loving him would mean in real life. Reaching up she kissed him on the forehead. As the quiet man's rich hair blew in circles with the wind, Ray held Dana Ann Arbor's newly braided hair in his hands as she lay comfortably against his sexy, hairy chest. Ray kissed the top of her head as they watched the roaring water of the seas in silence, in the dark, together. She knew that Ray was not talkative and that he was perhaps not as quick as other men she had known, but there was no doubt in her mind that what she was feeling for this man was unique. Every muscle in her body wanted him and every feeling in her mind said that she could make it work. From what he had said to her, it was clear his mother was a dominant force in his life. With her background however, she had dealt with far worse situations. After a few hours together, Ray told Dana Ann about Carla Jeanette Scott. He told her about Joe Bullet, his father and his brothers and his grandmother, Mattie and all of his relatives in Tulsa, Oklahoma. He wanted her to know the important details of his life, especially about his mother. With all that he said, she was not challenged by his mother's dependency on him; rather she could see clearly how the lonely woman could latch on to her son, needing him because she believed she did not have other resources. To her, his mother was co-dependent and she would always respect her need to be with her son and she would do whatever it took to have both of their love. When the time was right, Dana Ann was sure that with the help of God that she could handle his mother. Right now Ray was the only man she wanted and she was glad to be with him at this very moment.

"It was a great surprise to see you with Dillon today. Did he tell you I wanted to see you again, Ray?" Ray smiled. He looked at her with a special radiance in his eyes. He exhibited a sweet, innocent shyness to her that made her easily excited.

CAROL D. MITCHELL

"Well, I wanted to meet you too Miss Dana Ann. "I mean again," he corrected. They both laughed.

"That was so sweet of you to bring me here," she said, holding onto his arm.

"Don't even worry about it, Dana Ann. There is no other place I want to be more than right here with you," he told her.

Feeling comfortable with Ray, she knew she had to tell him about her failed marriages to Dr. Frank Michaels and Zim Danube to get that out of the way. She even told him about the baby and how Grace killed her unborn child when she pushed her down the stairs, during her sixth month of pregnancy with Dr. Michaels. The doctor's mother Grace made Ray think of his mother, Rovella. He wanted to protect this precious flower more. In his thoughts, he told God he would never bring any harm to this gorgeous woman, who had been abandoned then raised in an orphanage. He reached out for her and he sheltered her in a tight manly grip that made her feel secure. Looking down sweetly into her eyes, all he could do was thank God that he waited his entire life only for her. Tonight he gave her his passion, his warm hugs, his sincerity and the raw beginnings of his untested love.

"Sorry about everything you have been through baby," he said. He was deeply affected by her and Dana Ann could feel his passion most intimately. She worried that she had given him too much information about her past and because he liked her so much, that hearing all of this would be too much for him to bear. She watched a warm tear of sorrow fall onto his left cheek, and she snuggled against his chest tighter.

"I like that," he stated, responding to her move. She smiled.

"It's kind of hot in here, huh?" she asked.

"Yeah, but it's okay. I'm so moved by you," he smiled. She kissed his chest.

"I know a man ain't supposed to cry. But, Dana, I would never hurt you and I ain't gone let nobody else hurt you either. I will never leave you," he promised.

She believed him and made sure he knew that his tears were nothing to be ashamed of. When Ray told her that he would not be able to see her a lot because of his three jobs, she was relieved at the change of pace of their conversation. She dried his eyes with the tip of a yellow napkin and then opened the car window to let some steam out.

"Are you working so much to forget about your needs in life?" she asked him.

"No," he answered.

Rovella Starr
The New Love-Starved Bitch
Author's Gold Edition

"It's a long story, baby. I promise I will tell you everything you want to know about me one day. Right now let's get out of this car and go out and look closer at the beach," he said. She agreed and had quietly admired the way he had taken the lead and had called her "baby."

Within the midst of the shadows of a darkening eve, Ray and Dana Ann walked hand in hand out to meet the roaring waters amidst a wonderful multi-colored sunset. On the sand Ray admired her and he wished he could change time to be with her more. Earlier, he and Dillon had arranged to cover his work. He had arranged to get home by early morn in time to double back to San Francisco to be at his shipyard job by early morn. Ray knew that seeing Dana Ann was going to be the challenge of his life. He watched the drifting moon form a spotlight on her cheek. With her back leaning against his chest, he rubbed the back of her head, feeling sorry she had ever felt pain and regretting that his father would never meet her. She understood what he told her about his life. It was hard to tell her he had never talked about his mother before to a woman. When he told her about the shooting, Dana sided with Rovella, telling him that Rovella loved him too

While Ray was having the time of his life, Rovella noted Ray's absences from work and she regretted that Dana Ann Arbor was spending all this time with her son. Without Ray home, Rovella had been watching Jerry Springer and Maury Povich. She knew if she pushed Ray too hard about Dana Ann that she could lose him forever. What she saw on those shows to her was horrible, how a family could be torn apart if a parent approached her child the wrong way. One transvestite told Maury that he wanted to become a woman because his mother was such a bad one. She had heard children call their parents all kinds of nasty names and threaten never to see them again if they didn't accept some of the trash she saw people with on these shows. After the shooting, Rovella stepped back to let Ray have a little more freedom. When the weeks turned into months and Ray showed no signs of backing away from this star writer; Rovella worried that she had to advance her charge to win Ray back from this woman. By her own wicked estimate she had to reverse Ray's course of love before her dearest companion left her

—84—

CAROL D. MITCHELL

alone and out in the cold. Realizing that Dana Ann was a woman of resources and unthinkable means, the only person who could help Rovella with a plan to end this love madness was the unsuspecting, Joe Bullet.

By May 2000, one month before her upcoming tour, Ray and Dana Ann were madly in love. On this night, Ray rented a room for them at the Marriott Hotel in downtown Oakland, California. He had not been taking his pills for months now in anticipation of making love to his woman. For all the time they had spent together, Ray still could not have sex with Dana Ann. Before she went on her long tour around the world, Ray wanted to consummate their love tonight. Ray went to his first job where Clay E urged him to follow his heart through the night! Later, they had dinner at His Lordships on *Jack London Square*, where they dined on deep-sea lobster, fried corn and crab cakes. Later, he took her out to Lake Merritt for a scenic walk around the lake where they ended up at the beautiful presidential suite of the Marriott Hotel. In order to please the woman of hi dreams, Ray used half of his secret savings for hi Harley Davidson to pay for this night. He was happier to spend the money on his new love. She looked beautiful in her black, simple spaghetti strap Bob Mackie gown and neither of them could wait to go to bed and make love.

Inside the suite, Ray took off his clothes and to Dana Ann; the man had the body off a twenty-year old athlete. The masses of curly hair on his forty-four inch chest complimented his strong, masculine frame. His stomach was washboard flat and his legs were long, shapely and well-toned. To him, her body was youthful looking, well-toned and the lipo-suction she told him that she had done on her stomach last year gave her the same look he was sure she had when she was twenty-five. Her large, natural 38DD breast stood to attention and her waist was a small twenty-four inches that spilled into her strong shapely thirty-six inch, sisterly behind. Tonight as they checked each other out a long time, the two lovers were glad to end up together inside a red whirlpool sauna shaped like a heart. Nearly six months into their love feast, they had wanted to make love; but never had. They hoped that tonight the long effects of medication on Ray's manhood would finally take a back seat to their love.

They kissed and washed each other's body, Ray used a pink face towel to gently massage Dana Ann's soft body. As she lay on the king-sized bed, he smiled down at her and with each stroke of the towel, he felt as she did, special. No other man had ever bathed her or showered her with this much attention before and Ray had never seen a woman with such naked splendor as her. Tonight Ray took a small bottle of French, Pierre Armagnac Fragrance lotion out of the bathroom and starting from her feet up he very

–85–

Rovella Starr
The New Love-Starved Bitch
Author's Gold Edition

gently oiled her body with it. Dana Ann was on fire for him and he was on fire for her. Soon after the lotion was glistening on her body, Ray gently lay next to her on the bed. He kissed her gently on the mouth, igniting a fire that aroused them both, making it hard for her to wait to feel his manhood inside of her body. To heighten the mood, Ray carefully placed his lips on the edge of her hard, left nipple. Taking his time, he sucked her breast one at a time until a rich white fluid drained from her vagina. Then, when the ultimate time came for him to please his woman, it did not happen.

Ray tried everything he could to make it work and he had been doing this for months now and nothing ever happened. It started out working ending limp each time. He tried several more times to make it work and after three tries, Dana Ann told him it didn't matter because Doctor Jeffrey Watson told them it was going to take some time and that they must be patient. She was with the man she loved and that was all that mattered to her. For months, she had been happier with Ray than she had ever been in either of her marriages. With her arms around his waist, she pulled him down on top of her and he cried against her breast. She understood. She knew about Rovella, the medications she had him on and the psyche games she played with his mind. Ray had never lied to her about anything. She knew that she was the center of his life and he was the center of hers. She recognized the goodness in Ray as a man She had assured him that she felt all the residual of his efforts and that she would never leave him because of this. His going all the way would have been to many women the icing on the cake. To her she had the man she wanted and all she had to do was to wait. With what she had gone through with men and their little games, she was prepared to wait for as long as she had to for the man she loved. In Ray, Dana Ann had the kind of love she had never mastered in a man before. What happened in bed did nothing but make her love him more.

When Ray drifted off to sleep this night, she put her arms around him thinking there was no other place she wanted to be in this world but with him. She found herself regretting going on her upcoming tour to Chicago, Atlanta and Singapore. Watching Ray sleeping so peacefully next to

CAROL D. MITCHELL

her, there was no other place she wanted to be than in his arms and that was the truth. They both felt that way about each other. Later, when Ray woke up in the middle of the night, Dana Ann was resting right next to him with a big smile on her face. She was as happy as a lark; and when he saw how happy she was, Ray was truly overwhelmed. The last time before her when he could not get it up for a woman she left like a thief in the night. He never saw that woman again. Looking at this beauty brought tears to his eyes. He was sorry he had not been able to please her as a man. All he wanted to do was make love to her showing her how much, he cared. She was resting so comfortably. In a few days, she would be going on tour for three months and he would miss her dearly. He was aroused now for her, but he knew that if he tried again he would fail again; as he always had. All he could do now was pray.

"Baby, I will never leave you, ever. You don't have a thing to worry about, Ray. I have watched you throw your whole being into making me happy and nobody has ever done that for me before. Your endless wonderful gifts and surprises have made me feel special and you have given this all to me at great risk. I can see love for the first time in my life in your eyes," she offered. Moved by her love, he rolled over next to her and kissed her right cheek.

"You console me when I am sad, you bath me when I am tired and you listen to me like everything I say to you is important and vital," she said.

With that, Ray caressed the little woman to his chest like she was a little breakable doll. Tonight, as she willed her love into his chest, Dana Ann Arbor thanked God for her happiness and what was the love of her life. With his head buried over her shoulder, she looked to the heavens and asked God what had-she done to deserve a man who was so kind to her.

Soon as Ray felt that his relationship with Dana Ann had legs, he told Eric and Shane everything about his new love and they were glad that finally their brother was leading a normal life and all of them wished he would marry this woman and finally leave home. Eric and Shane both admitted to their brother that the woman was a great catch. With all of her success, her fame was not important to them so long as their brother was happy. He was.

Rovella Starr
The New Love-Starved Bitch
Author's Gold Edition

This Miraculous Love

Against all odds, the relationship between Dana Ann Arbor and Ray J.T. Starr was a strong love that was founded on shared emotions of love and neither of them could ever get enough of seeing one another. As Rovella Starr stayed in the background of her son's new life – she was quietly seething that all of Ray's love went to Dana Ann Arbor. For months, Rovella had been watching Ray from afar, as she carefully planned her next desperate move. For Ray and Dana Ann Arbor, the challenges of their love formed a unique bond between them and a solid relationship. He and Dana Ann took a boat from Jack London Square to San Francisco or onto the Peninsula. They went to Sausalito for lunch coming back in time to have dinner on the East Bay sometimes in Oakland, or Walnut Creek or Concord. They walked hand in hand along the pier at Jack London Square where they often rented a dinky at night and sailed on the Bay water. Many of their long nights out ended at Lake Merritt, where they ran or walked the Lake together. On Saturdays, they watched marathons or the lake boat races from the city sidewalk or they marveled at newlywed couples who often used the lake's scenic backdrop to take wedding pictures after getting married at the big white Cathedral across the street from the lake. Ray discovered that Lake Merritt was her favorite place and as often as he could he hooked up with Manpower to hire a janitor to cover his second job. Eric and Shane both sponsored dinner and entertainment for the happy couple in their homes to ensure Ray was happy and would sustain this very special relationship. Rovella turned down invitations to dine with the happy couple.

With the advice of his brother Shane, Ray was careful about what he told his mother. He was walking a tight rope to make sure everything he was

CAROL D. MITCHELL

doing stayed as normal as possible. And when Dana Ann set up appointments for him to see a urologist in Oakland's pill hill he was quiet about that too. Doctor Wellington was Shane's friend. He was an expert fixing problems like what Ray was having in bed. Oftentimes the two of them visited the doctor together and after seeing the results of a battery of test that the doctor had done on Ray Dana Ann Arbor understood the complexities of what he was going through a lot more. Doctor Wellington confided in Ray that Dana Ann's reaction to his problem was a rare response and that he was truly lucky to have found such an understanding woman in her and Ray knew that. Even without what many couples consider is the ultimate pleasure, this couple was strongly made for each other. Together they made such a handsome couple that people often stopped them on the streets to tell them how great they looked together. On Sunday, the couple often prayed at Rays' parent's church: Evergreen Baptist Church; or they went to Allen Temple Baptist Church, where Ray was friends with Pastor Smith. With faith, love and the promise of a glorious future together, the only thing that could stand in the way of their love was Ray's mother, Rovella Starr.

Rovella Starr

The New Love-Starved Bitch

Author's Gold Edition

Something Fishy Going On

    Joe Bullet felt he was a disappointment to his family and that was the reason Teresa Bullet passed away on him shortly after his conviction. Peter Bullet met some nice white girl about twenty-years old. He married her then he moved her to Los Angeles. Still blinded by being put in jail over a crime he did not commit, life had not dealt Joe Bullet a fair hand. In the only trip to the prison Peter ever took he showed up to tell his only child he was guilty and he hoped Joe Bullet rotted in hell for raping and for killing that white woman. Teresa, God rest her soul, sold her house and had not left him any financial support. The aging Joe Bullet had faith in God. For fifteen-years he was tortured, raped and beaten into becoming the prison preacher. He summed up his misfortune by believing that God needed him more in prison than he needed him on the outside and that was why he had to pay such a hefty price in this life. As Joe Bullet sat on the plane from Los Angeles to Oakland, California, he wondered why Rovella Starr wanted him to come to Oakland so bad. She said she was not feeling up to snuff in her old age, but Joe Bullet knew her better than that. She was a bitch, but Joe loved her all the same and right now he needed some cash badly and he knew Rovella had it to give to him. Let the truth be told, Rovella and Ray was the only somebody that wrote to Joe Bullet the whole time he was incarcerated in Tulsa. When you are a lonely man with a beautiful woman who you know ain't gone wait no twenty-years for your ass, getting any kind of letter from anyone is gonna make you like that person a whole lot. On the holidays, Rovella and Ray sent him fruit baskets and money for personal items for every year he was in prison. In their letters, she promised to get him out and to find out who really committed the crime. Although her promises never came into fruition, knowing she cared enough about him to say these things

CAROL D. MITCHELL

made a big difference to Joe Bullet. In the letters, Rovella talked about Ray as if he was the man of the house or a little boy and she kept him up on everything Ray ever did. Ray asked questions about women and guy things. Joe answered him regularly like a father. To Joe it sounded at first like Rovella was turning Ray into some kind of fruitcake. In her letters, she rarely said anything about Ray having a girlfriend, or even male friends for that matter. She said little about Shane and Eric other than that they were married with kids and were happy. Ray said Rovella made it hard for him to leave home. Joe wrote Rovella in 1980 to tell her that he heard her mother; Darnetta had been stabbed to death in an Orcutt Bar. When Rovella received the letter, she didn't flinch. To her it was, fuck the bitch." The evil motherless daughter never followed up on her mother's death, other than to collect her share of the poor woman's property. Darnetta lived in an old two-bedroom shack that wasn't worth a thousand dollars. When Rovella found that out, she told Eric to fly down there and let the State have the property so they could pay the taxes on that bitch's land, so it wouldn't fall back on her. She wrote Joe back telling him time had not made her like that white bitch Darnetta Jackson one bit more and not to ever mention her in his letters again. With that, Joe didn't tell her anything about her Tulsa relatives again.

As Joe Bullet relaxed in his seat on the Southwest Airline plane, all he could think of was the night of the rape back in 1972. He had not raped that white woman and as far as he knew there had been no way to ever prove that. He had heard about this new thing out now that was brought up in the OJ trial, called DNA. Maybe, someday this would prove to the courts that he did not rape and murder Emily. Right now all he hoped for was that Ray would be on time to pick him up at the airport.

By the time the limo dropped Ray off at the house on Market Street Rovella was out on the lawn waiting for him to ask him some questions:

"Well, look at this. I guess you got it like that where you can be sported around in a limo now?" She looked at Ray and continued…"Ah huh!"

"Customer from the bank came by to give me a ride. That's all," he lied. The one thing Ray did not want to do was rub his relationship with Dana Ann in his mother's face.

"You know Joe is gone be waiting for you at the Oakland Airport at Southwest Airlines. I called you job and Sam told me he would give you the message. You was supposed to come here from work at 1:00 and here you bring your old rusty ass up in here at 4:00. His plane lands at 4:30 and you're gonna be late picking him up the way you're moving, Ray!" she screamed.

Rovella Starr
The New Love-Starved Bitch
Author's Gold Edition

The once lovely Rovella Starr had let time and her insidious nature drive her once movie star looks down with yesterday's sunset. Rovella Starr was nowhere near the beauty she had been the day she married Zebbie on June the 4th, 1943, the day Mattie Starr righteously kicked that ass. Her once long black hair was still pretty, but straggly and winter white, but she had Lady Clairol to help her with that. Her shape was frail and emaciated and her former coke bottle figure was loose and gave way to straight, sagging, breast that touched her stomach pronouncing the tiny spare tire around her waistline. Her once smooth yellow skin was now blotched with brown liver spots that covered her face, neck and hands. Trying to hold onto a son who should have long since left the house was work and being a low down bitch was a lot more work. Ray ran into the house to get the keys to the Green Jeep Cherokee. He was brilliant now at blocking his mother out. With plans to leave this hell hole in three short months, he had determined that putting up with her for a few more days was not going to kill him. As soon as his girl got back from her tour he was going to ask her to marry him. With his private stash, he had bought her a ring from the Diamond Center. For months now she had been asking him to move in with her – but he was going to surprise her and say yes when he gave her the ring. Amidst the fiery storm of his mother's bitter anger, Ray hopped into his Green Jeep Cherokee – stopping only once to say hi to Shane and Eric's wives and his little nephew Zebbie, who had come by to see Rovella.

CAROL D. MITCHELL

Honesty Between Friends

As soon as the plane landed in New York City on what was a beautiful June day, Ray called Dana Ann. He reminded her that her connecting flight to Singapore the next day was at 10:00 A.M.; she thanked him for being so attentive to her needs and told him she loved him. He said he loved her back. Later, after they had talked for a few minutes more and Ray mentioned that Joe Bullet and his mother were getting along fine and had not argued since he got there, a cold chill raced through Dana Ann's body and the horrible thing about this feeling was that she had no clue as to why. To date, she had not met Rovella or Joe Bullet. There was no reason for her to worry. She dismissed her feelings as being foolish. Having promised the Morgan's that she would call them soon as she got to New York, Dana Ann ate a light dinner of salad and diet coke and then she sat down in the lounge chair to make her telephone calls. Leaving a message for the Morgan's Dana Ann relaxed and she remembered the many special moments that she shared with Ray. She missed him already. She thought about how Ray had no patience for loudness, violence or disruption of any kind and people like Joe Bullet really scared him. Now the thought of him being in Oakland, California scared her. With Ray having been a victim and prisoner of circumstances, all of her friends had been warning her that Ray was no match for her and that she was foolish to love and hang her coat on a man with all of his physical and mental problems. Dana Ann had time now to reflect on the concerns her friends had intimated to her; but none of what they said or believed would change her mind about Ray.

Some of her friend's said, best thing she could do for the both of them was to leave him alone. As Dana Ann shifted in the chair, she was reviled by how people could be so judgmental about somebody they didn't even know. People told her that Ray would end up being a viable detriment to her career. As she turned these opinions over in her mind, she concluded that none of them, including Dillon had anything positive to say about Ray. They told her they worried most about the Starr's lack of communication devices. Ray had no cell phone or answering service, which to other's proved that he and his mother both were out of touch with the times. Or they told her that she could not take Ray on the Hollywood scene because he was

—93—

Rovella Starr
The New Love-Starved Bitch
Author's Gold Edition

slow, his vocabulary was limited to simple verbs and nouns. And they asked her how she would explain especially to a literary genius that she was in love with a lifetime Mama's boy, who was part vegetable. They asked her too how would she tell the mass media and professional people that her man was a janitor for the Government of Alameda County and that he worked two other service jobs on top of that because his mother had told him to. They reminded her that people could be cruel. The tabloids had already drug Dana Ann Arbor through the mud when her doctor husband married the double amputee, Missy back in the 80s weeks after his mother, Grace caused Dana to have that much talked about fall that killed her unborn child. Beatrice reminded Dana Ann that it took her months to recover from those hot news items. The people who said these things to her had obviously not ever experienced love the way she had with Ray. He was precious to her a that she loved him too much to ever leave him. She was going with the flow and every waking minute of each of her days and all of her nights belonged solely to Ray. She had even tattooed his name over her left breast. She smiled because when she went to that place in Pittsburg, California to have the tattoo done; Ray told her that he was worried that the needle might hurt her. Looking around the beautiful hotel site, she didn't care a bit about the foolish things people had told her about Ray, she was only sad that he was not here to share the beauty of New York with her. The thought of him brought a rush of tears to her eyes. Ray with all of his difficulties was the most caring individual she had ever met. Thinking about it now, she had never set out to meet a man who was slow, or who was living with his mother, and the only problem she really had with all of this was that Ray did not have a cell phone. She didn't like any of that, but she loved him and there was no way she could verbally tell anyone the profoundness to which her feelings had reached for this man. She did however know one thing: Ray was going to be her husband one day so help her God.

    Later, it was weird for Dana Ann to call Beatrice Griffith and the first thing to come out of her mouth was Joe Bullet's name.

CAROL D. MITCHELL

"Girl, I call to tell you how nice New York is and how much I miss my man and you want to talk shit?" Dana Ann asked Beatrice. They laughed. "Come on Dana Ann. You told me this man has a scarred face and is a jailbird cousin of your boyfriend's mother who raped and killed a white woman in the south and that he is in town and the mixture of him and her and Ray don't mix. Ray's mother is Oakland's big, bad monster and to me it sounds like trouble is brooding on Market Street. I'm sorry. I am worried about you, Dana Ann!"

"Oh? Don't be silly Bee. Ray told me Joe Bullet was in prison for something he didn't do. You know how those southern white women holler rape and the cops seize the first nigga they see to make the white community feel safe. Girl it's the same OLE soup warmed over. You know the deal Bee. Come on girl, you're much smarter than you're sounding tonight, and I won't even mention the cigarette thing," she said, referring to the habit Beatrice picked up again. Beatrice had promised Dana Ann that she was going to quit smoking again. But, she couldn't stop smoking. It was a weakness that Dana Ann threw up in her friend's face when she lost patience with her, like tonight. It was fair game.

Ray likes Joe Bullet. He didn't act like there was anything strange about the man being in town so why should I? You have been reading too many of my novels, girlfriend. You're a true fan," Dana Ann joked.

As the tone of the conversation changed to a serious tone, Beatrice Griffith had watched this sorry relationship go on long enough. If being friends meant being honest, then this was her call and she was going to seize the opportunity, whatever the consequences would be. In her heart, Beatrice really didn't feel that her talented friend's love relationship with this lame janitor could ever work out for her. She thought that sometimes when people don't hear you straight, you have to come at them from a different angle, even a brutal angle in order to save them from continuing in the wrong direction. To Beatrice being honest marked the efficacy of what true friendship was all about. She deadened the first cigarette into the ashtray at her bedside. With the palm of her right hand she hit the bottom of the More cigarette box for the next cigarette. With her husband out at a Union meeting and her boys fast asleep, smoking was once again a way for Beatrice to relax. She put the cigarette between her shaky fingers; she tried once and missed the light; the second time, the fire burned crisp into the tobacco. She hit it, and then she breathed out.

"Dana Ann, do you really want a man so bad that you are willing to compromise everything you have worked so hard he asked. Dana Ann felt as

–95–

Rovella Starr

The New Love-Starved Bitch

Author's Gold Edition

if she had been hit with an Ali punch. She was so shocked by Beatrice's comment, that she found herself at first unable to respond. Beatrice continued...

"Do you have to sink so low that you are willing to accept a man like Ray whose mother controls his every move and whose co-workers play tricks on him to tease him because at birth he was born brain damaged and they consider his ass slow. Damn, that crazy bitch over there is totally responsible for the man not being able to have sex with you and that's not to mention that people on his job call him retarded. You love this man? How could you love a man that works three jobs, that does not have time to be with you as a man? For Pete's sake, and on top of all of that, you said his mother shot him! You said that she almost killed him. Surely, there are a million men out there you could go after that would love you and be a great companion and compliment you?" she asked.

The author was not shocked to hear this opposition regarding her relationship with Ray coming from her best friend. Her tone, her actions, her refusal to accept Ray and judge him this way only made her sick. Bee had been her partner in crime for over twenty-years. She supported her through two bad marriages and some difficult times in her life. Beatrice threw the baby shower at the Hilton on Hegenberger Road for a baby whose grandmother had killed it by pushing her down the stairs, The grated tone Beatrice used tonight was stern, uncaring and evil spirited because Beatrice had been through too much with her and wanted all of her unhappiness to end yesterday. This only hurt Beatrice badly because she loved Dana Ann Arbor. As she sat on the couch looking out into the beautiful New York skyline, she listened to her enraged friend and tried to figure out her role in this conversation. Understanding her friend's pain didn't mean she supported her opinions about this relationship. In fact, while Beatrice raged, she wanted to give in to her pain and hang up in her best friend's face. However, that was not going to ease the tension in her heart. It was time now after all of these months to put an end to the slights she had gotten from Beatrice over her relationship with Ray. Yes, she would tell her how she truly felt about this

CAROL D. MITCHELL

man. Next, she would hang up the telephone and never mention Ray J. T. Starr to Beatrice again. Unexpectedly, tears rolled down her cheeks. She held back her sniffles because she did not want Beatrice to hear how badly her negative words about Ray had sliced at her heart. When her cell phone, which was ringing from inside her purse, rang, she got up and reached in her bag and turned it off. With no way now to hide the rising emotion that was seeping from her heart, Dana Ann's pain would be undeniable to Beatrice. Dana Ann defended her love for Ray in a quiet, serene manner that she merely hoped would make her best friend understand the complexity of her love relationship with Ray better.

"It's almost midnight, here Bee. So it must be about nine there. I am tired, but I have to say this to you so you'll understand. First of all Frank Michaels was a doctor, Beatrice. Look what he and his mother did to me. Ray is on the other hand a janitor, and that man has been more of a man to me than Frank was the whole time I knew him. From the time we met to the end of the marriage, Frank gave me five-years of hell and he had an affair with another woman. He was not sensitive. That man never held me and didn't want me sexually. He did not bath me or call me to make sure I was in the hotel safely during tours. It was about the money with Frank and his mother, Grace. They were greedy white folks who could not square up to having a black baby – so they killed my baby and got away with murder because of their name. What about Zim? His biggest dream was not to be traded to a losing team and then he was traded to the Golden State Warriors and that was it and enough for him to drink and drug himself to death. That marriage was a sham. My husband couldn't love me because he couldn't love himself. What were Frank and Zim's reasons Bee for acting retarded? Were they slow? Were they Mama's boys who couldn't leave the house? She asked. Realizing that Beatrice was listening, Dana Ann continued to preach to Beatrice her love for Ray J.T. Starr.

"Bee, I was not looking for it. It happened on a cold day in December at a place I was not supposed to be at then and there he was. It was as instant as a hot cup of Sanka, in the early morn. There were no trite lines or tired games; nobody said a word. Our hearts found each other. His eyes did the talking and mine answered. The love was immediate, Beatrice. Inside Dillon's car, during our ride back from downtown Oakland, I tried to turn away from it, but you cannot walk away from true love, Bee. I know about the formidable tasks he has to face in this life and I know entirely who this man is. You see, Bee, when God sets love in front of you, you don't stop and ask God what kind of package it is or how perfect it has to be for you. If that was the case, Frank and Zim both would have never been my husbands.

Rovella Starr
The New Love-Starved Bitch
Author's Gold Edition

God lets you know when a person is right for you and if you wait on God he does not produce mistakes in humans, humans make mistakes of themselves. Our love, Bee is a natural kind of love that is fluid. Ray is the man that God put me on the planet to be with Beatrice, and that is why he took my baby back because he knew that I was not ready to have Frank Michael's baby. I know that as sure as I know my name that I will not leave this earth loving anyone except for Ray J.T. Starr. No matter what you or anyone else thinks about him, his mother or his challenges, his makeup is mine to regard, not anyone else's to decide for me. And, if I am lucky – Ray will accept me for who I am. And, that my friend is all that I can ask of him," Dana Ann defended. The smoking aside, Beatrice dried her tears. As she listened to what Dana Ann said, it was clear to her that this proclamation of love she gave to her for this lame man was heartfelt and sincere. Dana had always been sensitive to others and that was displayed in her many charitable legions of giving. True enough, it was the overall beauty of Dana Ann's unconditional love for people that made her the incredible writer she was today. Beatrice soon apologized to her friend, thereby ending their call.

"I'll call you in a few days. Have a safe trip, Dana Ann."

"I will," she told Beatrice, sounding very sad, but resolute.

The words, "God's creations," were perfect for him had resonated with Beatrice. After all, she had given up a cabinet position in Clinton's *White House Administration* to be with her "garbage man" husband. Dana Ann was right. This was her relationship to work out. Beatrice felt terrible that her words had come off so raw to her best friend. At least she knew now that she really loved this man and that she was perfectly willing to accept him exactly the way he was, while everybody else who knew about this wanted her to drop Ray and take the easy way out. Ray truly was a lucky man indeed to have found a woman like Dana Ann. With all of her crying and caring for her friend, Beatrice knew that she would have to be very strong indeed, to see her friend through this relationship.

CAROL D. MITCHELL

When Love Calls

"So…Who were you on the phone with? Was it Ray or Beatrice" Dillon asked Dana Ann.

"It was Bee, Dillon. I'm gonna have to cut it short because I am tired," she groaned.

"I know. Just calling to let you know that your flight has been changed to 1:00 P.M.," he reminded her.

"Good! That means I could use the extra three-hours, Dillon. Thanks. I will talk to you tomorrow.

The last call of the night was to Carol Morgan, who proudly told her daughter she was bringing in two more children. After making sure all was well with the Morgan's in Chino, California and saying I love you to both her parents, Dana Ann was done with telephone calls for the night. With calls behind her, Dana Ann got ready to climb in the bed until she remembered she had to call Brenda about some rewrites, and she did. Later, she thought about calling Beatrice again, but decided a nice suds bath sounded better. After soothing her tension, the Dana of New York City – eased out of the tub into a flowing pink gown by Jovan of Paris. She then sat on the pink ottoman and she sipped on a chilled glass of apple juice. Next, she looked out of her high-rise onto the Twin Towers, and then she looked over to the beautiful sky high rises in Manhattan and she admired all that was significantly New York. Later, as she lay along the side rail of the windowsill, she remembered the special moments she had shared with Ray back in Oakland, California. Tonight, Oakland seemed to be a million miles away. She smiled as she remembered all of his calls today. He wanted to make sure her flight was safe. Later, he wanted to make sure that she had eaten; and then he wanted to make sure her flight arrangements were right. It was amazing how attentive of a man he was. When she got to the room tonight, his yellow roses he sent were the first things to greet her eyes. He told her that she was too far away from him for him not to worry about her and he told her that he had something very important to ask her when she got back from her tour in September. She missed him so much so that she didn't know how she was going to make it three-months without him. Now she was used to his

Rovella Starr
The New Love-Starved Bitch
Author's Gold Edition

protective arm being around her at night and she loved the way he had a habit of pulling her to his back, the way he did when she rode on the back of the motorcycle with him. Missing Ray meant tears and tonight those tears turned into rivers and the mere thought of not having him made her dizzy. She had to catch herself because she felt like she was going to faint. When she closed her eyes, magically, it took her to visions of all the happiness they had enjoyed over the past few months since they met in December. What she felt inside her heart tonight was what she had always wanted to feel for a man; but, never had. Now she felt love more strongly than she had ever imagined was possible. It seemed like each obstacle she met regarding Ray made her love him more. Missing him meant she wanted him to quit the three jobs he was working and marry her. She knew that Ray was a proud man. He hated it when she spent money on limo's or when she took out her credit card to pay a restaurant meal. He told her months ago that should they ever marry, that he wanted to keep his job with the Government because the benefits were good and it had been hard for him to get that job and he didn't want to lose it. Ray made it clear without saying it that he never wanted to depend on her money and she knew this. The whole time she knew him he had never asked her for a dime or how much money she had because it simply was not important to him and she knew that too. Now, as the clock struck 2:00 A.M., Dana Ann knew she had to get some sleep in order to catch her flight on time tomorrow afternoon. Hearing the tap at the door of her suite reminded Dana Ann that she had forgotten to call the bell boy to pick up her dinner cart. She grabbed her white robe. Next, she picked up ten-dollars off of the dresser to give to the bell boy. She reached for the door and turned the knob and when she opened it she could not believe that he had come.

Ray looked like a dream model dressed in a dapper gray flannel suit with matching gray shoes. He topped his look off with his signature black cap and he was wearing a foot-long smile on his face. He looked as if he had run from Oakland, California to New York City. Never waiting for her to say

CAROL D. MITCHELL

hello, Ray grabbed the petite woman, pulling her off of the floor, up to his chest.

He kissed her. "You glad to see me, Dana?" he chimed. She was so overwhelmed, tears landed on his cheeks. "You smell like a rose," he said, smiling. She smiled back and her eyes continued to spill tears of joy. She hugged her man so closely. Ray hugged her back and he could feel her love and hear her little heart knocking at his. Looking down into her beautiful, tear-filled eyes – he was glad that co-worker and friend Clay E had gone to the Post Office on 14th Street in Oakland, California with him to help him get a passport to travel abroad. He had been right when he told Ray that he was going to need travel papers one day. At the airport, he thanked Clay E profusely for the valuable education he had given him regarding women and he thanked him more for convincing him that it was indeed the right thing to do to go be with the woman he loved!

Rovella Starr

The New Love-Starved Bitch

Author's Gold Edition

Poison

Sixty-four years old Margaret Fisher was born at the County hospital in Oakland, California, on July 4, 1938. From the time she first saw a soda pop can blow up in her mother's hot old station wagon, at their old East Oakland home on 62nd Avenue, the only child born to Rita Mae and Manchester Fisher wanted to be a chemist. Margaret's field in the life left many calling the flaming red hair girl, with the big hazel eyes, crazy. With a fascination for weird kitchen mixtures, Margaret was nicknamed by her mother, wine-stein and because she always had wet stains on her clothes from all of the explosions, she created, the kids at school called her among many other names, *"the absent-minded-bed-wedder."* They threw rocks at her on the playground forcing the smart, thick-skinned Margaret to get back at them by blowing up the school's lab turtles or slicing wild rabbits before the teachers could cut them open for the biology class. Frustrated that nobody paid attention to what she thought were prodigious explosive creations; and paralyzed in getting others to accept her for her growing scientific genius, Margaret got everyone's attention, especially, the Oakland Police, when she blew up a pair of gophers in the neighbor's garden creating a blowout that lit up the entire block of 62nd Avenue in East Oakland costing the city over $200,000.00.

During the 50s in what she called – her pre-grad school days, Margaret studied and had desired to pattern her life after distinguished Black 20th Century scientists like Lloyd E. Alexander – who roamed the hills of the mountains of Virginia to figure out what made plants and animals grow. She claimed to be a keen study of Herman Branson – whose specialized studies

CAROL D. MITCHELL

of x-rays and their effects on small worms was particularly interesting to her. Margaret was also said to have discovered the rapidity of how phosphorus was used by the body. In court documents, she said she wrote her scholarly theories in math languages to explain how much phosphorus was used in each of these stages. Later, for her conjectural doctorate at Yale, Margaret, a self-proclaimed twenty-four year old chemistry ingénue said she studied biophysics as practiced by the best chemist around the world. To advance her love of the sciences, Margaret claimed that she had developed and wrote three comprehensive studies on illusive undetectable elements that were indiscernible to man's most innovative lenses. While scientist around the world were trying to describe protein phenomena, Margaret Fisher, the East Oakland talent was said to have created concepts where she formed exact structure or formations of protein molecules. In her Creations, specifically her home produced formula called Reversal of Love (ROL); Margaret developed over a period of twenty-years, hemoglobin, and life's vital fluid designed to morph inside the blood stream as rhepholin. Her veiled formula, which she said took her two decades to produce, was developed from a pure green substance into a yellow cell that in the place of Hemoglobin carries oxygen from the lungs to other streamlines in the body. The object of Margaret's home creation: ROL was to erase love from a human's memory. In the process of love removal, instead of the molecule giving blood its' red color, in both of Margaret's creations: **Reversal of Love (ROL)** *and* **Creation of Love, COL** Ruephorin gave human blood a green color, which is formed generally after the drug's thirty-day incubation period has arrived.

Margaret's presumed ostensible overall thirty-year long study and creative chemicals in ROL and COL were a direct scheme to DNA and she said in court records that she formed her unique elements in order to graduate with honors from Yale and to fool the United States Government. In keeping her formulas invisible to human detection, Margaret produced evidence to her skeptics that proved researchers around the world described and sought to emulate her genius. When Margaret filed papers in Alameda court contending that the US Government was trying to steal her chemical components, the local Government labeled Margaret a crazy zealot, with possibly a hazardous drug that the Government had to keep an eye on and they did.

Each customer had to make an appointment at least three-weeks in advance and upon arrival answer a few questions and sign a twenty-page disclaimer that pretty much said if the potion fucked somebody up that they could not and would not ever sue Margaret Fisher. One of Margaret's high-

Rovella Starr
The New Love-Starved Bitch
Author's Gold Edition

priced San Francisco attorneys assured her that the ROL & COL contracts were court proof. And, Margaret trusted them that it was.

It was the tenth day of August, 2000 when Rovella Starr and Joe Bullet arrived on time at Margaret's house to pick up their order of Reversal of Love, (ROL). Margaret didn't care what Rovella and Joe were buying the potion for so long as Rovella Bullet and the frightening looking man she was with that she called (husband); Joe Bullet, had the money to pay for the extravagant substance. When they got out of the car, the man had got out first; Margaret pulled back her expensive drapes and saw his face from afar and breathed:

"My God!"

When Joe Bullet and Rovella Starr got closer to the front door, Margaret almost dropped the two expensive laboratory vials of ROL. Out her front picture window, Margaret held on to her drapes an she witnessed that this poor man's face was shaded two distinctive different colors of brown that were separated with a straight line that went straight down the middle of his face. Even as a self-proclaimed researcher of natural science, she had never seen a human's face so distorted, and discolored as this poor man's before. Only rock ground surfaces contained more craters than this man's face did. Catching her reaction quickly, Margaret gathered herself. The woman, who she presumed was Rovella, was a good-looking, beautiful, trim woman, with eyes so green and evil looking that Margaret met the deep green hue of them a block away. Out of the car, the woman positioned her straight nose in the air dressed flawlessly in a dark tailored Jones of New York pin-striped pantsuit, accented with red high-heeled Gloria Vanderbilt shoes. Rovella was working her model figure from side to side, like this bitch in the ghetto was a Paris runway strip. She had literally stopped traffic. To Margaret, this Rovella bitch carried herself like an original bitch. Margaret had always been good at reading people. It took a bitch to know one. And, she could tell by looking at this bitch walk that Ms. Rovella Starr was one of those OLE southern high yellow worn out bitches – which had caused people a lot of trouble. Perception aside, the fact that she would buy toxins

CAROL D. MITCHELL

and create more havoc before they threw her ass under the ground though, was none of Margaret's business, she thought. She examined the man with the scruffy modified natural, who looked dispirited and pitiful in a cheap white cotton shirt that was missing the third button and hung loosely at the butt of his worn blue Dockers. His old school, blue and white Nikes were cracked, crusty and run over. When they knocked on the door, Margaret slid away from the window and dropped them drapes in a hurry to make sure she was there to greet them in her most cordial manner. She opened the door, inviting them into her luscious, fresh smelling unprecedented living surroundings.

"Well, come on in Mr. and Mrs. Bullet and thanks for being on time. I got your $12,000.00 check via *Federal Express* this morning. Thank you," Margaret offered. The couple thanked her back and then walked into Margaret's expensive, tastefully decorated white den where Margaret pointed them to take seat on her clean ivory, plastic covered furniture. Margaret stared at Rovella with distrust for the woman that was growing. An impulsive woman, Margaret had the urge to call Rovella a bitch – but she didn't. Instead, she offered them something to drink. Both of them declined. Margaret had supplied incarcerated, eager, rich and famous customers her potions and with each sale, she tried not to pry too much into their personal lives. After all, this was a business and to her it was all about the dollars. However, she had suspicions about this woman. Rovella had told her that she had taken a second mortgage out on her home to finance getting the potion. Margaret had spoken with Rovella on the telephone a dozen times before making this appointment. Before the date of the sale, she had always screened her customers carefully to make sure the purchase was what they wanted. Partly, because she was so good at fooling people herself –Margaret could tell when people were lying to her and Rovella had lied to her about a lot, even about her marital status. Rovella told Margaret she wanted the ROL potion because she was dying of cervical cancer and she wanted her husband, Mr. Bullet to take the potion to forget about her in thirty-days so that when she died he would be free to love again. She said Joe Bullet had been a great husband to her and her three boys and that she loved him so much that giving him the opportunity to love after her death would be her infinite gift to him for all of the good that he had done for her and her boys in the past. When Margaret asked Rovella exactly how long she had left to live, Rovella told her six months. Five minutes later, she cried and told her that three months of living was not going to be enough time for her to say goodbye to someone she loved as much as she did Joe Bullet. To Margaret this was the biggest lying ass bitch she had ever met and for a second she had thoughts of not selling

Rovella Starr
The New Love-Starved Bitch
Author's Gold Edition

her the potion at all. The poor scrawny man sitting in front of her with the horrible two-toned face was a pathetic, poorly dressed man who to her looked like he had recently got out of the pen or something. It was clear to Margaret that Joe Bullet was a nice man who was being used by this evil woman. Now all Margaret Fisher wanted to do was make the sale and get this evil bitch and her sorry-looking co-conspirator out of her house.

To Rovella, Margaret Fisher was most peculiar. *"Look at this house,"* she thought. *"It's so hot in here you could fry an egg on the floor! If that flaming red-haired poison-making bitch spent nearly as much time and money on herself as she did creating poison she might look like something. She keeps looking at Joe like he is the scum of the earth. If she say something crazy about my cousin we won't buy shit from this crook."*

All Rovella wanted now was to complete the sale, then send Joe Bullet back to Tulsa and put this drug inside of her son to bring him back from the abyss that Dana Ann had put him in. Now, this so-called scientist bitch wanted to prolong her quest to get it on with all of these silly questions.

"You know this part of the process required that you sign all the pages of the disclaimer. I noticed you left out three-pages. Just sign there, there, and there," she said, pointing to the yellow markings, she continued: "Then you'll be on your way," Margaret promised. The whole time the signing took place, Joe Malcolm Bullet refused to look at Margaret. A heavy sweat seeped down the sides of his and Rovella's faces as Rovella wanted to ask Margaret more questions about the potion; but, was more eager to get out of the woman's house and get home. As if the woman had read her mind, Margaret explained the incubation period of the potion to the couple.

"Look, I know you're in a hurry; but, there are a few things you need to know. ROL takes thirty days to work. This strong potion chemically repels the endorphins that give birth to and sustain love. After the total reversal process, a new person can only initiate the reinvigoration of love for the treated subject, or should I say an exclusively new love interest. Again, I must say, the rejuvenation of love will undoubtedly never be the same love you had before. Each customer is allowed only one bottle of potion per love because you cannot seek more potions for the same subject twice in a

CAROL D. MITCHELL

lifetime. The human body is chemically designed to reject a second helping of ROL. On the thirtieth day of the love change process, the subject's skin will darken for one-half hour. Afterwards the skin will readapt back to its' normal hue and that will be your guarantee that the potion has reached its' full reversal course, allowing full amnesia to thereby take effect on the subject. The recipient of the potion will then go to sleep for at least two-hours. Afterwards, he will awake into the exact person he was before he fell in love and he will not remember the person he once loved; not by picture, association or anything. It is preferred that the subject takes this potion at the same time each day inside a mixture of either Gatorade or Tonic water only. No other substance will work with ROL. There are side effects to ROL, even death; however, the pie chart on page six of your documents show you that this drug boast a 99.5% SUCCESS RATING," Margaret bragged.

Rovella heard the word death and took some time out to read the papers. As much as she wanted to reverse Ray's love for Dana Ann, the side effects were something she had to think about for a minute. After short contemplation, Rovella shoved the potion contract over to a shaking and reluctant Joe Bullet for him to read. Joe, who was on Paxil and Xanax for emotional problems raised his hand and shook his head, meaning no thank you to the papers Rovella tried to get him to read. With Joe's refusal to sign, Rovella looked over the papers a second time before signing the contract and shoving it back to Margaret who then called her secretary into the living room to pick up the contract and make a copy of the signed contract for the Bullets.

"Now, who will get the potion?" Margaret asked. The restrained Joe Bullet was holding his head in his hands when he heard Rovella nominate him to receive the potion.

"He will," Rovella answered for Joe. Rovella smartly rolled her eyes at Joe. They were supposed to be doing this together and to Rovella, he had done more than enough to show Margaret that he was not a willing partner in all of this and she was going to cut off his pay for his disconnected performance. Joe knew her looks and finally, he signed the papers. Later, when she had the potion and the copies of the long contract in her hands, Rovella was glad to leave Margaret's house.

In the car, Rovella tried to keep focused on her driving. She would not have been able to do this without Joe Bullet. Since the sale, he had been eerily quiet. Back at the house, he would not look at Margaret or any of the paperwork, and had signed nervously with his eyes nearly closed. Evil, but not a fool, Rovella knew she could not really tell him what a coward he was

Rovella Starr

The New Love-Starved Bitch

Author's Gold Edition

because the last thing she wanted Joe Bullet to do was go tell somebody what she was up to with Ray. She looked at him sitting next to her in Ray's Green Jeep Cherokee wanting to go by Sears and get him some new clothes. It had been at least twenty-years since she had seen him before now. To her he was the one who looked like he had cancer, he was so thin. She thought, what an idiot he was to let Tulsa, Oklahoma and that damn crazy ass Judge Brossard try him for a rape and murder that he had not committed and steal his life's spirit away. Joe was not the same as he had been when they were growing up in Tulsa when people used to tell Teresa how cute her boy was. Joe Bullet was at one time the best dressed person, in Tulsa. Today, he looked like one of the drunks hanging out at the corner store on East 14th Street, in Oakland. Joe Bullet was a shrinking violet, a shadow of the happy boy he had been during their childhood and younger years in Tulsa. Not only had the prison system stolen his life, they had stolen his soul. Now to her he reminded her of Mattie and Zebbie. Obviously, what happened to him behind bars and the comments people made about his ugly face over the years had turned her cousin into a bitter, repulsive man. Sadly, Rovella did not know Joe Bullet anymore. As they drove up East 14th Street in Oakland, California, Rovella tried to keep focused on the road. It was a warm day in Oakland and she had run a red light across 73rd Avenue, where she was gearing to make a right turn towards the Oakland, Airport. As the summer day got hotter, Rovella was tense at all the money she had spent on the potion. She convinced herself that she would not have been doing this had it not been for Joe Bullet. After all, he was the one who had learned about Margaret from lifers in prison who took the drug successfully to forget about loved ones they'd never see again. It was merely a coincidence the mad scientist Joe Bullet mentioned in his letters lived in Oakland, California. She had initially called him out here to kill the writer. A simple gunshot wound to the back of the skull would have sufficed for her, but Joe Bullet told her that he didn't want to kill anybody because he had never killed anyone before. He said he did not want to go back to the pen a second time. He told Rovella that he was

CAROL D. MITCHELL

not gonna kill Ray's woman and that he was only helping her do this because he needed money.

This morning Joe Bullet had tried to talk Rovella out of going through with this crazy potion thing. Joe knew Rovella well enough to know that once her mind was made up about doing something nothing could stop her. Today, he wished he had never told her about Margaret in the first place. Now that the baneful old woman had the tube in her hand, stopping her from hurting Ray would be futile and his only hope now was that she would not kill a third member of her family. After a silent ride, when they finally made it to the Oakland Airport, Rovella dropped Joe Bullet off.

"Where you going Joe?" she asked him. Joe got out of the car, ironing his pants, ignoring the question.

"Ro' you got a safety pin?" he asked, pointing to his shirt. Rovella shook her head.

"That's a shame that you would put something like that on today boy. You knew we had to meet with this bitch today," she said, looking in the glove compartment. "No. I don't have one," she told Joe. After that when Joe headed into the airport, Rovella begin to cry because Joe Bullet was wearing the pain of prison life on his face well, and she observed his natural, once shining and full was now dull and thinning. A once muscular man, Joe was only 140 pounds of skin and bones. He owned two shirts, one white and one prison blue. He was wearing the white one and it swallowed his small frame. He owned one pair of pants, some faded blue Dockers. One pocket on the left side was ripped at the thigh. Rovella felt an unusual rush of sorrow for her cousin, remembering a time when Joe would not give up the bathroom in Teresa's house until his natural was round as a glove. She called him back to the car.

"Joe, wait a minute," she hollered. Joe heard his cousin and he jogged back to the car.

"Get your bag out the trunk," she reminded him.

"Oh…I am sorry Ro'. Got a lot on my mind cuz," he said.

"Joe. I sold Aunt Teresa's land. Eric went down there and rented it out and then when they kept complaining about upkeep, Eric advised me to sell the property. I sold it Joe," she warned. Joe was out of breath. He never questioned a thing Rovella did. After picking up his bags, all he wanted to do was leave. The airport was crowded. He had wondered about the property, but did not care about such things anymore. He stayed quiet about it as he placed the denim bag holding his life's possessions over his shoulder. Rovella grabbed her purse from the back seat of the Jeep. While Joe stayed outside

Rovella Starr
The New Love-Starved Bitch
Author's Gold Edition

of the door, she reached inside her purse for a fat, gold envelope. She gave that to Joe.

"Here, I can mess over other people, but not you, Joe. You are family and I love you. God knows that I hate seeing you looking this way. Forgive me for that and forgive me for this," she said, pointing to the gallon sized vial in her purse. Rovella tried to assure Joe Bullet what she was doing would make Ray a happier man. She told him that the relationship as a whole had taken its' toll on Ray and that if she didn't do something right away to help him he would be permanently damaged by this love and lose all three of his good jobs.

Joe knew why Rovella was evil. He did not want to judge her or say words to make her feel worse. Instead, Joe Bullet gladly took the $10,000.00 cash. As she watched from the Green Jeep Cherokee, Joe Bullet quietly backed away from the car glancing back to see his cousin blowing him a kiss.

He waved. Then he turned around slowly headed to the Southwest Airlines booth to pick up his ticket back to Tulsa, Oklahoma. For all the grief she had caused on Joe Bullet, Rovella pulled over to the parking lot and she cried for God to save the loyal and faithful soul of her cousin Joe Bullet because she knew that soon Joe Bullet was going to die.

CAROL D. MITCHELL

Is It the End

At 22 Orange Grove Road in Singapore, a peaceful, loving couple, who were authentically perfect together - enjoyed vacationing at the center of Singapore's business and social life. It was as if they had not a care in the world. With Ray in Singapore to keep her company, the thrilled Dana Ann released her staff to their own vacationing while together she and Ray took off for Singapore where the games began. First, they shopped for light summer clothing in anticipation of what promised to be a vacation that would be filled with many outdoor activities. Later, they dined at La Fete du Cuisenaire, where they ate French Cuisine in a cozy romantic setting. Three days into their vacation, Dillon and Brenda surprised the happy couple by arranging for them to spend the day at the Singapore Crocodilarium. With his love of science, reptiles and such, Dana Ann and Ray spent the day ardently observing literally hundreds of crocodiles up close, before ending an eye-opening tourist day at the Singapore Zoo. Later, they danced all night at a disco on Boat Quay, and then they ended their night hugged up inside Cup page Terrace where they hungrily dined on exquisite Northern Indian Cuisine.

From one book signing to another, Ray supported Dana Ann and she found that doing her tours was far more pleasurable for her with Ray there to support her. From New York to Singapore the tranquility and peace of what had turned into a two-week long vacation for Ray and Dana Ann was coming together. With no more vacation time left at his Government job, the obligated Ray prepared to tell his Dana good-bye. When Rovella called that morning, Ray's nervous sounding mother told him that Joe Bullet had left town early and that she did not know why. Then, the agitated woman stressed to her son the importance of his coming home immediately. When he told her what was up, Dana Ann understood Rovella's plea. Thankful for all the wonderful days they had spent together, she wanted Ray to go home to see about his mother. Heartbroken that the beautiful days and nights that she and Ray had spent together were going to come to a close, Ray did all that he could to hide his anguish over having to leave Dana Ann here, while he had to go back to Oakland. He promised her that he would meet her at the San Francisco Airport in South San Francisco, on September

Rovella Starr

The New Love-Starved Bitch

Author's Gold Edition

15, the last day of her tour. Then, her precious love promised her that he would spend all of his free time with her and her alone. With plans to be home on the morning of August 15, 2000, Ray and Dana Ann said a long goodbye at the crowded airport in Singapore and he promised her that he would call her every day. Soon as the plane lifted off the ground, a tormented Dana Ann allowed her worst fears to surface. She prayed that her love would have a safe return home. With Rovella needing him badly enough to call him in Singapore, Dana Ann could not help but think that Rovella Starr's call meant trouble.

CAROL D. MITCHELL

The Truth Is No Lie

On his plane ride from Oakland to LAX instead of Tulsa, Joe Bullet developed dreadful feelings about the deal that took place at Margaret Fisher's house. With the generous amount of money he got from Rovella, he decided to make a stop in Los Angeles to see his father, Peter, who lived in a house on Cambridge Street. He had thought that getting away from Rovella would make him somehow forget about the awful potion she was going to give to Ray; but, he felt worse. In fact, the further away he traveled, the more worried he got. In the middle of his thoughts, Joe heard the pilot announce that the plane would be landing in Los Angeles in fifteen minutes. Now he wanted to go back to Oakland and be a man and put a stop to what Rovella was doing. In the middle of his thoughts, a beautiful sister asked him what on earth happened to his face and he was glad she asked the question. Answering her question took the sting off of the dreadful events of the morning. When he told the pleasant looking woman that he was born with a two-toned face, the woman smiled at him politely. Then she got up from her seat to go sit somewhere else. Joe was used to people treating him like this. He reached inside his white shirt pocket to take his third Xanax of the day. The fact that the beautiful sister was frightened of him might have bothered him in his younger days, not now though. Children ran from him, animals stared at his peculiar face and dogs barked. Explaining how he looked to others was not a problem; however, Rovella Starr was and Joe Bullet knew that it would be in clear defiance of his belief in God to let this go without doing the right thing.

After the plane landed, Joe Bullet walked over to Southwest Airlines to ask what time did the next plane leave for Oakland, California. When the attendant told him Joe thanked the kind woman. He sat down in the waiting area to wait for flight 9678 that was due to leave LAX for Oakland, California in two hours. Doing the right thing had bitter, repetitive consequences for Joe Bullet. The last time he did the right thing by someone, he ended up caught inside a long prison sentence. The time before that left him holding on to an old secret that he was sure to take to his grave. For the first time in years, Joe Bullet had time to think about the significant right in his life that not only cost him over twenty-years of his life; it also caused him to lose the

−113−

Rovella Starr

The New Love-Starved Bitch

Author's Gold Edition

faith and trust of his own mother and father. Ironically, the only person who ever believed in him or his innocence was Rovella Jackson Starr.

The night Joe picked Emily up off the side of the road, to help her get away from her rapist was a bad move. Having turned the corner on Greenwood near the Cultural Center, in Tulsa, Oklahoma, with Teresa Ribs, he should have gone straight home. However, when he saw her that dark night in Tulsa, poor Emily had been savagely raped and dropped off in the path of Joe Bullet and all that he was taught as a child by his mother left him no choice but to do the right thing by that white woman. As his thoughts trailed to the events of that night, Joe was shocked when the restaurant attendant tapped him on the shoulder from behind.

"I'm sorry sir," the man said, "But, you can't sit in this area unless you order some food," he stated. Joe was scared. The last time somebody tapped him from behind, they were taking him to jail. Recognizing that his fright was a flashback from the past, Joe profusely apologized to the man. He was not thinking about eating. However, over the years Joe Bullet had learned to play it safe with white folks. With that, he got up to pick up a banana and a bag of pretzels. After he paid for the food, he sat down in the eating area again, where he relived what happened the night he was trying to help a person in need. Could he do it again? Could he risk his freedom to save Ray from his sick cousin?

On the night of July 17, 1972, Joe Bullet went to the south side of Oklahoma to get his mother some ribs because she said the Tate Place ribs wasn't no good no more.

"They have something good, (I mean niggas); yes I said it. And then they go and fuck it up," Teresa said, speaking of black people. Joe Bullet had heard this story a million times before. In order to keep the peace in his mother's house, he agreed to go to the south side at 1:00 in the morning to go get her some good ribs. Joe had the ribs and was on his way home when he saw a young white woman flagging him down in the middle of the street. Without thinking about it, Joe pulled over to the side of the road to help the white woman in distress. Behind the woman a young white man speeded off in a white late model Cadillac Biarritz. Joe tried to get the license plates of the car, but it was dark and by the time the car sped off he couldn't see anything. Anyway, his concern then was about the bleeding white woman who was standing right at his windshield. Her hair was so matted with blood that what wasn't dripping had dried in clumps all around her face. Her white dress that was colored red with her own blood was shredded. Her bloody hands were raised above her head in a defense motion. With her last bit of energy, she said: "Help!" And then she collapsed. When it looked like nobody was coming to help the woman, Joe Bullet got out of his car in time for the woman to tell him her name was Emily. She then passed out for good. Joe picked up the heavy set white woman. He put her in his truck right on top of Teresa's bar-be-queue ribs. Thinking the woman was going to die, Joe raced to the hospital and on the way he begged Emily to hold on for a few more minutes.

"Don't die Emily. I'm gonna get you to the nearest hospital. Just hold on lady!" he hollered. At the emergency room door, Joe jumped out of his red truck. He opened the passenger side and pulled the fat woman off the ribs and with all of his strength; he tried to save the woman's life. Once inside, the team of emergency doctors took Emily away on a stretcher and just minutes later, the doctor told his staff:

'Don't worry about wheeling her up to ER. She's dead," he said. With that, Joe Bullet felt a lump in his throat. He didn't know Emily and he didn't think she would die, but he felt sorry for the woman from his heart. Thinking there was nothing else he could do, Joe Bullet turned around and to his surprise a pair of handcuffs was clipped to his wrists from the back-side.

"Sir, you are under arrest for the murder of Emily Brookfield." As they read him his Miranda rights, Joe Bullet wished he could turn back the hands of time and go home.

At the trial, which took place a month later, Joe testified about what happened and one white man who was blind in one eye said it was Joe Bullet he saw driving the white Cadillac that the police found with all the blood in it. They accused Joe Bullet of switching cars to take Emily Brookfield to the hospital in order to cover up his crime. And one man lied and said he even saw Joe Bullet raping Emily.

"He was in that there alley by 38th and Trenton Avenue by the court house and I saw him humping away. When I got out of my truck to ask that man with that awful face, what the hell did he think he was doing having sex with that white woman, he hopped in that red truck and drove away!" the man lied.

Rovella Starr
The New Love-Starved Bitch
Author's Gold Edition

"With a face like his, who could forgit. Tell me your awner' who could forgit that face? I cannot the blind eyewitness told the judge.

The signs from the all-white jury told the whole story. They didn't care that Joe Bullet had helped this woman and was trying to get her to the hospital to save her life. They didn't care about the discrepancies in the testimony or whether Joe was guilty or not. To them, Joe Bullet was an ugly nigga who raped and killed a white woman in the pitch of black in Tulsa, Oklahoma and they were gonna make this nigga pay. Joe's looks and his race played right into the hearts of those white folk's fears and anxieties. The jury only took a record fifteen seconds to put Joe Bullet behind bars on a life sentence.

As a free man Joe felt lucky when the warden told him, "The judge said go home." He didn't ask any questions. He was free. Today, he sat in the airport waiting for his flight. For the first time in twenty-five years Joe cried. What Rovella was threatening to do to Ray, tore at his heart strings making him debate whether or not he had it in him to go back to Oakland to try and save another life. In his heart, with all that he had gone through saving Emily Brookfield, he reasoned that he had done the right thing and if he had to do it again, he would have. When his flight arrived, Joe Bullet changed his mind. He was sick and was too embarrassed about it to tell Rovella. So he was going to 2046 Cambridge Street in Los Angeles to see his father. Inside the yellow cab Joe Bullet laid back in his seat. For the second time, he opened the gold envelope that Rovella had given him. He counted the money, while tears of frustration and indecision rolled down his cheeks.

CAROL D. MITCHELL

Reversal of Love

Rovella picked Ray up from the Oakland Airport with an attitude, but she was smart enough to know not to push it with Ray. For two days he stayed in his room and didn't say a word to her. Rovella was glad to have Ray back in the house and she was not going to assail him or ask him why he had not told her he was leaving for Singapore for two weeks. He had covered his tracks. The money was coming in on time, the bills were getting paid and Ray had made sure that all of this was done in a timely fashion so that he would not have to hear his mother bitch about it.

In a few days, Dana Ann would be home and he would finally be free from this hell on earth. However, right now he and Rovella were getting ready to watch Rain Man and eat some fresh popcorn and Rovella told him that she had made him a big picture of Gatorade. Tonight, the Gatorade didn't taste as sweet to him as it had the night before. Ray excused himself to go to the bathroom. Later, from his room he called Dana Ann. After they talked and he assured her that everything was okay at home, he returned to the living room, where he sat on the living room couch with his conniving mother. As his eyes watched the movie, tonight it was Rovella's favorite, Spike Lee's Malcolm X – Ray did not feel well. As his eyes closed, he thought about Dana Ann while Rovella watched him closely. She began to think that putting the potion in his Gatorade had been easier than she thought it would be. As her son drifted into something Rovella thought was more deep than what you would call sleep, Rovella combed Ray's hair and she promised him that in a few days he would be okay and that things would be back to normal again. Already she had to start telling people lie about his fatigue. The day before when Shane and Eric asked why Ray seemed to be so drowsy, Rovella told them he had not recovered from jet lag yet and that the trip to Singapore had worn him out. She told her sons that the author could not appreciate Ray's real medical condition and that she was putting too much pressure on him physically, with all of her trips, outings and book activities. Considering that the ROL potion was having a domineering effect on Ray's mental health, Rovella was forced to pray to God for intervention.

Rovella Starr
The New Love-Starved Bitch
Author's Gold Edition

As tape one of Malcolm X ended, Ray passed out on the living room couch. Later, when Dana Ann called to say goodnight to Ray – Rovella answered the telephone.
"Hello?"
"How are you Mrs. Starr" Dana Ann asked her politely.
"I'm fine Ms. Arbor. How may I help you?"
"May I please speak to Ray?"
"Oh, I am sorry dear. Ray passed out on the couch. Since his trip with you, he has not been up to much. Maybe, you should wait a couple of days before calling him again. I will tell him you called, though," she promised.
"Click."
Rovella hung up. "The bitch," she thought. This was her time with her son. Had it not been for that bitch she would not be putting her son through this horrendous potion. And if that solution made Ray to much worse than he was at this moment, Rovella had a good mind to call the other bitch, the Einstein wannabe, Margaret and give that tax evading bitch a good piece of her mind. Rovella fantasized about the things she would do to Margaret if her potion killed her son. **"Boy, I would have a drug dealer knock on that red bitch's door over there on 62nd Avenue and knock that bitch smooth off,"** she thought.

Three more days into the potion Rovella called Sam at Ray's Government job to tell him that Ray would be off for a week because of a death in the family. He gave a fuck. Sam thanked her for calling and slammed the phone down. Soon as Ray woke up he asked his mother if Dana Ann had called. Feeling tired, and more lethargic than he had two days before, he asked his mother to call his job.

"I already called that drunken Sam before you got up Ray. I was barely finished talking before he slammed the phone down in my face," she complained.

He asked her again…"Did Dana Ann call?"
"She called Ray. You were sleep and I asked her to call you back in a couple of days," Rovella said, defensively. She then turned around to avoid Ray's

face. His hair was falling out in clumps. And Rovella was picking it up from right behind him. His skin was turning ashy gray. It was hard for her not to notice the variation of changes that the potion was putting Ray through. With each day she noticed another change in the way he looked. Terrified that this drug would kill Ray, she consulted the manifest that Margaret had given to her several times a day.

On this day, Ray walked slowly down the hall then into the kitchen to get something to eat, when he fell on the kitchen floor. A frightened Rovella raced to his side. Ray pushed her away.

"Mama, leave me alone. I can help myself!" Ray screamed.

"I would have told you she called, but you were asleep and I didn't…" Ray cut her off.

"Mama, I ain't even asking you about Dana Ann. I don't mention her around you because I don't want you to hurt her or cause her any pain. Don't you ever hurt her Mama," he pleaded. As the frustration of his growing limitations left him numb, Ray asked Rovella to help him up off of the cold kitchen floor. Instead, the uncaring unfeeling woman watched from the kitchen bar nook as her son pleaded for answers. She thought: *How dare he try to imply that I ran Carla away and that I caused harm to his crazy ass grandmother and his Daddy. Zebbie took that jump on his own."*

"What's wrong with me Mama? Why is my hair falling out and why am I so tired to do anything for myself?" he asked her. He continued… "I can't even fi myself anything to eat," he slurred. Sorry now that she had started giving Ray the potion, Rovella didn't want to hear Ray sounding slurry and being defensive towards her. It was clear to her that the potion had distorted his personality, but her latest discoveries of where he was going with this relationship made her even madder. She saw the expensive receipt Ray had in his nightstand from the Diamond Center. How dare that rich bitch steal her only means of emotional support away from her? It was one thing that she had his heart. Taking away her means of companionship meant all-out war.

"Ray, I told you yesterday that you are gonna be fine. You need to rest. You don't need to be hopping on every plane in the country chasing behind that writer. You ask me what's wrong with you. That's what's wrong with you. Once you start losing jobs over this woman maybe you'll straighten up and stop seeing her," she said. Ray fought with all of his strength to reach up at his mother. He raised his hand up to her and she slowly backed away from Ray. This time when he fell down, she did not budge. She made no reference to his fall.

Rovella Starr

The New Love-Starved Bitch

Author's Gold Edition

"We need to talk Ray. I was holding back on what I think about this silly relationship long enough." Tired, Ray was not able to defend against his mother. He laid his head on the cold floor closing his eyes to search for the strength he needed to tell his mother off. Still, impervious to the fact that she was poisoning him, Ray willed himself to spill out his guts to his mother. Lifting his tired body off the floor, he reached up to the counter where his mother was sitting. Using the silver iron bar around the bar nook, to pull his body up, the weakening man found enough energy to erect himself, at the bar. With his hair providing spaces where one could see chunks of his scalp, Ray stared at his mother through crimson red eyes, with yellow foam seeping out of the corners of his mouth. Had it not been for his innate need to defend his love, Ray would have stayed numb on the kitchen floor. What she saw was frightening, but Rovella had total resolve to see Ray through the entire thirty-days of the ROL potion.

"Mama, you ain't the only good woman in my life anymore. I love this woman, and you will have to accept that," he demanded, through gritted teeth. He continued...

"Clay told me when I got back that it was selfish for you to think that I could live out the rest of my life in this house with you forever. Clay has a lot of experience with women, Mama. I don't have a lot of experience with women because you don't like anyone. You have been running females away from me beginning with my own grandmas. You have made me feel like some stupid punk. I am a man. I have been so happy that sometimes I can't believe I am really living the love I have for Dana Ann. She pulls out the inner soul of me and she surprises me when she defends everything about you. She doesn't have a selfish bone in her body because she loves me and she sees you as part of the package deal. Dana Ann is too smart to dislike you. She tolerates the way you pull me away from her. I am going to marry her when she gets back from her tour. Deal with it Mama. I am getting married in May. Until then, I don't want to talk about this to you anymore."

A sad Rovella watched a glazed Ray eloquently defend his love and to her if any of it was true, she'd be happy for him. To Rovella, a woman

CAROL D. MITCHELL

who wouldn't know love if it crashed on top of her, it was a sad melo-drama and a little too much for the morning time. She thought: "Fuck the bitch!" She was going to be the one with the last laugh when this was over. When Ray labored to walk down the hallway to his room, Rovella looked at her watch. Ray's soapbox antics didn't move her. Three more hours before he was due for the next dose, she thought. She couldn't wait to silence his madness over Dana Ann. As much as she didn't want him with her, the big splotches of hair he left behind on the kitchen floor made her want to cry; but because of his grand standing, she laughed. She laughed at what a fool her son was. Soon as she heard his door close, she laughed again. She knew she had to hold on for a few more days, and then her newly profound Ray would be back to his slow stupid self – the way he was before he ever heard the name, Dana Ann Arbor.

Rovella Starr

The New Love-Starved Bitch

Author's Gold Edition

When the Lights Go Out

In her suite at the Four Seasons Hotel in Chicago, Dana Ann Arbor had dinner with Dillon and Brenda and tried to pretend that not hearing from Ray in two weeks not bothered her. Next year an important tour was coming up for them in Hong Kong and she thought it would be a good time for them to brainstorm their signing plans early. It was Dillon's and Pat's twenty-first wedding anniversary and Pat had flown from Oakland into Chicago this morning to be with her husband. Four-hours into their private hotel festivities Brenda called it a night. Next, Pat got drunk and left, telling her husband that she would see him later after his meeting with Dana Ann Arbor. For the still happily married couple, Dana Ann gave Dillon and his wife the keys to a customized yellow Rolls Royce. When Dillon and Pat saw a picture of the car they were to pick up in Oakland, they knew that what Dana Ann had did for them this time was over the top. All night they thanked Dana Ann profusely for her incredible generosity. After making sure that his wife made it to their suite safely, Dana Ann asked Dillon for a meeting. Covering up her ill feelings over Ray's peculiar absence was no longer an option for her anymore.

"Dillon, I need to talk to you for a minute, if you don't mind," she asked. Dillon checked on Brenda and pat to make sure they were safely in their perspective suites. Keeping what she felt about Ray inside of her burned like a wild fire in her soul. The calls to Rovella's house were fruitless and always ended with her telling Dana Ann that Ray was sleep or that he was not home. Beatrice though supportive, was sublimely distant on the topic of Ray; therefore, Dana Ann turned to Dillon, who was always compassionate and understanding and could lend advice to what was obviously

-122-

turning into a precarious situation at best. As she reviewed last month's cover of the National Reviewer with her and Ray on the cover, Dillon eased through the door.

"I remember that issue," he said. "A few people from the Government said that Ray was retarded and slow, but at least they didn't say he sleeps with Gorillas," Dillon joked. It was the only time Dana Ann had laughed in two weeks; and she was glad that she could count on Dillon' sense of humor during this time of her increasing grief.

"Who cares what any of them say?" Dana Ann asked Dillon.

"Then what's up Dana Ann Arbor?" he asked her.

Tears swelled in the author's eyes. She twisted the large rock Ray had given her around her finger and held her head down to her chest. As tears welled up in her eyes and dribbled onto her orange Brenda Mars Cassini suit, Dillon searched his heart for the right thing to say. They sat down together on the sofa.

"I called over there three times today," she said, looking worried. Dillon had never seen bags like these under her eyes before until now. Her emotions were pitted in this relationship and he had to find a way to save her heart from being crushed this time. Easing up from the black leather otto-man they were sitting on, Dillon rushed to the bathroom for some tissue for Dana Ann.

"Here," he offered.

"Thanks Dillon." Dillon sat next to her on the sofa. He put his arm around her and begged her not to talk anymore. But she couldn't be quiet about this.

"I don't think you are hearing me, Dillon. Something is wrong. Rovella has done something to Ray. I call at respectable times, one in the afternoon, two or three when he should be at work or home. He hasn't called me and that's not like him. Without a cell it's never been easy to contact him on his other jobs," she lamented. She took a deep breath, and then she blew into the tissue. Dillon patted her on the back. With a few more weeks left on the tour, he knew he had to hold Dana Ann up to professional obligations they had long ago committed to. In silence he came up with a plan to call Ray's brother Eric at his law firm in downtown Oakland. Next, he'd call Shane and ask them to go over to Rovella's and do a safety check on Ray for him. He told Dana Ann what he was thinking and she agreed he should do it.

"He is closer to Eric than he is to Shane. Shane has a tendency to go off. Call him first. Please do that," she repeated.

Rovella Starr
The New Love-Starved Bitch
Author's Gold Edition

While Dillon looked for telephone numbers in his pocket-sized Rolodex, Dana Ann eased up off the sofa. In a daze the beautiful, polished woman paced out onto the balcony into the tepid night air of the anteroom of her master suite. There, her heavy heart looked down onto the glistening diamond engagement ring that Ray had given her when they were in Singapore. It had only been two weeks ago, but it felt like a thousand years since she last saw his smile. Suddenly tears of frustration over his absence turned into a bitter feeling of pain that forced hot tears to form in her eyes, then down her cheeks. Looking behind her, she was glad that Dillon was with her tonight to make the calls. As h not wipe the tears away fast enough before more tears reminded her precisely of how much Ray Starr meant to her heart. Now, as she wondered what happened to the man she loved, all she had were the memories.

Ray J.T. Starr and Dana Ann Arbor had finished having dinner at Boat Quay on a large yacht called, Vanilla Rose in Singapore. The lovely couple was in love and everything about this night felt right to each of them. Both of them sat at a booth in a cozy restaurant in Singapore, where Ray told Dana Ann how good the Chinese food was. Laughing from her belly, Dana Ann agreed. He could have told her the sky was black and it would have been right, she felt so good. Six porcelain doll geisha girls dressed in red and black velvet Jeanie outfits danced around her dinner table while a quartet of older Chinese women played authentic Chinese love songs on harpsichords for them. Later, a well-dressed waiter decked out in a fine black and white silk bullfighter's suit, placed a special chocolate mousse desert and black velvet box on the table in front of them.

"What a beautiful couple you are," he said, using a thick accent. They both thanked the man in unison as he walked away from the table carrying the dessert tray over his head in a special artistic manner. Ray then stared into Dana Ann's eyes, flashing his signature wide smile, as more entertainers watched Dana Ann opened the shimmering black velvet box that had been hidden beneath her chocolate mousse dessert. One of the dancers was so moved by the viscosity of their love that she left the table in happy tears. Suddenly, the bright yellow lights on the boat shimmered, and then dimmed into the background of a burnt orange sunset. Without hesitation, the words came out of his mouth clear and sincere. These were simple but cherished words that many women want to hear;

—124—

that had the power of changing a woman's life. With six instruments joining into the precious sounds of the light harpsichords playing softly in the background of the shadows of a picture perfect eve, Ray J.T. Starr, her prince, eased out of his chair. He got down on one knee to sounds of light gasps over those who witnessed the special moment. Next the fine looking man gently took her manicured left hand into his then his eyes glistened as he civilly fought back tears of joy as he popped the question.

"Will you marry me Dana Ann Arbor?" Ray asked. This was the happiest moment of her life and the first time she had ever been proposed to properly. She answered his question with great pride.

"I will," she said.

All who heard the proposal agreed that they were struck by Ray's love for Dana Ann and his uncanny sincerity. Proposals took place all of the time on the yacht, but none they ever witnessed had outdone this one. Tonight Ray touched her heart in a way that sealed their love.

Dana Ann looked behind her into the suite. With Dillon steadfast on the telephone, she viewed her relationship with Ray philosophically. Being smart had not ever guaranteed her love before or happiness. For the two weeks that Ray had been gone – suitors sent her cards, flowers and idealistic yearnings for her company. Professionally, she obliged spending some time with a rich man in the entertainment business whose name we all know. He told her within five minutes of their dinner that he wanted to make love to her before the night was over. Following his insulting remark, Dana Ann left. This man's disparaging behavior moved her to close her eyes right there where her hungry heart picked up the source of its' fuel via images of the man she loved. Ray was right for her, he was everything John and Carol Morgan told her that love would be. His quiet, pleasing demeanor and respect for women had not allowed him to assume the callousness that she had seen in other men she knew. As Dillon called her name, she looked at the blue sky one more time. Wiping away her tears, she hoped that Dillon had good news for her concerning Ray.

"Just needed a little break there, sorry," Dana Ann told Dillon.

"It's all good, Ms. Arbor. I'll handle this for you. Now, what we have is…Oh, Eric wasn't home. His wife said that Rovella told her to tell Eric to find janitorial coverage for the family bank contracts for a couple of weeks. His wife said when she asked Rovella why, Rovella told her that Ray was not feeling well. "Nothing serious," she said, Rovella told her. She summed it up to being a case of overseas food poisoning from when Ray was in Singapore with you," Dillon said. Dana Ann sat down on the black ottoman to contemplate what Dillon said.

Rovella Starr
The New Love-Starved Bitch
Author's Gold Edition

"What do you think?" she asked Dillon. Dillon didn't tell Dana Ann that he was afraid of Rovella and that her history proved that she could be capable of anything, even murder. He didn't tell her that Eric mentioned she had spent some time with Joe Bullet, and Joe left town shortly afterwards. His role in Dana Ann's life had been as an employee and her protector. Securing business overseas in her profession was not something they could cancel and walk away from. People in the publishing industry were not as forgiving as those were in the movies and music industry. After all, Ray is a grown man and if he failed to handle his mother, Dillon was not going to allow his dilemma to adversely affect his boss' stellar reputation. That was his job.

"Let's be square my sister. You only have until September that is less than a month, left on this tour. Deal with Ray's problems when you get back boss. His Mama ain't killed him yet. Believe me he will be there waiting for you when you get back. Right now, the man has endorsed some serious zeroes for you to be here. Chicago awaits your genius and the fine reputation you have built in the literary world. You were a smash in Singapore. We sold your titles to Buddhists, Confucians, Taoists and Christians, girl. Your man Ray was standing right there, wearing his signature cap, with that toothy smile, supporting you every step of the way. He probably doesn't want to disturb your peace. Now, how many writers can say they had bestsellers translated in Chinese? Believe me, as your agent, you don't' want scandalous publicity and if something is wrong, don't let yourself be dragged into it now. Look at your ring. One day you will spend so much time with that nigga, you will not be able to stand his ass," Dillon joked. "So, let's compromise. I know you love the cat. I can see your pain Dana Ann. Ray is a great catch. I been knowing that brother since high school, but he should have left Rovella's house back in the day when she ran his father to that bridge where he took his own life to get away from her. If we don't hear from the brother by the end of next week, well, it's on!" he promised. Dana Ann knew that Dillon's wise words were sounder tonight than her emotional judgment. She knew that Dillon was saying all of this partly for her own protection.

CAROL D. MITCHELL

"You're right. I don't know if I ever told you this before Dillon," Dillon walked over to the sliding glass door where she was standing, where she had not taken her eyes off Ray's engagement ring.

"What's that?" he asked.

"Carol Morgan, my mother always told me when I was eleven-years old and beyond that no matter how bad a man's mother is to always respect her. Kids have unconditional love for their parents and Carol said sometimes kids never develop the objectivity to see their parents the way they really are," she ended. Dillon agreed. He kissed her on the cheek and he told her to get some sleep.

"We have a big day tomorrow, Dana Ann. Let it go. Get some sleep and I will see you in the morning," he promised.

Rovella Starr

The New Love-Starved Bitch

Author's Gold Edition

Closer and Closer to Death

"Peggy Ann Smith? Why does that damn telephone ring and ring? It is starting to get on my nerves. I have told Sam and the people at the bank and at the ship yard in San Francisco, that I have a sick son here. I ain't got nothing else to say to nobody because I have already told them that Ray is bad off! Rovella screamed.

Rovella hired Peggy Ann Smith when Ray stopped talking after his throat puffed up to the size of a tennis ball. Peggy, a Certified Nurse's Aide, who claimed she knew "medicine," and whose official claim to fame was that her husband is black, met Rovella twenty-years ago at Merritt College, in Oakland, California, in a Certified Nursing Certificate night class that Rovella attended for only two days, before she dropped out. Peggy was the only so-called friend Rovella had in life. When Ray took a turn for the worst, Rovella hired Peggy on as a nurse for Ray because Peggy was a disgrace before God as she was and she knew how to keep her stupid mouth closed.

"Just bring me the Gatorade and shut up!" Peggy said to Rovella. Peggy had her nerve. Nobody in their right mind talked to Rovella like this. Peggy had to be the only human alive who could hang with Rovella's shit and she was at the end of the rope with the woman. As a white woman who had been in and out of Santa Rita for selling drugs, not even a hard core woman like Peggy could stand too much of Rovella. On this day, Peggy was tired of hearing about the telephones that kept ringing and all of Rovella's talk about following the contract.

Today, while Rovella was in the kitchen whipping up Ray's daily potion mixture, Peggy wondered why Rovella didn't put this man in a nursing home. It was obvious to her as a trained Certified Nurse's Assistant that Ray was going to die. Last week when she told Rovella how bad she felt

CAROL D. MITCHELL

about what she was doing to her son and his girlfriend by giving him this stuff and all, Rovella called Peggy a **_"Sorry White Bitch!"_** and told her to mind her own fucking business, then she chased her out of the house with her shot gun.

For seven days, Rovella held a bed watch over Ray whose face was coal black and was now unrecognizable. He lay in the bed twisting and turning. Inwardly he could hear everything that was taking place around him, but his body held him prisoner inside a comatose brain that was preparing to suppress every feeling that he had ever possessed for his love. This form of forgetfulness would mirror retrograde, but would be slightly different in that Margaret had chemically designed ROL so that it would retard his memories singularly to his body's redaction of endorphins toward his only love, Dana Ann Arbor. Accordingly, after the thirty-day incubation period his memories of his family and friends would be fully sustained.

His gray bedroom walls were plastered with pictures of the stunning Dana Ann. A life-sized poster of her posing with Vanessa Williams hung directly over his bed. Colorful book covers from every book she had written were carefully organized inside expensive gold frames, decorating his newly painted gray and orange walls. Today, Rovella put a blue knit cap on her son's head like the one Johnnie Cochran had on during the infamous O.J. Simpson murder trial. Unable to open his eyes fully anymore, Ray shook violently whenever he saw Rovella. Fifteen days into the solution, his breathing was shallow and to console herself over what was happening with her son, Rovella marked off each day on the calendar with a black marker. Rovella, who was a slow reader, read the papers Margaret had given her many times and still did not fully understand the instructions all that well. Ray's coloring, his behavior, his inability to speak was all chronicled perfectly in Margaret's contract. As horrifying as Ray's condition was, Rovella was not worried because she knew that by Fall Ray would revert back to the way he was before he met Dana Ann Arbor. And to Rovella, the good thing about that was that he would not have a trace of memory of Dana Ann Arbor ever again. If Ray saw her on the street, she'd be to him after this, another pretty chick passing by.

"Here it is Peg. I can't do it today. Just lift his head and pour the whole thing down his throat honey," she said. As Rovella watched Peg pour the spiked Gatorade down her baby's throat, she reveled at the rewards that would come at the end of all of this.

"I'm going home after this Rovella," Peggy said, in her annoying, squeaking voice. Rovella scanned the bitch. "He looks mighty awful to me. His face is all black and his body is stiff and to tell you the truth, he looks

Rovella Starr
The New Love-Starved Bitch
Author's Gold Edition

dead. I think you ought to call 9-1-1. He has a tendency to swipe at ya' violently sometimes and every time I put something in his mouth, or try to brush his teeth, he bites my hand off," Peggy complained. Out of nowhere Rovella socked Peggy in her back, causing her to drop the red empty cup that she had taken out of Ray's mouth. The assaulted woman opened her mouth in shock. Rovella looked at Peggy like she had lost her goddamn mind, talking about her son that way.

"You talk too dam much, Peggy and I' starting to think you are the reincarnation of that damn Mattie," Rovella pushed her.

"Here's your money," Rovella told Peggy, as she reached inside of her purse. Peggy backed away from the mad woman.

"I don't even know Mattie. But I am sure I ain't nothing like the woman!' she defended. Everything she ever heard about Rovella from others to her was true. Glad that this friendship had stalled she grabbed her things off of Ray's nightstand and left the red cup on the table. On her way to the front door, Peggy pitied Ray. The bewildered woman wanted to take her fist and jam it down Rovella's throat. Instead, she scanned Rovella back like the bitter old woman had completely lost her mind. In a moment of spontaneity, Peggy spoke her mind.

"You too old to be playing these kinds of games with people's lives Rovella," Peggy stated. Rovella, with her hands on both hips stared at Peggy as she was anxious to hear what Peggy had to say. With the sun from Ray's bedroom window hitting her dead in the face, Rovella squint her eyes.

"Haven't you had enough of this wretchedness" Peggy asked Rovella. Rovella gave Peggy the finger. Walking towards her slowly, Rovella stuck her tongue out at Peggy. Then she asked her if she was through.

"You have had your moment of truth and I haven't heard a thing," Rovella yelled.

"I'll tell you this Rovella. I ain't coming back here no more!" Peggy shouted. Peggy, her gold hair in a Jherri Curl standing on the top of her head, strutted outside in her second hand 99 cent red white and blue jogging

CAROL D. MITCHELL

suit; her payless clad feet, beating the pavement like she was crazy to her beat up black BMW.

Rovella traced her steps down her driveway, thinking to herself: *"Now that is one sorry ass white bitch. I this day and age, knowing all that we know about how hard it is to be black in this country, from show like "Roots" and the Autobiography of Miss Jane Fucking Pittman, why the hell would that fat sorry ass white woman try so hard to be black."*

By August, Ray J. T. Star's mind and body were savagely trapped into human bondage. Done for by an indiscernible, invasive drug that his mother poured into his body, soon a once striking man looked like a monster. Weeks of cerebrum confinement left him fatigued and often he was dead inside a constant sleep like the one a patient is in after taking high doses of Demerol. Two weeks into the drug, fatigue morphed into an inhibiting type of liveliness that kept Ray awake at least twenty-one hours a day; however, physically he was not able to move.

Realizing that few people if any knew of the poisoning, surviving mental incarceration was indeed a monumental task for Ray to get through every day alone. Nevertheless, he had to find a place beneath the surface of his infliction to commit memories of Dana Ann, same way a squirrel would store nuts for its' young ones. Further, he could not allow ROL to sedate his love for her permanently, no matter what those papers his mother read to him said. With that, Ray was no longer worried about how he looked or that his hair had fallen completely out or that his muscles had atrophied, leaving his body twisted into a pretzel. Skillfully, his worst thoughts towards his mother had morphed into so many things, she could not figure out how he felt anymore. Even picking up his own limbs presented to be a challenge; so picking up the telephone that was a foot away from him for help was not to Ray a rational thought. Ever since taking ROL, the hot flashes had formed a waterway through this body that rendered his emotions out of whack. The body now functioned as an entity that was autonomous, and had literally little if any connection left with his brain. Crying, releasing bodily fluids visit him without warning; yet, Ray could clearly make out each sound that was going on around him. He could see things normally and he had memories that were intact, but the human body as we know it, defied all that represented who Ray was now and when he struck out at Rovella violently, there was no way for him to tell it was going to happen. When Peggy was there to care for him Ray yearned to plead to the woman for help. Nothing happened, for he soon learned that he could not perform the action that would cause his mouth to open. He could not move his hands because his eyes twitched.

Rovella Starr

The New Love-Starved Bitch

Author's Gold Edition

Tragically, when Ray figured out which brain command worked for a specific motion, the idea only worked for that action one time. When his face twitched, silently, Ray could not will it to stop. The work of controlling his bodily actions made him clearly see how selfish we are as normal functioning human beings and it made him see how much it is that we take for granted. Thirty-days raced through Ray's mind. When worst came to worst and Rovella walked into the room with the Gatorade and a dogs muzzle to put over his mouth, Ray passed out. For at this time, in this place, he simply could not take it anymore.

CAROL D. MITCHELL

Ending in Chicago

"Joe, when you go to Chicago for that book signing you told me about, make sure you stop at the South side of Chicago and say hello to Pullman Village. You know we got a world famous African American Labor History Museum over there. You never know when something is going end," Peter told his son. Soon as Joe Bullet was ready to leave, he promised his father that he would do that.

The visit to Los Angeles to see his father would be the last time Joe Bullet would see Peter Bullet. In his 90's now, Peter was remarried to a nice southern white woman in her 70s who had shown Joe Bullet great hospitality the entire two weeks he stayed with them in their lovely small home on Cambridge Street. For days. He had vacillated on what he was going to do about Ray. Each time he called Rovella; the phone rang and rang. He was worried. Doing the right thing took such considerable work.

After a nice send off by his father and stepmother, the plane ride to Chicago had been most relaxing for Joe. In Los Angeles, he and Peter had shopped for new clothes and Peter talked his son into getting a fresh haircut and two brand new pair of Nike tennis shoes. He was feeling better not than he had in years. The extra money Rovella gave him would afford him a nice hotel room and the additional $5,000.00 Peter gave him would give him a fresh new start in life. Finally, Joe Bullet was going to get the chance to have a needed break from mayhem and enjoy his stay in Chicago and then Joe Bullet was going home to Tulsa. Joe got lucky one day when he went to the newsstand and saw Dana Ann Arbor's picture on the cover of the Chicago Tribune. Inside, he read the press release, and found out where she was going to be and he marveled over how beautiful the woman was. He had told his father, that Dana Ann was so beautiful that she looked like the God of African Beauty had created her and then dropped her on this planet.

From his hotel suite, Joe enjoyed he comfort of his fresh smelling room at the Hilton waiting for tomorrow to meet one of the nation's Most talented writing stars. He had read Dana Ann's books in prison before he knew her. To him the author wrote with vivid imagination, grand skill and creative intelligence. She was a versatile writer who had not been pigeon-holed into one prolific genre. She wrote love stories, westerns and well-

Rovella Starr
The New Love-Starved Bitch
Author's Gold Edition

researched time and period pieces with the same fashion and fervor of being the dedicated professional that she was. The Chicago paper described Dana Ann as being a multi-faceted talent with respectable credibility in everything she put down on paper. There was even a picture of her with Ray on the society pages. As Joe unpacked his things to settle down into a relaxing evening, he placed the letter he wrote for Dana Ann on top of the dresser, and then he stuffed the rest of his things in the top drawer on top of the Holy Bible. He was only going to be in Chicago today and tomorrow. By the 3rd and 4th of September, he planned on flying back to Tulsa, Oklahoma, where Peter had set up an interview for him to get a job with the train station. After unpacking, he made one telephone call before picking up Dana Ann's novel "Missing Person." When he found it at the flea-market in Los Angeles, the book brought back memories. The book was so popular in jail; there was a waiting list for the book. He finally would read Dana Ann Arbor's second novel. It was an intriguing eight-hundred page epic about a Russian who was stripped away from his family at birth. All through the epic, Joe was involved. He remembered being hooked on the ideal of the main character finding his loved ones. *In the end when the tired Russian, Rashmani is eighty-years old, one of his brothers finally put the pieces together only to get to Moscow the very minute that Rashmani dies. The man saw his seventy-eight year old brother coming slowly towards the slat on which he lay and he tried to hold on to life's precious breath for five more seconds. Rashmani panted and struggled to stay alive. As Gushmani edged closer to him, Rashmani feverishly stuck out his trembling hand to receive the flesh of a brother he had been looking for for sixty-years. He was inches from completing that arduous lifelong journey before death got selfish on him and snatched Rashmani away from that meeting permanently. The story ended with his brother sobbing helplessly over his long lost brother. Others who had read it told Joe Bullet that he would cry when the end came. Joe denied it. However, after he closed the end of that great epic – he knew that all of her books would be bestsellers.*

With the famous author stuck in a dilemma of her own, Joe was eager for tomorrow to come to go to the book signing to meet Dana Ann and to let her know what was happening to Ray. The decision for him to be

CAROL D. MITCHELL

here had not come easy, but doing the right thing could not be compromised and that was his final decision. Brutal prison life, his inward secrets, and his mother's death had changed him and Joe Bullet felt that he did not have anything to live for anymore. Alone he had thought that since he and Rovella had been so close growing up that she would have mellowed with age, but to his disappointment that had not happened. Now Rovella was more treacherous than she had been back in Tulsa, Oklahoma. In her quest to maintain her son's sole devotion and love, she was too impaired by a lifetime of insanity to rationalize the cruel repercussions of her actions, in his opinion. Those being said, Joe Bullet knew that he would have been derelict in his responsibility to his family to go back to Tulsa without handling this first. He had not told Rovella this, but he saw what happened to Fuzzy-Hussy, a friend of his in prison. Fussy's rich uncle bought him Margaret's ROL potion. It passed the sensors. They gave it to him. He took it and thirty-days later he never remembered one iota about the bitch Hazel that had left him two weeks after he had been thrown into the slammer. He knew first hand that Margaret Fisher's formula worked. Hell, the woman was a universally known chemical genius who was taken seriously by scholars, professionals around the world that is all except for the United States Government. Truth be told Margaret Elizabeth Fisher was far more threatening whipping up her chemicals from her house in East Oakland, than she would have been working for the CIA in Joe's opinion.

By morning time, Joe Bullet was not feeling well. He did not know what it was. The book signing had been put off until tomorrow because the President's wife was visiting the hotel. With much time on his hands, Joe took a cab from the hotel to Chicago's South Shore Cultural Center. Forgetting the name of the place his father asked him to visit, Joe Bullet toured the cultural, historical and architectural treasures of the city's largest African American arts communities. Today, a gospel group was performing outside. He did not know the name of the group, but the music was beautiful and the tunes brought back memories of when he and Rovella was so close back in Tulsa. Sitting down on a bench Joe Bullet dreamed of the kid who Zebbie once called, *"The Pretty Girl"* with the big green eyes who had always defended him; who no doubt loved him. He remembered the day he last saw his Aunt Darnetta, she dropped Rovella off on his mother's steps screaming:

"Here you go Teresa; you take your niece, this little evil bitch. I have done all I can for her!" Darnetta screamed.

Not once in his lifetime did Rovella Jackson ever say anything about his ugly birthmark and one time she rubbed lotion on his face and she told him he was the prettiest looking man that she ever knew. Those were the

Rovella Starr
The New Love-Starved Bitch
Author's Gold Edition

kindest words he had ever heard in his life. He had never betrayed Rovella before and he was in the greatest pain of his life at this very moment, but he knew in his heart that his cousin came first. Nobody loved Rovella more than he did. For over fifty-years they were confidants and they were each other's best friend and protectors. However, what she was doing to Ray and Dana Ann was so wrong, it was like a cancer of Joe Bullet's heart. Sadly, he was convinced that no matter how much he loved Rovella, he could not be her protector anymore. Caught up in his love for Rovella and doing the right thing, Joe Bullet could have put a quick end to his dilemma by calling the police, but his own unfortunate experiences with law enforcement and his horrifying events behind bars quickly made him decide against reporting Rovella to law enforcement. He did however have to put an end to this madness and he knew telling Dana Ann about it through his letter was the right and the safest thing for him to do for everybody concerned.

That night at the hotel, Joe treated himself to a king's dinner having two bottles of White Zinfandel wine, the house T-bone steak well done and buttery, garlic mashed potatoes smothered in brown gravy with scallions. He had candied yams. Buttered scalloped potatoes, broccoli covered with heaps of freshly churned butter and cheddar cheese; and, for dessert, he ate a hunk of double fudge white and dark chocolate cake – with two scoops of Swiss Malted Chocolate ice cream. After clearing his conscious with good thoughts, and having filled his belly with good eats, the exhausted Joe Bullet called housekeeping to come pick up his empty tray. Before lying down to nap, Joe Malcolm Bullet took all of his medication. Next, there was a knock at the door, one, two, and then three knocks. When the door was swung open, the caterer said:

"'I'm here to pick up the dinner tray." The gorgeous lady who answered the door gave the caterer a generous twenty-dollar tip. She thanked the servant. He thanked her back, and next Rovella Jackson, who had dialed 9-1-1 closed Joe Bullet's hotel door.

CAROL D. MITCHELL

Time to Take Action

With about thirteen more days left on the tour, Dana Ann had become a pro at keeping her emotions in check. To forget about the pain of not seeing or hearing from Ray, the busy author concentrated by putting her words on paper. With a staff to run and engagements to fill, she was simply going through the motions. Not a day passed by when she didn't worry about Ray. Sometimes she felt he was talking to her telepathically, and telling her not to worry about him. After all, with only ten more days left on her tour, she would be home soon enough to find answers to all of her questions regarding Ray's strange absence. Rationalizing what she was going through had not kept Dana Ann from suffering the physical ramifications of her pain. She could not sleep and had lost ten pounds. The days had been too long and hard. Secretly held up in her hotel suite, she dared tell Dillon how depressed she really had been. Secret calls to Doctor Watson in Oakland went undetected by her staff, as the ever suffering author did all that she could to uphold her staff and to maintain the normalcy amidst the most horrendous pain that she had ever felt in her entire life. It was no secret to her at all that the enemy was Rovella Starr. Having always relied on her solid pragmatic good sense, Dana Ann hired Lance Dupree to privately investigate Ray's absence. For the past two weeks, Lance reported to the author that he could not get one shot of Ray going in or either coming out of the house on Market Street. Each night Lance Dupree sat across the street from Rovella's house and he shot one picture after another of what was going on in that house. He had called Ray's Government job and got nothing because of California privacy laws. Nevertheless, he gave Dana Ann a horrifying picture of Rovella sitting in her chair at the living room window aiming the barrel of her shotgun directly at the front porch. Lance then recorded her daily activities, where she spent considerable time in the back rooms of the house. On Thursdays, Lance reported that Rovella shoved a large green garbage can filled with empty Gatorade containers to the edge of the sidewalk for the garbage man; but, one day Eric was the one who pushed it out there for her. With weeks of information that Lance had gathered, it gave Dana Ann little comfort of Ray's well-being. It left little choice for her to determine that

Rovella Starr
The New Love-Starved Bitch
Author's Gold Edition

somehow Rovella had Ray held up somewhere in the back of the house where she was spending a lot of her time.

  The book signing that took place a day after the President's wife left the Chicago Hotel had been sad for Dana Ann. Her staff absent Dillon, who had returned to Oakland days ago for a family emergency - told her that one of her fans, a man had been found dead in his hotel room and that he had left a fan letter for her on his dresser bureau. They said that the letter had been given to the Chicago Police and that they would in turn give her the letter following the investigation of the man's death.

  When Rovella Starr could not wake her cousin, Joe Malcolm Bullet up after the lovely dinner they had shared together, she called 9-1-1. Joe had called her the day before saying that he wanted to talk to her about her giving Ray Margaret Fisher's ROL potion. Having long since blocked the reality of what was really going on with her son out of her mind, Rovella believed that the potion she was feeding her son was really medicine, and that it would help him to return back to his old self. Feeling sorry for Joe Bullet, who meant the world to her, the deranged woman could not understand why Joe didn't believe this. The reality of Joe's bad state of mind, was reasoning enough for her to jump on the first plane to Chicago. Joe Bullet had always been of great concern to her and she didn't like the way he sounded now. He had kept telling her on the telephone to do the right thing and not to hurt Ray. He cried that he didn't kill Emily. Rovella didn't know why Joe was rambling so and repeating things to her that she already knew. **His early release from prison had more to do with her than anyone would understand. Her sacrifice to get him out of prison was merely another testament to her love for Joe Bullet, but no one ever had to know this.** With all of this crying and rambling, Joe reminded her of Zebbie the way insinuated that she would hurt Ray. The morning following Joe's agitated call, Rovella raced to Walgreen's on High Street in Oakland, California. There, she bought a pad lock for Ray's bedroom door. At home she drilled the pad lock onto Ray's bedroom door, and then she gave him his dose of ROL, promising her near death son that she would be right back because she

CAROL D. MITCHELL

had to leave California to go tend to Joe. Just hours after he died, a depressed Rovella Starr told the Chicago police that she was stunned that something like this could have happened to her first cousin. She told the police that when she couldn't arouse Joe Bullet she called them right away, and had thought it was them at the door when the bell boy came to pick up her and Joe's dinner trays. When the police asked Rovella what she was doing in Chicago, Rovella did not lie. She told them she told her son Ray, who had been ill, that she had to take a flight to tend to her cousin Joe, who had taken ill in Chicago. Joe had called her that morning sounding depressed. Joe let her in the room later and together they ordered dinner thinking he'd feel better after he got something into his stomach. "After dessert he said he was tired and he would talk to me later, and then he went to sleep. When I saw the white stuff coming out of the sides of his mouth, that's when the door bell rung. I paid the man for taking the trays. Next I tried to wake Joe up again. And then, I called the police," Rovella stated. A sad Rovella Starr told the truth. She went on to tell the investigators that they couldn't take Joe Bullet because the police said he was "Dead on Arrival."

"Who couldn't take him?" asked a mean cop.

"The ambulance, who got there before the police couldn't take him," answered Rovella.

"So, later, a white truck came and took his body to the morgue. And, then you guys brought me here," the bereaved Rovella stated. At the 18th District Precinct at 1160 North Lara bee Street in Chicago, Illinois and the Chicago police deserted Rovella Starr in a cold lobby.

The chilled precinct in downtown Chicago was dusty, old and was made to intimidate the city's slew of crime doers. The old wooden chairs in the lobby were made of rickety – splintered wood and the avocado green counter tops were scratched and the sliced Formica counters were high enough to keep the undesirable people of Chicago effectively at a distance. The inquisition seat Rovella was sitting on was hard, it was too low for her and it was made of rusted tin and was uncomfortable. The precinct gave the innocent the feel that they had done something wrong and that if they didn't tell the truth they were going to jail. Rovella had seen *Columbo* and *Mannix*. Back in the 70s, she and Ray watched all of those shows together; and she knew from looking at those shows this was a rife police department. This afternoon she eyed this place suspiciously. She knew she had to be cooperative with the cops out here. She wasn't a reader, but Peggy had told her that her niece, who was a Chicago prostitute, had died in a chokehold in a Chicago police precinct. She said the Chicago Police were worse than New York and Los Angeles put together. Now, Rovella knew that she had to be

Rovella Starr
The New Love-Starved Bitch
Author's Gold Edition

cooperative with these cops or they could do dirty things to her and throw her away in one of their many precincts and nobody would ever find her again. Because of the injustices that her own cousin Joe Bullet suffered, she knew about red tape and how if you weren't careful enough or if you were black that you could end up all wrapped up in some bullshit you had nothing to do with.

This afternoon this bunch of tired, craggy, no caring ass cops were an especially dirty looking bunch to Rovella. She had to be on her guard to handle these dirty ass bastards though. Two of these sorry ass no good mutha-fucka's had dropped her off inside a cold lobby that felt like a meat freezer and had still not offered her any words. All she wanted to do was finish answering the fucking questions, and get out of here. She needed to go tend to Joe's remains and then go home. However, this bunch of assholes would not even let her make a telephone call to Eric or finish her statements. Too much business was going on. People were being slammed, thrown, pushed, and shoved around like dogs. It was noisy and the 18th Precinct was nasty. Rovella wanted to leave right away. As the wait in the lobby got longer, Rovella surmised that for the most part these were some mean looking lazy ass pigs mostly in their late thirties and early forties, who spent too much time chasing God knows what and eating fattening, greasy doughnuts that had left them all with deep brow lines, spare tires and pop bellies. Time, crime and crooks, low life's low budgets, had borne mean looking specimens with the title of "Police."

White doughnut boxes with the word "Doughnut" spelled out in blazing red letters was sitting on every table in the place. Rovella thought these cops were routinely greedy freaks of fucking nature to the tee. "Slam," (*doors closing*) "Shut the fuck up" (*Too much cussing*) and "Save it for the judge."

Just plain old disgusting words spilled out of these cop's mouths from various ends of the entire station. The chorus of cops reading the Miranda rights: "You have the right to remain silent…" blurred into a chant that Rovella was sick of hearing by now. She knew this was not the place to fuck around; but, this was not the place to look for sympathy either. One

CAROL D. MITCHELL

mean ass black cop held a thin, frail prostitute by the collar. Her needle mark riddled arm was pulled over the top of her head to the snapping point by a cop. He talked to the woman like she was a dog. The woman cried so hard that black mascara ran down her cheeks and her crying and resistance to the cop made him terrorize the woman even more. Rovella had never heard terror like this before. She heard the snapping of the woman's arm like a green bean. "Ouch!" the woman cried. Then that mean son-of-a-bitch tossed the woman's emaciated body to the counter where she was processed, as someone took her belongings, put them in a brown bag and then the cop tossed her into a tiny cell with some more hard-looking whores and dope fiends. Again, nobody was talking to her. Rovella felt like she had been forgotten about.

After four more long hours of waiting, a cop finally took a depressed, cold, Rovella into a tiny freezing room with no windows. Inside she was slammed down hard into a brown metal chair that screeched across the concrete ground, causing her to cover her ears. The room as small as it was reminded her of a broom closet and was dusky and was filled with cigarette butts and smoke. The concrete floor was laced with hard rock pebbles that rolled beneath her black house shoes. It was hard for her to breathe and in her evil mind the growing disenchanted Rovella called the Mexican cop a bad name under her breath. He asked her what was the last thing Joe Bullet said to her, in a thick accent that Rovella could barely comprehend; and, when she asked him to repeat the question, that son-of-a-bitch slapped Rovella upside the head. Rovella looked at this cop like had had lost his mutha-fucking mind.

"You fat ass mutha-fucka!" Rovella screamed. With no witnesses, no windows and free will to do her however he wanted to – Officer Jimenez took control.

"Sit down you yellow, black bitch!" he hollered. Rovella hated him right off. She began to feel the shock of what happened to her cousin. Surprisingly, she found it difficult to face the reality of what had happened until now. She couldn't respond to the questions and in her evil mind, she was calling this this fat ass Mexican every name but the child of God. She had surmised that she would never call this Mexican a "Wet Back" to his face. But to her that was what he was and she didn't appreciate the tone of his voice at all.

Joe Bullet was the only relative she had other than her children and grandchildren. She wanted to say something. No words came out of her mouth and she surprised herself when she started to cry over Joe. Flashbacks of their lives touched her heart. The tears rolled down her cheeks so fast that she looked ten-years older, however stunning she still remained. She was

Rovella Starr
The New Love-Starved Bitch
Author's Gold Edition

getting frail now and only weighed ninety-pounds. She felt horrible over losing Joe. She kept crying and trying to find the words to answer the questions, but her voice cracked until it was gone. The cop was going to have to draw on his expertise with this resistant bitch, he thought. Recognizing she was out of sorts, Officer Jimenez cased the beautiful woman like he was a lion in a mouse's den. With all of the skills of a seasoned cop, he then picked up the drooped head of Rovella Starr using his fat right hand. He then fooled the bereaved woman with something that felt to her like compassion.

"Look. I know this is upsetting to "Jew." But, we really need for "Jew" to tell us what "Jew" cousin say to "Jew" before he died, Mamacita," the rogue cop asked her. It was hard to do, but Rovella took in a deep breath. She felt dizzy, but she was going to answer the questions so that she could get to the morgue and then to the airport in time to catch her flight back to Oakland, California.

"He said, he said," Rovella cried. Jimenez gave her a tissue from out of his pocket.

"Take jor time Mamacita," he offered. Officer Jimenez knew right away that Rovella was no guilty of killing Joe Bullet. A sixteen-year veteran with the Chicago Police Department he knew that he would have let her go along time ago had she not challenged him; however, he was going to play this one out for procedural sake and to teach this bitch not to talk back to the police. Doing their job faster now with the help of automation and computers, the Chicago Police Department had looked up Joe Bullet's past and they really didn't care about him. They didn't have enough evidence yet to prove that anyone had reason to kill Joe Bullet of if it was really a murder at all. But because the President's wife was in the area and a world famous author was in the hotel, they had to do everything about this death right, so that it wouldn't come back on them. The officer left Rovella in the room to cool off for a minute. When he came back an hour later, he had more questions for the fatigued, still gorgeous woman.

CAROL D. MITCHELL

"They said the letter he wrote to the author said he was worried about Ray. Who is Ray?" Officer Jimenez asked.

"Ray is my baby son. That's why I am here to make sure that Joe was okay. I have always been there for Joe when he needed me. He had sounded so bad, I couldn't turn my back on him," she cried.

"Why was he so upset about jure son?" Jimenez asked.

"It was the medicine, I think," she answered. Ray is taking medicine to make him be well, like he was before. He had started to have some side effects that have kept him in the bed for a few days. Joe went with me to a lady's house in East Oakland for the medicine; but, Joe thought the medicine would do something bad to Ray. We both were concerned," Rovella stammered. Rovella was telling enough of the truth for the cop to believe her because what she was saying was the same concerns that Joe had expressed in the letter to the author. Only Joe had called the medicine, ROL. There was no such thing and Jimenez didn't have any reasons to believe an ex-convict who had done twenty-years in a Tulsa prison for brutally raping and murdering a white woman.

"Ms. Starr was there anything else on Joe Bullet's mind that would have caused him to take his own life" Jimenez asked her.

"No. I can't think of anything," she lied. "Why you say that? I mean, why you say he took his life?" she asked. Jimenez didn't answer Rovella. Next, a black cop walked in and to Rovella he was prancing around like he was John Wayne. Rovella couldn't believe this mean ass bastard. So, who the fuck did he think he was?

"Did you know why your cousin killed that white woman in Tulsa in August, 1972?" The black cop asked Rovella. This Officer Prescott bastard had come from nowhere with that question and it was not fair to Rovella. To her Joe had never killed or raped that white woman and what happened to her cousin to her had always been an injustice because nobody knew him better than she had. Joe wouldn't kill a flea, and he couldn't fish when they were kids because Joe couldn't even hook a fish. She was seething when Prescott asked her this horrible question. Her emotions had been unbalanced before; but, now she was livid. Yes. She had lied about not knowing everything, but she didn't have anything to do with Joe's death. Teresa Bullet, as mean a ho' as she was; had never raised her or Joe to kill anybody. How dare this black ass mutha-fucka insinuate that Joe killed that white woman and this was the first time anybody had put this in her face. Who did he think he was taking her cousin's good name into vain so soon after he died? She believed 100% in Joe's innocence. And, every day he was in that prison she lost a little bit of her heart for him. Privately, now she knew that if she lived

—143—

Rovella Starr
The New Love-Starved Bitch
Author's Gold Edition

to be one hundred she was going to erase this bad mark from Joe Bullet's record, so help her God. Hurt by the officer's question, Rovella lost track of time, where she was and everything. Holding her head with her hands, she breathed hard to hold back her anger. The frail woman then leaped out of the chair. She then jumped up into Officer Prescott's face, and then she slapped this nigga square on his left cheek. Officer Jimenez, acting like an East Los Angeles Street gang member, pulled the woman off Prescott. Jimenez then slammed Rovella down hard onto the metal chair. With blood racing out of his nostrils, Prescott raced up to the chair where Rovella sat and the forty-one year old rogue cop beat the holy shit out of Rovella, as he strategically hit her in select parts of her body where you couldn't see the bruises with the naked eyes. Sheer evil forced the semi-comatose Rovella to stay focused. Strong, Rovella shook this nigga's blows off. Holding both of her arms to her chest, the beaten woman heard everything Officer Prescott said.

"Bitch what are you doing? Don't you know I can throw your black ass in the slammer for assault on a police officer bitch?"

Rovella didn't say a word to this bastard. She felt strong enough now to place a hooker on that Mexican cop too. With what they said about Joe, she didn't care about herself anymore. Feeling bruised and sad over Joe's death, she would tough it out until these bastards let her go. They would let her call Eric and he wouldn't have been able to make it here in time to do her any justice, anyway. As Eric always did in defending her, she knew that he would have told her to be quiet and answer the questions yes or no or I don't recall.

Later, Prescott and Jimenez both tried to break Rovella down even more as her body went from being hot to cold. Not offering her even a drink of water, the questions kept coming hard and fast. But this was the same Rovella whose own Aunt couldn't beat her down with a switch. Drawing back on this strength, Rovella stayed the course. They asked her about Joe

CAROL D. MITCHELL

Bullet, Teresa, Dana Ann, Peter, Darnetta, Mattie, Zebbie, Ray, Eric, Shane, cousins, Peggy, all of that. Though people had called her dumb all of her life, Rovella proved to these tough cops today that she was nobody's fool of punk. They had gone too far. These cops and she dared say anymore to them than yes or no. At the end of this questioning marathon, the cops concluded that Rovella Starr, however violent, dumb and contentious, loved this wretched, convict, Joe Bullet way too much to have partaken in hurting him. Therefore it was Prescott, who was privately fascinated by the fine woman that let her go. Prescott even offered to take her to the morgue. He even waited for her to say goodbye to Joe Bullet and then he took her to the airport.

Back at the station, Officer Richard Prescott told Officer Jimenez that Rovella Starr, fine as she still is was hiding something; but, it was not murder. A superior court judge had actually called Prescott and ordered him to let Rovella go.

"She was too damn neurotic and too damn dumb to murder a flea. Most likely Joe was depressed. We found Xanax, Paxil and over the counter drugs in his room. We see a lot like him every day. They are like Vietnam veterans, some of these prisoners. They commit a crime, and then they convince themselves that they didn't do it and when they get out of jail, they are like war veterans. They have nightmares about the shit. I think she really did come out here to discuss family problems with the guy. Her son is supposedly engaged to the famous author, who is staying in the hotel where Joe Bullet died. Joe didn't say anything about an engagement in his letter. I haven't talked to the author yet. Anyway, I did talk to the victim's father, Peter. And he said his son left Los Angeles a few days ago depressed about some medicine his cousin had her son on. He did say that Joe told him he was troubled with his cousin Rovella, but after spending nine-hours with that crazy bitch, who wouldn't be? I called this Doctor Jeffrey Watson in Oakland who was filming a show at some Black Network called Soul Beat. He confirmed that he did prescribe Xanax and Paxil for Joe Bullet at the request of Ray. A general Practitioner in Los Angeles, named Carla Diane Starr said she prescribed anti-depressants for Joe too. Doctor Starr faxed over some records indicating that Joe Bullet was dying of AIDS. His medical records indicate that contracted the disease in prison. The guy was depressed about many things. I took his cousin to the morgue for a viewing of the body before dropping her off at O'Hare airport. Man, I ain't never seen a human face so scarred and ugly," Prescott said, referring to Joe Bullet.

"Well, while you were gone I did talk to the author," Jimenez stated. "She said she knows Rovella's son and that he had mentioned Joe Bullet to

Rovella Starr

The New Love-Starved Bitch

Author's Gold Edition

her once or twice a few weeks ago. She said that they are engaged. She described their relationship as being close, but oddly, she said she has not seen her fiancée in weeks. Everybody knows that Dana Ann is known to pick up the world's stray cats everywhere she goes. I gave her the letter that Joe Bullet came out here to give her. No way do I believe that woman would kill her son through some wild concoction made up by some scientist in East Oakland. Man, that's ludicrous. The man was on so much medications it's no wonder he was hallucinating. Well, I did not pry into Dana Ann's personal life. Her lawyer and wall-to-wall assistants and aides limited the line of questions and since she certainly didn't have anything to do with Joe Bullet's death, we left after five minutes of questioning," Jimenez reported.
Within five days of Joe Bullet's death, the Chicago Coroner's Office ruled it an accidental overdose/AIDS. Joe Bullet had mixed three different medications with alcohol, which contributed to his death via the complications from AIDS. The body was shipped to Rovella at Thompsons Funeral Home on September 9, 2000. Joe Bullet's will specified no funeral or burial. In honor of that, Rovella gave Joe's body to the Neptune Society. They cremated Joe's body and shipped the ashes to Peter Bullet. Peter flew back to Tulsa with his son's remains, where he poured Joe's ashes on top of his mother's grave in accordance with Joe's last will and request.

CAROL D. MITCHELL

The letter

Lance told Dana Ann that Rovella had given the Chicago Police so much hell that Officer Prescott said that they assumed send her ass back to Oakland, California – than inquisition her anymore about her cousin's mysterious death. While Rovella was in Chicago, Dana Ann paid Lance to go into the house to get Ray; but, there was a pad lock on his bedroom door and the Oakland Police said they had no grounds to get involved. Lance then made arrangements the next day to get a court order to get Ray out of his padlocked bedroom. Further, Rovella said to him that Ray was not a prisoner in her home. She challenged Lance to ask her son himself if he wanted to go. Escorting Lance down the hallway to Ray's room, once there, Rovella turned the lock. Next, she opened the bedroom door and Lance was truly shocked at what he saw. Ray, bald, thin and lifeless lay in his sterile bed on top of spotless white sheets with a huge smile on his face. Lance admired the tribute on his walls to Dana Ann. Ray's room was neat and was beautifully furnished. You could tell the room had been freshly cleaned by the fresh smell of pine sol. Fresh, colorful flowers had been carefully placed by his beside, giving the appearance that Ray was being well taken care of. However, the truth of the matter was that Lance's visit happened to come about the day after Peggy had made up with Rovella and had only moments ago cleaned Ray's room. Additionally, Ray's emotions had tricked him again. Ray tried to look sad to let Lance know that he was being held captive in his mother's house. Instead, of looking scared or sad – today Ray's emotions read as happy and a large smile was on his face. To Lance, Ray did not look like a prisoner. When Lance asked Ray if he was oaky, Ray's brain told him that he was saying no, but his mouth answered yes to Lance's questions. Case closed.

Rovella asked the good-looking detective if she could be of further assistant to him. Lance told her no. Since he had not complained about his mother caring for him during his illness and she had cared for him all of his life, why should now be any different. "After all," she said to Lance, "I am his monster." Still skeptical of Rovella, Lance drove downtown to the Oakland Police Department on Broadway in Oakland. There, the ex-police officer examined police records that revealed that nobody had reported anything to the police about a missing person or anybody being held against

–147–

Rovella Starr
The New Love-Starved Bitch
Author's Gold Edition

their will on Market. Later, an officer named John Jenkins told Lance that if he went back over o Market Street bothering that woman that he could be charged with breaking and entry, etc., Rovella Jackson-Starr truly had the law of the land on her side.

From her Chicago hotel suite, Dana Ann thanked Lance for all of his hard work. Then she called Eric and she was not surprised at how smart and skilled of an attorney Eric was. Eric assured Dana Ann that if anything was wrong with Ray that he and Shane would know about it. He told her that he saw Ray a week ago and that yes he was a little under the weather, but the trip to Singapore had drained him and with a little TLC from OLE mom's he would be okay. "Yes, he took some time off from work, but Ray usually did take a month off of work this time of the year. He did it in 98' too," Eric assured the pretty lady. When she asked him about the padlock that Rovella had drilled on Ray's bedroom door, Eric agree, "Yes, it was extreme, but not for Rovella," he stated. "Mama's always been over protective of Ray and it's no surprise that she secured the door before leaving down. She did the same thing to him during Joe Bullet's murder trial.
"Hey, don't worry," Eric laughed. "She was back from Chicago by dinner time!" Eric told Dana Ann that Shane was on his way to his mother's house to take the padlock off of the door. Eric told Dana Ann to relax and to hurry up and get back to Ray after her tour. Dana Ann had heard it three times now from Dillon, Eric and Lance that Ray was okay. With a few days left on her tour, she could live with that. As Dana Ann paced around the plush atmosphere of her suite at the fabulous hotel, she was suddenly turned off at its' sheer opulence. She was reviled at how people could be so dismissive at Rovella's host of lurid actions. No other person she ever knew got away with so much ruin. Suddenly, some of the most luxurious amenities in her life were blatant reminders to her how unimportant having nice things were if you had no one to share them with. She questioned her priorities as she scanned the expensive creased drapes and the cream colored counters that turned her off. None of this meant anything without Ray here to share all of this with her. Being rich was convenient in that she had money to use to

CAROL D. MITCHELL

make sure that Ray was okay. To Dana Ann, Rovella was a gifted thug. After talking with Eric, she saw with her own eyes how Rovella's manipulative ways were artful enough to fool such a skilled corporate attorney as her own son, shoe reputation as an attorney in Oakland's City Center was equal to that no less than a Johnnie Cochran. No matter what the detective, Dillon or anyone said, the truth was she was not going to be happy again until she personally could see Ray and make a decision on his welfare first handedly. Sustaining her day to day function had presented to her a great amount of difficulty keeping focused. She could not cope with Ray's safety being an issue that was on her mind all of the time. Love had bitten a hole in her heart and right now that love was biting its way to the very core of her existence. Her vision had left its' direction and it had turned her world upside down. When she learned a couple of days ago that the man that died was Joe Bullet, it was very unsettling to her. What was he doing in Chicago and why had he come could only be answered in his letter. Just days after his death, Dana Ann reached into the drawer next to her bed for the letter. This was the second time in days that she really had the time to read it completely from beginning to end without interruptions.

"Dear Ms. Dana Ann Arbor,"

> *My name is Joe Bullet. I am writing this letter to you because my first Cousin, Rovella Starr has given Ray a solution she bought from a lady in East Oakland named, Margaret Fisher. I know I ain't really supposed to be following you like this, but Ray talks so fondly of you. When he picked me up from the airport last month, he told me he was the happiest man alive and believe me I could see it all on his face. I had to take this trip to Chicago to see you to give you this letter. My cousin Rovella is like a sister to me. However, the last time I saw Rovella at the airport in Oakland, California I could see that she was out of her mind. I take the blame for that, cause my cousin lost her mind when they put me in jail for something I did not do. When Ray was born, he was born brain dead. He was his Mama's baby and instead of staying in Tulsa to have that baby birthed right by his granny, Mattie, she done took herself to Oakland, California in 48' where midwives don't be. They didn't think he was going to make it and when he did the doctor said his brain was lacking oxygen and that he was going to be messed up for the rest of his life and his mother kept all the women's of Oakland and the world away from Ray because of it. She was trying to protect her son and nobody understood that but me. You know that is a mother's instinct to protect her son. That's all and then you came along. When I saw your picture in that Chicago paper I said to myself you sho' is fine indeed. You are black and*

—149—

Rovella Starr
The New Love-Starved Bitch
Author's Gold Edition

pretty like his Mama, Rovella, only a few shades, darker. That what they say about a woman fine as you, back in the day. You changed that boy's life. You made him feel like the man people told him that he would never be even his own Mama told him that. She done him wrong by buying that stuff. But, I have to tell you the truth. Don't blame Rovella. Blame me cause I am the one who told her about Margaret Fisher. What happed was when I was in prison, (for something I didn't do) this cellmate of mine named Fussy Hussy he done took this potion by that lady in East Oakland. And when he woke up after thirty days, he didn't remember a thing about who his wife was and he tore up all of her pictures that he had and he said to me if he see her again he would kill whoever put that picture up there. Well, I don't want to keep rambling on I feel better with you knowing the truth about all of this since he love you so much and I knowed by what he say that you love him too. Soon as you get this letter, you had better go see how he is doing. Stop Rovella from giving him that poison. That's all I really have to say. I am going to buy your book today so you can sign it when I see you. While I was incarcerated, I read all of your books. And you are a darn good writer, if I must say so myself. Mysteries happen in life. People like you uncover them. Westerns and science fiction books are my favorite and you can hang with the best of them. Good luck with Ray. Call me if you need me in Room 122 of the hotel. Oops, I forgot. By the time you read this letter, I will have passed through your line. I might be back in Tulsa, Oklahoma, I am sure."

Sincerely yours,
Joe Bullet
P.S. Ray told me he loves you more than the morning sun. When I last saw his face, it lit up like a light bulb exposing an old secret. God speed and good luck.

Dana Ann read Joe Bullet's letter three times. His allusion to mysteries and secrets untold was interesting to her. Something inside of this letter appeared to her to be left untold and unfounded. She was sorry she could not have met this nice man. Determined to keep his letter, she placed it back in the envelope, and then carefully stashed it away in her luggage. During the Chicago Police official inquiry of Rovella after Joe's death, the Oakland Police called Dana Ann to tell her that they read Joe Bullet's letter. They determined that he was simply an ex-convict that had pretty much died of natural causes, considering he had AIDS. Joe had written the letter to get her attention because he was a fan. They talked about the many investigations on Margaret's so-called potions, telling Dana Ann that there were no grounds to arrest Margaret and for her not to worry about the supposed drug, ROL or COL The Oakland Police Federal Expressed samples of the so-called potion to the Chicago Police who came up with the same negative testing score that the Oakland Police had received from Edward's Evermore Laboratories. Despite all this evidence and all of this proof, Dana Ann considered other facts. Why would Joe Bullet re-route his life plan to get his letter to her? In her bones, she felt that something awful was going on with Ray and there was no reason at all to keep this on the back burner. Eric had told her enough to give her a small window into what Rovella Starr was about. To her Rovella, was a sick and demented woman who was hiding something making her afraid to let go of Ray. She had passed herself off as dumb, when in fact she had the ability to outsmart everybody and had in fact been that way all of her life. Lance had investigated this woman's entire life for Dana Ann and nothing he gave her indicated Rovella was dumb. She was manipulative, spoiled, selfish, and Rovella knew how to get her way without incurring liability for her conniving actions. However, to Dana Ann people like Rovella have their match. Now, Dana Ann was determined to put an end to this madness. Rovella had crossed the line with Ray and in her heart; Dana Ann knew that the time had come for Ray to get away from this miserable woman, before something awful happened to him. This was not the time for tact or decorum. If she had to get ghetto with Rovella, she could go there. The one person who could help her carry out her plan was Beatrice. Dana Ann called her right away.

"Hey," she said.

"Girl, it's all over town how Rovella smacked a Chicago police officer in the face over what he said about her dead cousin and for the beating they gave her. And, I heard the cop was a brother too," Beatrice chimed.

"I am not surprised," she said. "Beatrice, I will be back in Oakland in about five days. I want you to pick me up at the airport

Rovella Starr
The New Love-Starved Bitch
Author's Gold Edition

and go over to Rovella's house with me. Rovella has given Ray some strange potion she bought from some woman in East Oakland. I think the woman has something, but the police and the Government have dismissed the woman as being some kind of nut. Lance found no trace of her school records and the woman swears she has PhD. with honors from Yale. I think she passes herself off as a nut to sell potions to people. The real kicker is that I truly believe that the stuff works and I have to get home before it's too late."

"Get out of here, girl," Beatrice said. "You have got to be kidding. Yale graduate? You know she might be telling the truth! You never know," Bee said. "Wow! Sounds like material for your next book."

"No. I am not kidding and yes, Yale and a potion is her sell." Dana said.

"So, when do we hook up?" Bee asked.

"Meet me at the Oakland Airport, September 13, at 5:00 P.M., I will have a rental at the airport for you because when we pull up in her driveway, I don't want Rovella to know who we are," Dana Ann stated.

"You got it!" Bee stated. End of conversation

With the horror of 9/11 having taken place two days earlier, it was hard to make plane reservations. The nation was in mourning. Dana Ann could not believe what happened to the World Trade Center and the Pentagon. She had visited both places a dozen times. Her need to contribute had her calling the American Red Cross before noon on 9/11. From there, Dana Ann donated five-million dollars to relief efforts. Members of her American book writing club were calling her like crazy. Sadly, though, life goes on!

CAROL D. MITCHELL

A Mother's Love

"Ray, can you believe it's already Wednesday, September 13, 2000. And you go and fall in love with a famous, rich bitch that has set out to destroy you and your and your family. Ever since she been on that tour she been on all these TV and talk shows and last I heard she was giving away millions to the American Red Cross. Not once has she mentioned your name to anyone, not eve to Oprah, Ray. I never asked you why you put me in this situation. All I have done all of your life is fix shit you get yourself into. That's all, Ray. Fix it. Fix it. Fix it. Fix it. I ought to change my name to Rovella Starr Fixit it. Protecting, you Ray keeping you away from mean people and covering your tracks," she said, picking up the things that Ray had thrown onto the floor. "But, you have never been one to appreciate your mother. In two days, you gonna be okay and I'll bet when you waked up you ain't even gonna say thank you. Nah, you don't give a fuck. You don't care. That black ass cop in Chicago nearly killed my ass, and that Mexican cop was no better. I did that for you too. Trying to stop my cousin from ruining yours and my life. But when I am dead and gone Ray, then you are going to wish that you had listened to me better. I swear to God!" she yelled. Rovella tucked the laundered white sheets around Ray's bed unaware now that Ray had learned not to pay attention to her anymore. "You know," she said, finishing her tuck, "I ought to get out of your life, your business and go on and sit by and let you destroy your life. That's what you been trying to do anyway. It took Rovella forty-five minutes to clean up the mess Ray had made of his room. His skin was so blackened now that all Rovella could see were the whites of his eyes. The nights before, when he stopped breathing, Rovella called Peggy over. She begged Rovella again to take him to Highland Hospital. Rovella told her it would be over in a few days. She showed her again the page where *"loss of breath"* was a part of the incubation process. This time she showed the nosey woman the exact page that *"loss of Breath"* was on. Peggy looked at it. She then told Rovella that after the thirty-day incubation period she was surely going to call 9-1-1 for Ray. Rovella told her okay after the Certified Nursing Assistant successfully revived her son. After cleaning up Ray's mess, Rovella went into the kitchen and ground up several multi-vitamins would be okay after 12:00 P. It was already 3:00 and Rovella wanted

Rovella Starr
The New Love-Starved Bitch
Author's Gold Edition

him to quit frowning so much and be positive. So after she poured the days solution down his blue throat she read the newspaper to him. She told him not to worry because by Friday, he would be back to normal again. She was mad before, but she would always be here to protect him. After thoroughly cleaning his room, she fed him his dinner; tonight it was Chateau Sirloin Beef with rich white noodles and snow peas. Rovella wanted to share the news of Joe Bullet's death with Ray. She had not told him about what happened yet because the whole fiasco had been such a shock to her and the Chicago Police made her so mad she told anybody who would listen, even strangers about what the officer's did to her. Ray had certainly taken a turn for the worse, and the only reason why Rovella did not worry was because the papers predicted his condition word for word and so far, the ever-changing formula had not skipped one beat. Though Ray was deeply sedated, Rovella knew that he could hear everything she said, whenever she wanted a real reaction from him, all she had to do was put a picture of Dana Ann in front of him. But, in two days, that would not earn a mere noticeable mention from Ray. So far to Rovella, there was no indication that the ROL formula would fail her and Ray. With that, the paperwork Margaret gave Rovella clearly promised her that Ray as bad as he looked could recognize voices around him and that he could hear words that were spoken normally.

"Ray," she said, placing her hand on his shoulder, "I talked to Margaret Fisher about this growling you been doing at night. You ripped the muzzle I bought for you to shreds. You are acting like a caged animal. I didn't raise you to behave this way. You know that OLE bitch had the never to tell me that because the howling and growling are not on the last pages of the paperwork, that you might be having an allergic reaction to the ROL and or its dosage. The only reason why I didn't go over there and kick that bitch's ass is because; she promised me that the potion would work all the same. We have been through too much baby." She said. Rovella kissed Ray on his forehead. His body temperature was at 103.2 but a high fever was in the paperwork too, so Rovella didn't worry about that. "You know what baby?" she asked, in a cunning tone, "I noticed your girlfriend hasn't called

CAROL D. MITCHELL

you for some time. I guess she really did not love you after all. See I have been telling you all off your life about these no good ass Oakland women. Now, I guess I will have to include the rich bitch's in that too, huh? She asked him.

"Now that girl takes the cake. You mean to tell me, she has all of that money and has access to all of that technology and she can't come see about you? You should have known yourself that a woman like that would not be interested in you for too long. All she is worried about is money and making a lot of it. A few weeks ago, Peggy told me she saw her on one of those talk shows talking about her successful Singapore tour. You were with her, Ray and she didn't mention you once to that host, Peggy said. Peggy said she was waiting. Never heard a word, she told me. Peggy said when the host flashed a picture of you and her on one of those rag sheets, your fancy little love smiled and told that host she didn't believe in discussing her private life. Usually, those stars will say they have somebody special and they don't want to talk about it right now. But she didn't even say that. Dana Ann Arbor is too ashamed of you to confirm to the woman you had a relationship, "Rovella appealed to her son.

Ray's evil mother continued to coddle her son who knew she was making this up. Afraid that his body would belie the anger he wanted to portray, Ray lay still. He then began foaming at the mouth. Next, his chest heaved as he tried to will himself to attack his mother. "Ah, baby, relax. This tension is not good for you. Ride it out and it will be over before you know it, Ray. Your jaws are so tight. You laying over there sweating like you done run a race or something. Just listen to what I have to say and be careful next time. Yeah, baby, all it took was for you to get sick and she made herself scarce. Your own uncle even risked his life going to Chicago, to warn her about me? Did she care? No. But, don't you worry, baby," she said, pulling the covers up to his shoulders, "She won't even be a memory. Watch. Later, you will be out of this bed. And, you can go back to all of your three jobs. Love means sacrifice and that's what being a mother to you means to me, Ray. I have sacrificed my whole life for you. After your Daddy died, I gave up on men. I have been by myself ever since because I dared another man to tell me anything about you. You were born dead right in front of me and I will be damned if I let your life come into double jeopardy. I have given you everything you ever asked me for in life from motorcycles to DVD players. You have furs, leather and suede, all expensive. Mama gave you all of that baby. That little dark ass bitch you call yourself in love with she can't even wash your dirty draws. Soon you will get out of this bed and see clay E again and all of your friends at the Government, the Bank and the Shipyard. After

Rovella Starr

The New Love-Starved Bitch

Author's Gold Edition

this your mind will be clearer than it has ever been before and you won't have to have that sex hungry black ass bitch around pulling on your coat tail trying to make you into some kind of stud to suit her nasty ass purposes."

Ray's blank stare showed he wanted nothing more than to be able to strike out at his mother. He was confused about why she wanted him to remain her baby and why she could not leave him alone as she had Eric and Shane. Turning his head from side to side, he saw the tears coming down his mother's cheeks. All he could do was blame himself. He had always been a quiet person; therefore his mother never knew the full extent of his abilities as a man. With his eyes that he thought was closed, Ray felt his mother's fingertips combing his hair and he knew then that like his father, his mother didn't believe he was a man. He felt too that Rovella really, really did love him. Her evilness played out like a huge sacrifice to him now. The deranged woman must have gone into shock when he was born and the medical personnel told her that her beloved baby boy was dead. Ray knew that he had to leave his mother's house. All of this was his fault now. He believed that the potion was not going to work and take his mind off of the memory of Dana Ann Arbor. He was fighting hard to preserve his memory of Dana Ann Arbor. He was fighting hard to preserve his memory of his one and only love. Rovella held Ray's still hand. He was quieter and more still than he had been in days ago. He sank into his thoughts with an expressionless face. To Rovella that was all for the better for what she had been trying to tell her son all day. She pulled a chair up to his bedside. She then took a wad of papers out of the brown bag she was holding. Next, she placed the papers in front of her son's eyes for him to see. It was hard to talk about it, but she wanted Ray to know her pain. Ray was all she had left in the world really. Losing Joe Bullet was not something she had ever reconciled in her mind and his death was still a complete shock and mystery to her. He was sitting there with her eating this big dinner. He then laid on the bed and died

"This is about Joe," she said, in a very quiet tone. "Your Mama is strong baby and not too much in this life has put me down like this here paper. These papers came from the Chicago Coroner's office. It's a copy of the

CAROL D. MITCHELL

report. It says that Joe Bullet died of AIDS and a drug overdose and alcohol mixture," Rovella cried. She was so shocked about the Coroner's report and all of the things that was wrong with her beloved cousin. Rovella was so hurt over the Coroner's report that to Ray she was uncharacteristically subdued. Ray had never seen her without fight. Her spirit appeared to have lifted from her body. She was humble and the coming moonlight shone on her face tonight letting him know that his mother cared about her first cousin in ways he had not seen before. She was humble, she was beautiful, with the moonlight that was shining on his mother's beautiful face. He had never seen his mother this way before. She kept looking at the .papers as if each time she read them they would give her another finding that would somehow bring Joe Bullet back to life again. When her grief could not be contained anymore, Rovella laid her head on her son's chest and she cried. She showed love and remorse and regret with a depth that Ray had never seen her portray before. In his drug induced, ghostly, deadly way he had always known that she and Joe Bullet were very close, but there was never evidence to support to exactly what extent her relationship with her cousin was. For the first time since being on ROL Ray attempted to sit up. Nothing happened. When his head made a sudden movement towards his mirror and he saw his reflection, he told himself to scream and nothing happened. Not willing to force it anymore, Ray prayed that this surreal moment with his mother would allow her to transfer some of her new found love towards his love, Dana Anna Arbor.

Rovella Starr

The New Love-Starved Bitch

Author's Gold Edition

The Shot on Market Street

Because of bad weather coming out of Chicago O'Hare, Dana Ann's flight had been delayed for two –hours. She made it to the Oakland Airport at 7:00 P.M., and Beatrice Griffith picked her up in a brand new white Lincoln Continental Town car. Out of the airport onto Hegenberger Road, the ride to Market Street was only a few minutes away, as the rush hour traffic for this Wednesday had slowed. Beatrice sped down Hegenberger Road towards the 880 Freeway North, where the traffic was always a bitch.

"I can't believe we're doing this, Beatrice said. Dana Ann you have enough money, you know enough people out here to have somebody else go over there and do this for you. Why are you taking this risk?" Bee asked her. The fashionable author had not come here impulsively. For several weeks now, Lance Dupree's investigation and research had taken him into the bowels of Rovella Starr's past. This visit represented something to Dana Ann that no one could do for her. She had to face Rovella herself. She wanted Ray's freedom and she wanted answers to some questions that she had for Rovella.

While Beatrice drove her peace friend, Dana Ann meditated on her ideas. Beatrice wisely noticed her friend's withdrawal into a silence that was surely calculating the risk of their upcoming visit. Dressed in a white, smart two piece Bob Macke pantsuit, one of the nation's most famous and prolific writers looked as if she was on her way to a business meeting, that was anything but, with her hair gathered back into a neat, professional French roll. For all that this entailed, Dana Ann was too calm for words!

"Remember when we used to party at the End Zone" Beatrice asked.

"Oh, we must have past High Street, huh? Looks like we're headed up on our exit?" Dana Ann asked Beatrice. Not getting the response she

CAROL D. MITCHELL

expected from Dana Ann, Beatrice was worried that this focused look on the author's face was leading them into danger. Rovella Starr had a reputation and she was fearless from what Dana Ann had told her. The energy Dana Ann had put into this visit appeared to have been well worked out in her mind. To Beatrice, the author had taken leave. Somebody with a determined purpose and spirit was in this car with her tonight. When they turned up on Market Street, Dana Ann didn't say anything. She pointed to where she wanted Beatrice to park. Bee parked the car less than a block away from the house. Then, both Bee and Dana Ann got out of the car. For mid-September, the night was cold, but both women put on their coats as they walked one block to Rovella Starr's house.

To Dana Ann, it appeared that the dejected looking brown house on Market Street did not smile on top its' loft of forgotten hay colored grass and had not seen a watering in many months. What had once been a white concrete driveway was now peeking out of a blackened cover that consisted of years of spilled motor oil and gas leaks and cracks from the 1989 Loma Prieta earthquake. Further, up the driveway sat Ray's motorcycle and an abandoned, rusting 70s model gold LeBaron that was sitting on four flat tires. The side by side picture windows dared open up to sunlight, as the outside world was shielded by a pair of dough-colored blinds with the round pull strings. On the side of the house, each window was decorated with what was the theme of the entire neighborhood, black iron wrought bars that truly would not be challenged. Inside a neighborhood that needed protection, Dana Ann and Beatrice walked together up to the front door as gunshots rang out. Bang! Bang! Beatrice and Dana Ann backed away from Rovella's house. They took cover back at the sidewalk behind Ray's Green Jeep Cherokee. In a surprise move, it was Beatrice who assured Dana Ann that gunshots in this area were like flowers were to Beverly Hills. They held cover momentarily.

"Stay here until it's over," Beatrice warned Dana Ann. The two women ducked behind Ray's Green Jeep Cherokee. When the coast was clear, they pursued their walk again up to Rovella's front door. By now, a light was shining behind the thick blinds and a black shadow was walking by the window. Suddenly Dana Ann remembered what Ray had told her about Carla Scott. She was the last woman Ray had to walk up this driveway. Finally, they were on top of the stairs that lead up to the house and they had not been there long before Beatrice freaked the fuck out. Already the neighbor's lights had gone on one by one. Dana Ann got the feeling that the entire neighborhood had their eyes on her and Beatrice and she was right.

Rovella Starr
The New Love-Starved Bitch
Author's Gold Edition

Ray was in his 50s. He was a man who the word "woman" did not go with well as far as this neighborhood was concerned. So, two nice looking well dressed women creeping in the black of night up to the craziest woman in town's doorstep was news. Word was out that Rovella Starr was not to be messed with period. Few people took the outright chance to come on this woman's lawn; much less did anyone dare have the nerve to come up here and go in her driveway, walk up the stairs and then knock on Rovella Starr's door? Hell no! With each step up the stairs, Beatrice became unsteady in her steps. Dana Ann quieted her friend's growing anxiety by bringing her finger to her lips knowing that this was not a woman that you wanted to shock.

"I told you to be quiet. What's wrong now?" Dana Ann asked her. Beatrice pointed to Rovella's picture window.

"Look, Rovella is sitting in a rocker. Look at what she's holding," Beatrice pointed out as she referred to Rovella's shotgun.

"Don't be silly Bee. She knows who I am and shooting me out and out would be too much of a risk for Rovella to take. This is a calculating woman. She ain't no joke. She had a bad time with those Chicago Police Officers, when Joe Bullet, her cousin died. She's crazy, but stupid she ain't. Chill out. I'm gonna ring the doorbell," Dana Ann stated. Dana Ann nervously touched the loose eye of the rusted, corroded gunk that had got on her fingers. With her heart beating fast enough to blow out of her skin, Dana Ann was scared. A loud "plop" let her know that the years of service had long since been over for Rovella's door bell. Now the round part of the doorbell had fallen out of its' socket. Beatrice pulled at Dana Ann's shoulder, hoping they would not be killed. Dana Ann intercepted her question, but not before Rovella yanked open her front door, scaring the hell out of the two ladies.

"Go away bitch!' Rovella screamed to the top of her lungs. The women didn't move. They shook like hell, but they did not move. They stood their ground waiting for whatever.

"Put the gun down, Rovella" Dana Ann warned. Rovella slowly aimed her gun between Dana Ann's eyes.

CAROL D. MITCHELL

"Look bitch, take this other bitch and both you bitches leave or I will shoot," Rovella warned.

When the women did not move, Rovella hollered.

"What the fuck are you waiting for ho, a cab or something?" Rovella cocked her head to the right of her shoulder. She eased down one stair and got more serious with each crinkle of her dark brow.

"If you don't leave here in a minute, I will pump a bullet in the both of you for trespassing on my property," Rovella screamed. As the women continued to be still, Rovella aimed the barrel of her gun at Dana Ann's chest, this time. With finger on the trigger, sweat seeped down the sides of the author's face as the trembling Beatrice held on tightly to her right arm.

"This bitch is crazy!" Beatrice shook. "Dana Ann let's go," she pleaded. Dana Ann shoved Beatrice aside. With a look of serious consternation in her eyes, the fierceness of her demeanor could not be mistaken. Not even in the dark.

"I'm sorry Ms. Starr. I came here to ask you to let me take Ray to the hospital. There are a few other things I want to discuss with you too. First, you need to back the fuck up. Next, you need to take your finger off the trigger. Then you need to put the gun down," Dana Ann spoke. Rovella ignored the warning. She used the butt of the rifle to back the women off of the front porch, as her attention had been quickly, diverted to another matter. Maxine's white French Poodle ran up the steps making Rovella angrier than she had been before. Losing interest in the women before her, Rovella chased the dog to the end of the driveway until the little dog jumped up into Rovella's face and bit the shit out of the tip of her nose. Rovella cussed the dog out. "I told that bitch to get you a leash!" she screamed. Thumping sounds were coming from inside of Rovella's house and you could hear muffled screams coming from the side entranceway. Then shrieks rang out loudly from the back of Rovella's house. Unable to figure out what to do, Dana Ann and Beatrice both prayed that the dog would run.

"I am tired of Maxine letting you come out and shit and pee on my lawn. I have told that drugged out bitch time and time again that one day I was going to kill your ass if you ever came on my property again and now you done bit me in my face. You piece of shit!" Rovella screamed. Rovella aimed her gun at the fearless little mutt. "Don't shoot!" cried Dana Ann. Beatrice covered her face and cried. Above the horrifying yells, Rovella aimed to shoot and kill this dog.

"Don't do it. Please don't shoot that dog Rovella, please!" screamed Dana Ann. Beatrice joined Dana Ann on the lawn, pleading for Rovella not to shoot, but it was too late. Rovella had warned the dog three times to get

Rovella Starr
The New Love-Starved Bitch
Author's Gold Edition

off of her lawn. Then she shot the dog. After the gunshots rang out, the neighbors turned out their lights one by one – while the poor little French Poodle lay on Rovella's yellow grass dying. This was the ghetto. Gunshots had rung out all of the time for a number of reasons and nobody cared.

"I can take your rich ass right here bitch. I can tell the cops you were trespassing like that dead dog out there was. I want to blow you away right now. God knows I do, but I'm a be nice and ask you and this other bitch to leave my property. Ray ain't going nowhere. I got it all taken care of. In forty-eight hours he won't know you from diddly shit!" Rovella offered.

Dana Ann looked at this evil woman dead in her hateful green eyes. She knew how crazy she was – but seeing her in person was a bit too much.

"His doctor's name is Margaret Fisher huh Rovella? Are you still pouring ROL down Ray's throat every day thinking that he will stop loving me" Did you think that the Chicago police weren't gonna give me the letter your cousin wrote me? Did you think that I would stand by and let you hurt Ray this way? I know that you love your son, Rovella, and I know what you did to Joe Bullet too!" Dana Ann surprised her. The shocked Rovella cased her front porch again as Dana Ann and Beatrice slowly approached the stairs again. It was a dark, creepy, cool night in Oakland and quiet outside of a few gunshots.

"Rovella, what happened in Tulsa back in 1938?" Dana Ann asked a now mortified Rovella, who had now turned herself around to face the aggressor, Dana Ann Arbor.

"Leave me alone and stop the sixty-four questions, or I will shot. Go away. Nobody knows about that!" Rovella screamed out in pain.

"Oh…but, you have pushed me lady. I am here to get Ray to UC Medical Center in Davis to reverse what you have put him under. Rovella, Joe Bullet took you deep into the heather's golden marshes one day when you were both only nine-years old. Do you remember what happened that day?" Dana Ann asked a shrinking Rovella. Beatrice's mouth flew open as she watched Rovella change into the defensive mode.

"Shut up about that! Rovella screamed. She raised her gun again.

CAROL D. MITCHELL

"Don't aim that gun at me again you sick ass bitch. You're already in trouble for killing Maxine's dog. You lower the gun Rovella. Face the truth about what you did to your own cousin, Joe Bullet. The guilty woman slowly lowered her Rifle. With her head lowered to her chest she listened to a haunting tale that she was sure no one would ever discover.

"He told you he had a bucket full of corn liquor. You and Joe Bullet were going to taste your first drink of liquor together because you were close and had done everything together. Remember that?" Dana Ann asked her. The shocked Rovella slowly placed her gun down at her side. Standing at the front door, Dana Ann and Beatrice kept a safe distance from the deranged woman at the foot of the brown cracked steps of her home. Beatrice was surprised at how docile Rovella's flagrant demeanor had become. Rovella's shoulder's relaxed, and suddenly the pain and aggravation of what she did to Joe began seeping out of her body. That and the cold made the old thin woman shiver as Dana Ann continued to talk.

"You guys were playing and dancing in the heather's. Joe Bullet was a cute little boy then. His face was a normal smooth cinnamon brown on both sides. There was no line down the middle like now. In fact, people used to marvel and rave about how cute he was and how beautiful you are. Some thought you were twins. You were both two happy first cousins who loved one another so dearly, weren't you Rovella?" The question made it colder for Rovella and she could not stop shaking. She tightened her muscles, and then she closed her eyes and wished this was a dream. Dana edged slower up to her, as Beatrice followed behind. She continued: "You played and picked yellow peaches off of the green trees, at a time you were both innocent children. You plucked purple grapes off the grapevines with your beloved cousin and talked about your future. You wanted to be a teacher and he wanted to be a medical doctor. Then Rovella, you picked up the barrel that would kill both of your dreams. You playfully threw the contents of the acid onto Joe's face didn't you?" Dana Ann asked her.

Suddenly the bereaved Rovella Starr could not take this anymore. Against the will of her body she broke down to her knees on her front porch and for the first time in her life she cried as she had been carried back to a dark secret and a moment in time where innocence met tragedy in the most unsuspecting way. It was a time that created the monster of Rovella. Nobody could cover up the pain of the mistake of her youth. Even now, she had no words to defend the parallelism of this tragedy. There was no confession to give. The truth about Joe Bullet was written all over her face in the form of pain like none either woman had seen before. None of her actions could defend what she did to Joe Bullet. Beatrice felt terribly sorry for this woman,

Rovella Starr
The New Love-Starved Bitch
Author's Gold Edition

as fear glided into immense sorrow for Rovella. In front of Dana Ann and Beatrice, Rovella Starr was a broken woman. She had taken on the scars of Joe Bullet's face in almost every aspect of her life. She defended Joe and she punished herself daily for an accident that could have happened to anyone, however; because Rovella was still near her gun, Beatrice and Dana Ann both, kept their distance.

"Joe Bullet had picked up the wrong barrel. All their lives she regretted pouring what she thought was corn liquor, but was really acid on Joe Bullet's once beautiful face. There was no way anyone could have known about that," Rovella thought.

"Ray needs my help, Rovella. You have to let my staff take him to UC Davis Medical Center tomorrow at 9:00 A.M., or I will publicize what you did to your cousin and the spin will not at all look like an innocent childhood accident, as I know it was. I have hired a detective named Lance Dupree to look into Joe Bullet's murder trial in Tulsa. However, if you don't comply with my request, I will call off the investigation. Joe Bullet is your Achilles heel, Rovella. No one ever knew what the man meant to you and I know he meant enough for you to be willing to carry the burden of this accident for the rest of your life. Since the day you poured that acid on the left side of Joe's once pretty face you have been punishing yourself for it. Your own mother didn't even understand your pain. Darnetta never knew about the accident, nor did Teresa, the aunt that raised you. Joe loved you so much he never told a soul. But his letter told me there was more to the both of you that met the eye. Mr. Frank, who was a rich doctor offered to help you fix Joe's face, but his help was as conditional as the judge you screwed to get Joe Bullet out of jail. You had sex with that horrible man for years. It's tough to lose your virginity at nine-years old. And, it's tough to be labeled whore by a town who never knew you were an innocent child trying to fix a horrible mistake, without the proper guidance. That doctor would have died having sex with you had his wife not found out. You did all of this to pay for what you did to Joe. Joe Bullet knew your heart. He told his mother Teresa he lifted the bucket that scarred his own face for life. He said it was his fault

CAROL D. MITCHELL

and nobody ever questioned that manufactured lie. Even to this day – you are the only one who knows why Joe Bullet lived such a tortured life. I give you credit for standing by Joe, Rovella. You could not even steal his land because of this tragedy and you forked over his share of the money out of love and guilt. You never told your kids about it or your husband, nobody, yet they all had to pay for the sins of your youth. From the day of the accident, Joe never threw it up in your face. You had sex early in your life in trade to undo and to punish yourself for your wrongs. You served yourself up for a long-term sentence in life for what happened to your beloved Joe. Evilness gave you the balls not to care to assault and to hate. Your aunt became raucous because of your pain. What hurt you even worse was that Joe never held what you did to him against you because he loved you too much Rovella. You couldn't understand Joe's love because you didn't recognize love. He could have gone to the police over what he knew you were doing to Ray. Instead, the man came to Chicago, figuring I would talk some sense into you. And then he died. Joe wanted Ray to live, Rovella and he wanted you be saved, but he didn't know how to save you. So in Joe's honor, you have to stop what you are doing and began healing from your own pain."

As Dana Ann talked, she signaled Beatrice to go and get the car. Feeling safe now with Rovella, Dana Ann, she continued as she ignored Beatrice's tearful moans in the background.

"Nobody has hurt you Rovella, but you. You have carried this dark secret and the dreadful truth about Joe Bullet for your whole life. For people that gave Joe Bullet pain, you went after them. You haunted judges, and poisoned teachers that you make them learn to leave Joe Bullet alone. You even ran one teacher out of the Tulsa school district. It's time for you to let this go. Quit ruining the lives of the people who love you, Rovella."

Rovella Starr listened somberly to Dana Ann Arbor. A heavy weight dropped from her shoulders. The truth had come out of the dark subtleties of Joe Bullet's letter onto the yellow fading porch light of her home in Oakland, California. She did not have to hide it anymore. As the 71-year old woman stepped back inside her front door, she looked Dana Ann dead in the eyes and nodded her assent for them to pick up her son. Later, she looked out of her window as Dana Ann walked down the stairs to pick up the dead dog. Surprisingly the dog was still alive, but barely. Dana Ann stayed with the wounded animal until Beatrice finally showed up with the car. Dana Ann took off her white blazer and remained shocked that no police had ever showed up to this horrifying scene. Dana Ann wrapped her

Rovella Starr

The New Love-Starved Bitch

Author's Gold Edition

coat around the dog, as she put her cheek up to his face and begged the cute poodle to hang on to his precious life.

"You're gonna be okay little puppy. Hang in there," Dana Ann begged, as she hugged the little dog. Inside the car, Beatrice raced to a Vet that Dana Ann knew in the Piedmont area.

Later that night, Dana Ann felt that she had failed Ray. Her attempt to see him had done her no good. When Brenda called to tell her that Maxine said yes to her offer to buy Fifi for a thousand dollars that was the most promising news of the day to her. When Dillon called to confirm Ray's pickup tomorrow morning, Dana Ann gave him the details of the rescue mission. She told him she didn't think Rovella would give them any problems taking Ray and she was right. Dillon told her that he wanted to stay on the safe side and go in there for Ray when Rovella took her break from the house. The tired author told him to suit himself. Seeing Ray's Green Jeep Cherokee outside had weakened Dana Ann. She surprised herself at how much she still needed Ray. She could only imagine the pressures the drug had obviously put him under. The housekeeper had left her a pleasing dish of wild rice and stuffed Cornish hens with a note saying: "Welcome Home."

Dana Ann was surprised at how hungry she was. After dinner, she took a bowl of peach cobbler out of the freezer. She heated it in the microwave. Next, she sat back on the sofa. She looked up to the oil painting of her and Ray. Her love for him seemed to be getting stronger, for not even the food she ate had given her the strength to do anything but think about him. At one time, she lay with him and talked to him about their future beneath this picture listening to *Whitney Houston*. Then, things looked so promising for their love. Now Ray was in a cave of a drug induced illness. She could not penetrate the drug and despite her love for him, she would have to wait and see what the doctors at Davis said about Ray's condition. In a world where technology was flourishing, there were witch doctors like Margaret out there, who created lethal substances that the Government had not taken seriously. Prejudice and the sheer desire to stay out of the ghetto's reality had allowed Margaret to create substances that ruined people's lives.

CAROL D. MITCHELL

Can Ray Be Saved

The instructions according to Margaret Fisher said that if the formula's contraindications' worked the last day of consumption of ROL could therefore be forfeited. That meant that by the time 9:00 had arrived on September 15, 2000 Ray was 100% into his memory loss. With the help of Eric and Shane, who created a diversion for their mother to leave her house, the rescue team of Clay E, Dillon and Lance drove up to Rovella's house at 9:00 sharp to get Ray. Shane made sure the entry was open, while the team paced to Ray's room. They found Ray laying in bed with a nozzle over his mouth. Lance removed the nozzle immediately. Ray's skin was green enough for him to play the lead role as the *Incredible Hulk*. He was rail thin and easy to lift. Ray was highly medicated and totally incoherent. His hair had rejuvenated overnight and was hanging long past his shoulders. With a beard that was hiding his round chin, Clay E was moved to tears to see his friend this way. With no time to chance before Rovella came home, the rescue team lifted Ray into a red and white ambulance. Brenda, Dana Ann's assistant raced into the front room with a note for Rovella telling her where Ray was being taken. Dana Ann had doctors standing by at UC Davis Medical Center in Davis, California. She had pre-paid all of the doctor's fees for them to reverse the effects of the drug that Ray had been taken under. Dana Ann had Lance question Margaret who said she was sorry for what happened and that the best she could do was turn over her formula to the doctors. However, she stipulated to Dana Ann, that nothing the medical staff did would reverse ROL. Apologetically, she told Dana Ann that she would pray that Ray would be one of the few who simply would not take to the full effects of the drug, knowing that was not going to happen. Margaret ended their telephone conversation wishing Dana Ann all the luck in the world and not meaning it.

Later the day of the rescue Dillon reported to the author that the lead chemical doctor told him Ray's test all had come back normal. He said there was no sustainable chemicals running through his blood stream that would indicate he was under the influence of any drug. He told her that Ray was weak and sad. After the final examination conducted by twelve different doctors which Dana Ann had flown from various parts of the world, they all agreed Ray could go home in a few days. Rovella had called UC a few times.

Rovella Starr

The New Love-Starved Bitch

Author's Gold Edition

She said she would pick Ray up in three days. Whatever Ray had gone through in the past month left no traces of physical or mental impairments and he assured Dana Ann that Ray was the same person he was before taking the formula. Dillon told Dana Ann the first thing Ray asked for was his trademark hat. Then he asked about his mother, Rovella. He reported Ray asked about Clay E. Then Dillon told her the bad news. "Dana Ann I don't know why; but, Ray didn't ask about you." Not wanting to hear the rest or why, Dana Ann hung up the telephone. Now she had a sinking feeling in her heart. She had thought she was going to be able to purge Ray from her system if the news was bad. However, she loved him more now than ever. The saddest thing of all was that Margaret's formula worked. Dana Ann knew she couldn't begin to ask Ray to go through all of that again. Reality had to give her the reasoning to accept this fate and live for today. As difficult as all of this had been for her, she had Fifi to care for now. She wanted to be up to getting him well again. She had a career to nourish and she had to be 100% to meet her professional obligations. Feeling that the potion had worked, Dana Ann was not going to push it. She could not talk to Dillon anymore about it. When he called back to see how she was doing, she thanked Dillon asking him to leave her alone and give her time. The minute she hung up the telephone she pushed herself to move forward with her life. All she had ever wanted was for Ray to be back to his old self. She did not want to confuse him if he didn't remember her. She was not going to throw herself at his knees and make him remember a past that was erased from his memory. She was not going to show up at the hospital with his ring to remind him of a past they tenderly shared, one that he would never know again, that would point an ill finger at his sickly loving mother. Thinking of all of this was morose. She was deeply hurt at how shallow the police department was and she wondered how a person like Margaret could not be taken seriously for being the perilous chemist that she was. Dillon called back again to say that he showed Ray her picture and he did not say anything about it one way or another. When she asked Dillon if Ray had been awake

CAROL D. MITCHELL

when he showed him the picture; Dillon, paused for a minute, and then he quietly answered, yes. Ray was awake when he showed him her picture.

After hearing more sad news all Dana Ann hoped for was that one day when he needed her that he would remember their love and contact her. The pain of not being with Ray was played out in her heart fully yesterday, now she could feel the pain even stronger today, knowing at some point she would have to move on. Ray and his mother both had been through more in one life-time than she could imagine. When Dillon called her back a fourth time to tell her that he showed Ray a picture of the two of them together, he said Ray looked confused. Again he said nothing one way or another about the picture. Dana Ann surmised once again that the potion had done its' job. Now for the first time since Ray had given it to her, Dana Ann took off his engagement ring. She walked slowly to her room and placed the expensive jewel in the black velvet jewelry box. She did that at 2:00 in the afternoon. When the telephone rang again at 6:00 that evening, she was surprised that she was still sitting in the same spot where she sat after depositing her ring into the box.

"Hello!" she answered

He answered: "This is Lance."

"Lance?"

"Hello Dana Ann. I heard about…"

She cut him off. "It's okay Lance. I don't want to talk about it right now," she said. He understood exactly. "I have another job for you. I want you to find out all you can about Joe Bullet and the Bullet murder trial of Emily Brookfield. Lance please focus on who killed Emily Brookfield, in 1972 in Tulsa, Oklahoma for real. Meet me tomorrow at the Outback in Pleasant Hill, around 12:00 and I will give you more pertinent information. Okay"

"Okay!" He said back excitedly.

—169—

Rovella Starr

The New Love-Starved Bitch

Author's Gold Edition

Lance Dupree

    Lance had liked Dana Ann Arbor from the moment he first saw her at the Academy Awards the year before. A successful very wealthy man in his own rights, the handsome former Oakland Police Officer had acquired his extreme wealth through wise investments and ownership of a detective firm that covers all of the USA and part of Canada. At forty-five-year- old, the tall attractive man, normally compared to a younger *Billy Dee Williams* had some bad luck of his own. On June 5, 1975, Columbia drug king pin Carlos Mando Santiago, who had threatened Lance in 1974 for fingering him in a 3.5 million dollar drug bust, ordered five gang members called, "Manacito" to put a hit on Lance Dupree. Carlos's brother, Armando Rodriguez Santiago rented an apartment in Oakland's Rockridge section five miles from Lance's lovely, five bedrooms Tudor home. After casing the Dupree home for months, Armando picked a time when no one was home and planted timed explosives inside the master bedroom and inside the Dupree's daughter's bedroom. When Carlos, from his prison cell, gave him the go, Armando detonated a bomb from his own apartment that blew up Lances, house. Lance who was on his way out of the front door headed to work at the Oakland Police Department turned around as soon as he heard the boom. Next, he ran back to his daughter's room. His nine-year old daughter was standing in the door frame of her room charred from head to toe. When Lance touched her she crumbled. The situation for his wife Paris was far worse. Already, there was no way to identify her ashes. In his attempt to save his family, Lance incurred burns over seventy-five percent of his body. Later that evening when he saw the fire department bring out his family using shovels, Lance lost his mind on the stretcher as they were taking him to Alta Bates Hospital. It took years for Lance to recover. He quit the Oakland

CAROL D. MITCHELL

Police Department in 1989 to open up and head his detective business that grew so rapidly, several of his friends from the Oakland Police Department joined his business and made twice as much money with less of the danger of being a Policeman. On April 12, 1994, Carlos Mando was found dead in his prison cell. Reason for his death, was unknown. Prison officials ruled that Carlos died of natural causes. On September 24, 1995 Armando, Carlos' brother was shot on the 580 freeway in Oakland, California for resisting arrest and for pointing a firearm at a police officer with intent to kill. With a horrid past out of the way, and after years of counseling, Lance Dupree was ready to get on with his life. Known to have a knack for solving murder cases quickly, Lance was eager to fly to Tulsa for Dana Ann Arbor. He would get to the bottom of the Joe Bullet murder and he wanted even more to get to know Dana Ann Arbor better, but good fortune and the clever intuitiveness of his skilled private detectives had made Lance's job regarding the JB murder easy.

Today, when Dana Ann walked into Pleasant Hill's Outback Steakhouse heads turned. Autograph seekers met her at the door where they begged for her autograph. Popular in this part of town, the author stopped to meet her fans. Having successfully toured *Danville, Blackhawk, Walnut Creek, Concord, Antioch, Pittsburg* and neighboring towns, Dana Ann was surprised at how many people had read her books. Sitting steps away from the action, Lance had already gotten a table for their meeting. He admired the beautiful author whose striking features were difficult to ignore. She looked to him like a Nubian Queen and he loved the way she tossed her head high with confidence. Today she graced the stage wearing her shoulder length black hair in a shiny precision bob that bounced with each step she took She wore a beautiful hot pink cashmere sweater with hip-hugging white pants and pink and white open toed sandals that to him really set her outfit off. With the smile on her face, there was no hint of the trauma she had gone through. Despite a healthy appetite Dana Ann had lost nine pounds, but her sisterly treasures the breast, and the butt were still visibly in-tact and Lance could not overlook what a prize beauty this sister was. She sat at the table with him, then she handed Lance a check for $64,000.00 for the work he did on Ray's case. Then she handed him another check for $100,000.00 for his investigation fees on the Joe Bullet Murder trial. Lance accepted the money thinking that he was so anxious to meet her that he had almost forgotten that this was a business lunch.

"So we finally meet again Lance. It's been too long," she said extending her French manicured hand to the handsome man. Lance leaped out of his chair to be a gentleman, and to properly seat this fine woman. Lance had

−171−

Rovella Starr

The New Love-Starved Bitch

Author's Gold Edition

been doing steady duty at Gold's Gym on Grand Avenue in Oakland, California. In his forties, the good looking man had his pick of women but few had given him the impression Dana Ann had. To Lance, she was a seasoned professional, who was self-assured and he admired the way she had put up a brave fight to preserve her love for Ray. Having been there every step of the way including at the rescue; the whole time Lance observed Dana Ann he did not know why a together sister like her was fighting so hard for the janitor, Ray J.T. Starr. With time, he surmised that her fight for this man had to be born out of one thing and one thing only and that was love. Encouraged by her bravery and determination, the kind Lance Dupree had nothing but praise for Dana Ann.

"You look great Dana Ann. Congratulations on your book deal with ABC."

"You've heard about that already?" she asked smiling.

"You are the tops of the west my lady," he said, tilting his head to meet hers. Dillon was kind enough indeed to fill me in on you during the rescue mission," he stated. He scooted her chair up to the table. She smiled. Then she straightened up in her chair and thanked him again.

"Sorry about all of the cancellations. It has been months but, after what happened to Ray, I couldn't get it going Lance. His friends have called me to tell me that he has gone on with his life and that in four months he has not so much as mentioned my name. That the Government is not investigating Margaret for her chancy formula is beyond me. When I questioned Margaret myself, she assured me that if she had known what was going to happen that she would not have sold the formula to Rovella and Joe back then. Enough of that," she ended. "'Hey, you did a quick and bang up job on the Joe Bullet murder trial as you did on the acid part of the Joe Bullet case. I will be forwarding the results of your investigation to Rovella Starr soon. And because of your great work, I have added to your pay an extra forty-thousand dollars for your efforts," she said. Lance lowered his head:

CAROL D. MITCHELL

"Joe Bullet was good man. Many people felt sorry for him because of his face. They said being scarred was something the man handled with a great amount of dignity. All the praise for solving this should go to my detectives with the CB's" said Lance. "But then, I will take any compliments that you are willing to give me beautiful lady," he smiled. He leaned forward to take her hands.

Lance was sitting still now admiring Dana Ann. He did not like telling clients everything about how he solved his cases, but Dana Ann to him was special. He was starting to have feelings for the woman, but to him Dana Ann was clearly not interested in him. He had seen the memorial her Ray had in his bedroom of her. Impressive as it was, there was no doubt in his mind, that Ray really loved Dana Ann. He let go of her dainty hands. Then together they placed their white napkins into their laps. When the waiter came, Lance ordered a steak well done with a baked potato, butter and sour cream and chives and the house horseradish. She ordered the same.

"Stephan Little lives in a trailer park on East 14th Street in Hayward. When I was in Tulsa last month working on the JB case, I learned Stephan Little moved out here a year ago. He supports himself doing subcontracting work at a power plant in Antioch," Lance said, accepting coffee and water from the waiter, "Thank you," he said to the waiter. The waiter said thank you back.

"Nice waiter," Dana Ann commented. "So do you think this Stephan guy had something to do with the murder?" she asked Lance.

"Yes," he answered. "He called his friend Willie Smith in Tulsa Oklahoma every day, according to telephone records. DMV records show that Willie Smith, his friend owned a 1972 white Cadillac Biarritz that his mother gave him when she divorced his father in July of 72'. The car was first registered in Tulsa, Oklahoma around May of 1971. The minute you called me after Ray's rescue date, I flew to Tulsa and stayed there for two weeks investigating this crime. Like I said, people who knew Joe and Rovella praised Joe. The older guys in the bar talked about how fine Rovella used to be and how they all wanted to have a piece of Rovella, before she married the unlucky, Zebbie Starr. They said, Zebbie's side of the family never wanted to see Rovella again because of what she did to the town's politician, Mattie. I approached the police department about reviewing records about the Joe Bullet murder and I was put off by a request by a Judge Brossard. To tell you the truth, I felt they were trying to protect the real murderer," Lance confided. "My staff found witnesses to the murder who said that Joe Bullet was actually at a bar-be-queue shack at the same time Willie Smith picked Emily Brookfield up at a nearby bar. Witnesses said that the Tulsa police

Rovella Starr
The New Love-Starved Bitch
Author's Gold Edition

were not interested in their testimony for Joe Bullet. And, therefore little testimony on Joe's behalf was ever entered at the trial."

Sorry to interrupt again. I am your waiter. My name is Paul. Your order should be up in ten-minutes. Everything okay?" he asked, looking at the couple.

"Everything's fine," the woman answered. Lance nodded his assent to the waiter. Pleased that the couple was okay the waiter placed a basket of bread and some butter on the table before he walked away. Then Dana Ann remembered that she wanted some more water. She felt sorry that Joe Bullet had lived such a miserable life for a murder he never committed. She had been listening ever so closely to Lance and she felt that he had already solved the JB murder and she was excited to finally hear the status of his investigation. Because she loved Ray so dearly, helping his mother with this case had the elements of putting years of hatred on her part to rest. She was glad that being considerate to others needs was the way the Morgan's had raised her to be.

"Waiter!" Lance shouted. Paul doubled back as Lance pointed to the author.

"Could you bring her some more water?" Lance asked.

"Sure," he said, before taking off again.

"Anyway," Lance continued, "this Stephan Little person called his friend Willie Smith a month ago. They apparently planned to rob a Wells Fargo bank on Fruitvale in East Oakland, as to throw the suspicion on it being somebody black because the robbery was to take place in a predominantly black area. Anyway, Willie used a wide range CB radio to Stephan about a hoe he raped and killed a woman named Emily in Tulsa back in 1972 and was let off because his grandfather was Judge Brossard. He said if he could get away with something like that then robbing a bank would be a "piece of cake," he told Stephan. "Just so happens one of my detectives, Skip Mitchell picked up the confession and the robbery on his CB. Later he sought to find and question Judge Brossard, who died last year of lung cancer. Anyway, on the day of the planned robbery the police caught Willie and Stephan red-handed. Emily's body was exhumed for a DNA sample. So

—174—

CAROL D. MITCHELL

happens the rape kit sample taken at the time was preserved. DNA didn't match Joe Bullet. But, it did match Willie and bingo he admitted everything!" Lance said. "The case was in the bag!"

The surprised Dana Ann almost knocked over Paul's dinner tray.

"Rovella was right about Joe, too bad for him. You mean they did it and for all of these years, that judge convicted an innocent man. They let him rot behind bars to protect his own relative?" she asked. "I guess asking why he did not excuse himself from the trial would be a silly question?"

"You're right Lance. Unfortunately, the sins of the south go on," she said.

"What gets me," Lance said, leaning towards her, "Is that had they not planned that bank robbery over that CB radio – it would have been difficult to connect. The police wanted to catch them red-handed, so we followed Willie's and Stephan's roadmap. On the day of the robbery attempt, Stephan was gunned down by an armed security officer and Willie broke down inside the bank admitting o the Swat Team, the robbery, the murder in 1972 and another unsolved murder in Atlanta in 1975. During questioning Willie told authorities that he had told the Tulsa Oklahoma police back then that he had raped Emily and the white guy that questioned him told him to be quiet about it when he found out about Brossard connection," Lance said.

"Well, I will be damned. They would assume arrest a black man for helping out a woman, and then crucify the right man that did it because of nepotism. That's a shame. Rovella was right all along when she said Joe Bullet didn't kill that woman." the author said. The surprised writer was grateful to Lance Dupree for his incredible genius in solving this crime. Tonight, she ate her diner feeling good that something positive had come out of all her efforts. She missed Ray so much. As she sat in front of the handsome detective, her lost relationship with Ray submerged her in private thoughts of what could have been.

After dinner, Lance convinced the reluctant writer that she needed to take a break and get away for a minute. His home in Concord, California was only ten minutes from Pleasant Hill, California and, he had wanted to invite her to see his new house in Concord for some time now. He was never going to forget his wife and child but his mother who lived in Jamaica convinced him ten-years was enough time for him to mourn. She encouraged him to move on with his life. It was 9:30 when they made it to Concord, California's exclusive Marietta Court Dana Ann marveled at the richness of his property in the rolling hills of Concord, his was one of a few homes in the area with a private tennis court and golf course. When Dana Ann told him of her love for Golf, Lance promised to give her lessons at the game many said he was a

−175−

Rovella Starr

The New Love-Starved Bitch

Author's Gold Edition

pro at. Zelda, Lance's German maid greeted the nice looking couple at the front door. Soon the two of them were settled in his living room sipping tea out of imported silver in front of a lighted fireplace. Ahead of where they enjoyed Ancient Tea from China, Lance pointed her to a beautiful view of the scenic mountains of Clayton Valley hills and the serenity and peacefulness of this place was so soothing that once she was seated on Lance's white fur couch, Dana Ann took in a deep breath.

After tea and cookies Lance wasted little time telling Dana Ann Arbor how he felt about her. Sitting next to him was a woman of strength and valor rarely ever seen before. His smile let her know he was interested; but her pain let him know that she never would be. Lance understood her reaction immediately. To him she was the kind of woman he had been looking for to spend the rest of his life with. Her heart was so large that she was still caring for a dog that she literally gave another life to and she had given Ray a chance to start over again as well. She could, have gone to the hospital and claimed her love; however to him she sacrificed her true feelings so that his life would not be forever damaged by his horrific ordeal. She had even given his mother a peace no money could have given her. Soon Rovella would know legally that Joe Bullet had been innocent all of the time. The facts of these matters had not slipped from Lance at all. As she sweetly sipped her tea, Lance learned over to pour her another cup. He knew the time was right now for him to tell her how he felt about their friendship. With a flip of the controls, the lights in his living room dimmed and the blue stars from the black skies lit up that canvas. When he told her how he felt, his gesture though kind had not moved Dana Ann. Lance got down on one knee and he told her that he had only done that one other time in his life. Then he joked:

"The OLE knee cap is kinda going out on me now." They both laughed. She put her cup down then she held her stomach.

He reached beneath the couch. Then he pulled out a huge blue velvet box that held a huge engagement ring. Time for Lance was of the essence. He loved Dana Ann and did not want to wait until he felt she was ready. He

CAROL D. MITCHELL

knew that if she said yes, that he would make her the best husband she could possibly have. He looked into her beautiful brown eyes that seemed to tear up the moment he popped the question.

"Dana Ann will you marry me?" he asked, nearly crying.

When she did not have an answer, Lance understood that too. He was however, still on his knees and she dropped her head to her chest, as she was considering his question. Really, she was trying to come up with a nice way to turn the nice man's proposal down. Dana Ann was not impervious to Lance's worth. He was one of the most sought after men in the Bay Area. Only last year he dated a world famous runway model that loved him so much she threatened to kill herself when Lance dumped her.

"I'm sorry Lance. You know the situation with me. It's too soon for me," she said. As he prepared to take the lady home, Lance asked her to think about his proposal. His proposal had to Dana Ann been honest and sincere and she told him that. With an understanding in the works, the two of them enjoyed the rest of the evening until the butler called for her car.

A few minutes later her white Bentley let her off at her home. Inside a happy Fifi attacked Dan Ann. She picked up the dog, kissed him frantically, and then waved the healthy, happy dog back to his own private green corner in the house. Later, Dana Ann took off her overcoat laying it on the couch. Tired now; she slipped out of her pink and white sandals, leaving her shoes next to the white love seat. Later, she walked into their bedroom and then turned on the light. Next, she raised the bottom of her pink cashmere sweater up to her forearms then over her head, then off and away it went. When she saw that her sweater had landed on the floor she was too tired to care. She used the last of her energy to step out of her white pants. It was one leg at a time. Fatigue made her trip coming out of the second leg. When she was stripped and was sitting on her bed wearing only her black thong and pink lace bra, she read a note the maid left on her bed telling her that dinner was in the microwave. She looked at the gold telephone and was sad that Ray did not call her. She remembered Ray and the pictures of them being together here in her abode began racing through her mind. Fighting back tears, she reminisced about how Ray loved getting those notes from the cook. He told her always how thoughtful that was of her. He left her notes telling her how much he loved her. Looking at the oil painting of the two of them placed in the corner next to the closet brought tears to her eyes. Still, however, she promised herself that she was not going to cry. For four months now she had been crying. She was supposed to be moving on and forgetting about him. These feelings she had now had pushed

Rovella Starr
The New Love-Starved Bitch
Author's Gold Edition

through the doors of her heart, demanding to be seen. Why were these feelings so hard to shake? She wondered. In an effort to face reality without the tears Dana Ann eased up off of her bed. She raced to the front room for her dog. When he saw Dana Ann, Fifi leaped into her arms. She loved Fifi so much and she was so glad that Maxine let her have him that she mailed the kind lady an extra $5,000.00. She was laughing now. She thanked the dog for loving her, and then she carried him back to the bedroom with her. Without thinking one minute about Lance's proposal, the still broken-hearted Dana Ann closed her eyes to relive Ray's proposal. She then drifted off to sleep with Fifi right by her side. Dana Ann slept the whole night with a smile on her face. When she woke up the next morning on top her tear soaked silk pillows, she wondered how much time it would take for her to forget about him, if ever.

CAROL D. MITCHELL

Without a Trace

When one loses memory they will not seek that of which they do not know is gone. Six months after consuming ROL Ray J.T. Starr was normal as he was before he met Dana Ann Arbor because that was the way Margaret created the drug to be. Snatched out of the truth of his existence, Ray was going to meet his friend Clay E for a walk around the beautiful Lake Merritt at noontime. Today, Ray stood outside of the Government building where he worked wearing his signature black cap with white Puma emblazoned in the center completely unaware of lost time.

Ray's curly, dark hair rested on his shoulders and shined brilliantly against the backdrop of a perfect sun. Earlier this day, a woman from the law office across the street told him she thought he was the most handsome man she had ever seen. In a way that has always been characteristic of Ray, he thanked the kind lady and smiled. He was indeed a very good-looking man, but all he wanted to do was work and win awards proving to Sam what a good worker he was. Now instead of putting voodoo dolls in his janitorial closet, Sam had a photographer post pictures and press releases in his locker of a stunning woman that Ray knew would have never given him the time of day. People asked him where this woman was and how was her writing coming along? Tired of Sam's constant pranks, he couldn't answer their questions because he had never seen the woman before a day in his life. When he told Rovella about it, the woman never answered him and walked away or sometimes she told him to forget about these pranks of Sam's and move on, so that's what he was trying to do. If he had ever met a woman as beautiful as, Dana Ann Arbor, there was no way he could forget about her.

On this lovely afternoon, Ray was feeding breadcrumbs to the geese around the lake when Clay E showed up late for their walk. Today Clay E was wearing a red Fedora that he called his pimp hat, with a black suit, a red tie and brown snake skin boots. To Ray, who was a sharp dresser, Clay E was dated, but he was neat and clean and his crazy girlfriend Lozetta-Ann

−179−

Rovella Starr
The New Love-Starved Bitch
Author's Gold Edition

had lit a fire under his ass for an engagement ring and marriage proposal and Ray was glad to see that Clay E was happy.

"Hey man, you been waiting long? Clay E asked.

"Not that long." Ray said, turning his attention back to the birds. "Just feeding these birds and looking out at the water. A lake in the middle of a city, you ain't gone find that no place but in Oaktown, man." Ray said.

"Yeah, it's a trip ain't it man?" Clay asked . Ray smiled at him and nodded his head. Later, he looked at Clay with a big smile.

"So how you been doing man?" Clay E asked. Ray slowly turned his head back to Clay E's way. A slight wind made his hair whip the sides of his face.

"Why you always asking me how I been doing when you see me every day Clay E?" Ray asked defensively. Clay shrugged his shoulders and didn't answer.

"You been doing that for month's man? What's up with that?" Ray asked his friend.

Clay had been hoping for Ray's memory to come back. Months ago, he tried to tell him that the magazines and newspapers in his locker were a life he really had with Dana Ann. However, he stopped telling Ray about her when he realized the man had no memory of his lost time. Each day Clay E hoped Ray would remember the woman he so dearly loved and pick up with her again. In Six months Ray had not mentioned as much as a word about Dana Ann. To Clay E there was always hope. He had never been a pessimistic man. Otherwise, he would not have been able to work for the Government for over twenty-five years.

CAROL D. MITCHELL

"Since you don't wanna talk man Mama acting kind of funny since she found out Joe Bullet did not rape or kill that white woman in Tulsa back in the day, man. She had stood up to that crooked judge who was protecting his peeps from murder and her assault on him made the front pages. Federal Express brought her some papers and she cried. Mama keeps crying over his death. I try to remember when it happened, but I can't. I don't remember the funeral or anything. Sometimes I wonder what is wrong with me." Ray admitted.

"All man, Rovella will be alright. Your Mama ain't no joke if she challenged a Superior Court judge in a murder trial man." He changed the subject.

"Ray, you don't ever remember being in love do you man?" Clay asked.

Ray stopped feeding the birds. He looked out into the cold blue water off Lake Merritt when he told Clay about Carla Scott.

"She acted weird after meeting my Mama. And that wasn't cool." He answered.

Ray began to feed the birds again. Clay E took off his red brim to play with the black feather. When Ray was not looking, Clay E checked him out closely. It was hard for him to watch Ray go through life knowing what he had in Dana Ann Arbor. She was the love of his life. It was truly the saddest thing Clay E had ever seen. Clay E knew Ray well enough to know if he know about her he would be there. Ray was a man of few words, but he was sharp. Ray was not a man you could say things to without furnishing him proof of what you were saying. Pictures of her were not doing him any good. On the day of his rescue, medical experts at UC Davis assured the rescue team there was no evidence to support Ray had lost his memory and that ROL was simply a toxic mixture of Antifreeze, Ethylene & Gatorade. Doctors were certain his retrograde form of amnesia could be subjectively short term. They said, Ray would in time make a 100% full recovery. Other than that, there was no way to make him remember something that to him had never happened. To Clay there had to be something that would put Dana Ann and Ray J.T. Starr back together again. He still had the letter Dana Ann mailed to him in October. She told him not to confuse Ray by telling him about her. To Clay E, Dana Ann was one who wanted to protect Ray

—181—

Rovella Starr
The New Love-Starved Bitch
Author's Gold Edition

because she loved him. However, Clay E was not sure being quiet was the right course of action for him to take.

CAROL D. MITCHELL

I Do

Dana Ann concentrated on Lance for being a nice, supportive friend. He visited her regularly bringing flowers and gifts and his caring and kind words. For months his mother had been on a writing campaign trying to sell the idea of marriage to her. Ida Mae Dupree wrote beautiful letters telling Dana Ann how much Lance loved her and how glad she was that her son's life had changed for the better after meeting her. Dana Ann had seen enough of life to know that marrying a person for their goodness might not actually be a good replacement for love. She was never going to love another man the way she loved Ray, not again in this lifetime. However, that did not mean that she had to turn other prospects of marriage completely down. She was in her forties now and she needed companionship. She needed a man to comfort her to advise her to spend her life with. Nobody in this life would ever be 100% happy, why should she? Lance was asking for her hand in marriage. Now she had to take him seriously. As she weighed her options, she knew she was not in love with Lance. Nevertheless, Lance had been there for her during the most turbulent time of her life and it was not fair to turn a man away with his qualities. After all was it not enough that at least one of them was in love? Did she have to love him too to make it work? What if she married him liked, and respected him? Would that not be enough to make her happy? Everybody liked him. Beatrice Griffith told her that Lance was the man that she had always pictured her to be with.

Fifi loved Lance Dupree and all of the Hollywood stars thought Lance Dupree was well versed, articulate and fabulous. With the wedding date set for May 2001, there was planning to be done after she returned from a two week engagement in Southern, California. As Dana Ann stood on the balcony of her beautiful condominium with Fifi at her side, she thought about marrying a man that she did not love and the pain she felt in her heart towards the man she did love. For many days and nights, she asked God why he took Ray away from her. Dillon told her Ray was happy and carefree and had gone on with this life. Maybe it was all for the best that he did not remember the horrible ordeal that Rovella had put him through. She had thought of was she could approach Ray, but her many skeptics, including Beatrice warned her that she could do serious damage to Ray by approaching

−183−

Rovella Starr
The New Love-Starved Bitch
Author's Gold Edition

him at this time. When her friends asked her if she wanted Ray to be happy her answer to that was always yes. Whereas in the beginning it was easy for her to look at Ray's pictures since dating Lance she took the beautiful portrait of them out of her bedroom sticking it inside of her closet. She promised Lance she'd throw it out; but, she couldn't do it. Ray meant so much to her heart that she had not taken his ring back to the Diamond Center. Instead she paid off the account telling the store manager to return any money Ray paid on the ring back to him and that's what the Diamond Center did. When the money entered Ray's account he never noticed a thing.

Today the sun shone brightly despite previous days of cold weather. In one hour she would meet Lance at Border Books in Pleasanton. From there they were going to Whorter's to pick out wedding announcements. It was Friday. She was leaving for Los Angeles tomorrow. Looking at her watch, she picked up Fifi, she kissed him and then she put him in his green and white designer doghouse. Later, she went into the bedroom to get her taupe ski jacket. When she opened her closet the life sized photo of her with Ray fell out of the closet at her feet. Bending down slowly, she carefully picked up the picture looking at Ray's incredible smile. Nobody loved her like Ray. He was gentle, kind and happy, always to be in her company. Winds out of her sail, she sat on her bed. Next, she kissed the photo over and over again. Whereas she should have been all cried out over him by now; she was not. In fact, in her heart, she loved Ray J.T. Starr more now than she ever had before. She was grief stricken. When she closed her eyes, she thought of him; and when she opened her eyes, Ray was the first thought at the beginning and end of each of her days. Because they had not fully consummated their love, Lance was remanded to wait to have sex with her on their wedding day. Lance had not a clue that she had Ray's name tattooed on her breast; however, with enough going on in her life, she would think about that some other time. She only had twenty-minutes to make it to Pleasanton.

CAROL D. MITCHELL

A Time to Tell Him the Truth

"Man," Clay E said, shaking his head with a deep breath, "There is something I need to be real honest with you about, Ray. This is hard for me to do Ray because when I promise somebody something I like to keep that promise. But, there are some things that it is not cool to keep inside," Clay E expressed. Ray, not clearly understanding people's reactions towards him lately became subdued. He wanted his friend sit down on the white granite at Lake Merritt. Then he observed the troubled way that Clay E began holding his head in his hands. The walls of silence caved in on him and Clay E until heat entered the center of their aura when Clay E showed him a piece of paper. Clay had reached inside his pocket for his wallet and the way he fished that piece of paper from his wallet to Ray, appeared to be nothing but trouble. As he waited eagerly for Clay E to explain to him what this paper was all about, Ray sat next to him quietly. Privately, Ray had hoped that this was not about the beautiful writer that people kept telling him he was in love with. His main thought over the past few months was how could I have been in love with this woman and not remember a thing about her? He had asked Rovella about Dana Ann many times. However, here lately his mother dismissed the rumor by telling him that people were cruel; especially, she said, those that worked for the Government. She said Government employees were the unhappiest people she knew and all they had the time to do was complain and conjure up rumors about people's lives. And then Rovella said something to her son that gave credit to the rumor when she advised him: *"Ray, sometimes you have to leave well enough alone."* He had never told anyone about it, but the week before Ray saw pieces of a dream about a dark, lovely ebon woman with many books around her. His old high school buddy, who he had not seen in a while was in the dream. He remembered seeing Dillon at the Department of Records about eight months ago, but his memory stopped there and he chose to keep the rest his secret. Ray chose to not remember the conversation or whom Dillon was even with at that meeting. He was not much of a reader, except for science fiction books. Ray tapped on Clay E's shoulder with the thought in mind to protect sweet truths and to keep peaceful calmness in his life.

Rovella Starr

The New Love-Starved Bitch

Author's Gold Edition

"Man, don't worry. You and Lozetta Ann will be all right. Now she is a little wild, but what can I say?" he said, tossing his hands up in the air. Clay E wished that he could go along with the flow and pretend like Ray's past did not exist; but he could not. He had promised Dana Ann that he would not tell, but Beatrice's sister told Lozetta Ann that Dana Ann and Lance were soon to be married. Clay wanted to at least give Ray the benefit of knowing what was up.

"Man you have to find a way to remember her." He said. Ray gazed at his friend with a confused look on his face.

"Remember who man?" Clay turned around and gave the man direct eye contact. His eyes moved rapidly as he was desperately trying to convey to Ray that Dana Ann loves him and is the true love of his life.

"Dana Ann, the novelist, the woman who wrote all those novels, who has been on Oprah, Sally Jessie, Letterman and Jay Leno. Dana Ann is the woman who confronted your mother and asked her to let you go. She is the woman who loves you more than life itself and she loves you so much she has been willing to let you go. Your memory of her is gone and you have to get it back Ray," he confessed. Ray was confused. Clay E was still holding the crumpled letter in his hand. Sweat was pouring down the sides of his face. Ray picked his hat up off his luxurious mane to scratch his head. He conveyed to Clay E that he could not see the picture of him being with this Dana Ann person. Ray put his hat back on and, with his right hand rubbed his chin. He then looked out into the lake water at the white doves floating in a line. When Clay E realized that his confession had fallen flat, out of frustration, he put the letter back inside his wallet and then tucked his wallet back home into his right rear pocket. Knowing that the letter would only complicate matters more, Clay resorted to storytelling. He told Ray that Dana Ann was the love of his life. He told him everything he had told him about Singapore. As much as Ray trusted and respected Clay E he did not have anything to say back to his friend. As their lunch hour was coming to a close, quietly Ray did not doubt that his friend was telling him the truth. However, he could not act on feelings being fed to him by others who were

CAROL D. MITCHELL

aware of a life he had clearly cast aside. As Clay E looked out into the water, Ray hoped and prayed for the first time since his traumatic experience that he had not hurt anyone.

"Hey Clay E man, don't be so frustrated. Let us quit talking about women. Tomorrow I am going to the Art Festival at the Golden Gate Park. You wanna go with me man?" he asked. Clay E lifted his head. Looking at his friend, he merely nodded his head, saying yes he wanted to go. Then he spoke.

"Why not man. Why not." He smiled.

With his back turned away from the lake water, Ray watched Clay E until he crossed Oak and 14th Street. Next he closed his eyes and asked God, "I trust you will guide me when the time is right?" He asked the Lord.

Rovella Starr

The New Love-Starved Bitch

Author's Gold Edition

Changing Times

Eight months after the rescue of Ray, Beatrice was planning what she called, "The right One" for her best friend, Dana Ann Arbor. Glad that her friend had finally gotten some sense into her head and that she was marrying the guy that was her complete match, Beatrice was thrilled. No more rescue missions or crazy gun toting prospective mother-in-laws to deal with. And, no more crazy East Oakland women with formulas to deal with. Normalcy was here to stay for Dana Ann and nobody was happier about that than Beatrice. Through all of their late night conversations about Lance, Beatrice had to admit it to herself that Dana Ann was not in love. To Beatrice, that was the sad truth of the matter. However, as far as she was concerned, Dana Ann would learn to love Lance inside of the marriage. People did it all of the time. Sometimes it is not necessary to marry for love. She had heard that all the time on the talk shows. Two months ago Dana Ann invited Beatrice and her husband to travel to Santa Maria with her and Lance. Surprisingly, the whole time they were there, Dana Ann never touched or kissed Lance and each time he tried to show her affection, Dana Ann shunned his advances in front of everybody. To Beatrice, their Relationship was more like a brother and a sister relationship without intimate love. At night time Dana Ann convinced the two men to sleep together and she shared a room with Beatrice. Further, Dana Ann confessed to Beatrice that she was marrying Lance because he was the right man for her; but she reiterated that she was not in love with Lance Dupree. Today Beatrice was standing in line at Nordstrom's with her pink bridesmaid dress doubled over her arms, wondering why this marriage did not feel the way a happy event like this was supposed to feel. The day before at Ever Green Baptist Church, felt more like a wake than a wedding rehearsal. The only person smiling was Lance

CAROL D. MITCHELL

Dupree. Lance was sending for his mother in Jamaica. She was due to fly in at the San Francisco Airport tomorrow and Dana Ann told Lance that she wanted to pick Ida Dupree up so they could get to know one another. Dana Ann had invited Beatrice to go to the airport with her, but Beatrice declined because she had to attend a Union meeting with her husband. Beatrice paid for her dress and then she walked down Union Square in San Francisco, California to Market Street to catch the Bay Area Rapid Transit District, (BART). Bad feelings about the wedding caused her stomach to ache to the pint she wanted to call Dana Ann and tell her that maybe marrying Lance was not the right thing for her to do. For two months Dana Ann had not mentioned Ray to her, whereas before every other word out of her mouth was about Ray J.T. Starr. Now, she did not mention Ray's name at all in the telephone conversations. Beatrice made it to BART, next she walked down into the well on Powell Street to catch her train to the Oakland Civic Center BART Station. The escalator was broken again, so she grabbed a hold of the silver railing and walked down many stairs of the escalator to the East bound Platform. There she waited for a Concord train. When the Concord train arrived, Beatrice boarded the train. As the fast train raced through the underground tunnel beneath the water of the Bay, Beatrice looked at her watch. It was 3:00 P.M., she was glad that she had made it out of San Francisco before the rush crowd had arrived. Suddenly, Beatrice held her belly, not knowing why she kept feeling sick in the pit of her stomach. Truthfully, she felt something awful was about to happen, but what? Looking into the black spaces of the underground; Beatrice focused on how nice Lance was and what a perfect match he was for her friend, Dana Ann Arbor. Lance was rich. He was the perfect match for Dana Ann. She thought that he and Dana Ann complimented one another. Truthfully, Lance was not as handsome as Ray was; but to Beatrice, he was not a Mama's boy and Lance had a lot more going for him that Ray did. If only Lance could have the most important thing of all, Dana Ann's love. And then, to her, everything would have been perfect. When the train halted at its' first East Bay stop at the West Oakland station, the door opened and Beatrice was surprised to See Lance Dupree. He had been running up the stairs for the train and he was out of breath when he raced onto the car where Beatrice was sitting.

"Anybody sitting here?" he asked, pointing to the seat next to her.

"No. go ahead and sit there," Beatrice answered, smiling at Lance. Lance took the window seat and Beatrice admired the way Lance had gotten his hair done for the wedding. He had a perfectly trimmed beard and his hair was cut in a perfect fade. He was quite the catch in his black turtleneck and his black Levi's and his matching leather boots. The handsome 6'3" man

Rovella Starr
The New Love-Starved Bitch
Author's Gold Edition

looked like he had jumped right off of GQ Magazine. And, Beatrice noticed that he had a happy glow about him. Unfortunately, he was wearing the flow the bride should have been wearing and, was not. Lance told Beatrice that he was ecstatic about his upcoming nuptials; and, Beatrice could tell by his smile that he was happy.

"You look happy," Lance said to Beatrice.

"I am," she said back nervously.

"Yeah, this is the dress. You wanna see it?" she asked him. When he nodded his head yes, she took the dress out of the beige Nordstrom bag and unzipped the middle zipper to hold up the dress for him to see. Many of the passengers in her car commented on what a nice bridesmaid dress it was. Lance the agreed too that it was a very nice dress.

"That is a nice dress for a Maid of Honor. How did you like the wedding rehearsal?" he asked Beatrice.

She lied. "I liked it. Evergreen Baptist Church is going to be the perfect place to hold the wedding. You guys are extra lucky to get the choir too," she said.

"Well, 19th Street is my stop," she offered.

"We got here so fast. Time sure flies when you're having a good time," Lance gloated. She agreed.

"Great to see you Bee!" he shouted, waving bye to her.

"You too," she yelled back, Beatrice flew up the stairs with her dress and easily found her black Mercedes Benz on 20th Street in downtown Oakland, California. Before she got in it the bad feeling in the pit of her stomach was again a noticeable set back. Something awful was about to happen and she knew it had to have something to with the wedding.

Like any bride the day before her wedding, Dana Ann rushed all over Oakland, ending up today at Neldam's bakery on Telegraph street in Oakland, California. She was glad that she had stopped personally to check on the cake. Regardless of what people think about whipped cream frosting Dana Ann wanted a lemon chiffon butter cream frosting on the cake and the lady had it down at first as whipped cream. Having taken care of that, there still was not enough time left in this day to complete all of the things she felt that she should personally do for herself on her pre-wedding day. Lance wanted a large wedding and by the time the invitations were made out the list consisted of over two-hundred and fifty people including some very well-known Holly wood movie stars. Lance had hired the Bay Area' largest private security firm to check invitations for the wedding. Tonight Dana Ann was going to drive her red BMW to the San Francisco airport to pick up Lance's mother, Ida Dupree. So far the two of them had established a good rapport and they talked at least twice a week. To Dana Ann she was a nice woman, though somewhat egotistical and on the demanding side. Like most mother's do, she thought the world of her son; but, not to the extent that Rovella cared for Ray. She had told her many times that she could not have handpicked a better mate for her son than her. Ida had raised three sons in Jamaica and she was proud of all of them, she said. And, she commented that she was especially proud of Lance for putting hisself back together after his horrendous tragedy of losing his wife and child in the now famous Oakland, California explosion. When Ida Mae filled in the gaps of Lance's life, Ana Ann was concerned that Lance had not always opened up to her, but she reasoned that his reluctance to tell her everything had more to do with her resistance to open up completely to him.

This lovely sunny day in May 2001, Dana Ann was at least twenty minutes late leaving for the airport. As she prepared to go out the door, Fifi pulled at her trousers and refused to let her open the door. With only an hour before the arrival of Ida Mae's flight, Dana Ann found herself fighting with Fifi.

"Now, what's wrong with you tonight Fifi?" she asked, the cute little dog. Fifi began barking like he wanted to go with her.

"Fifi you know I can't take you with me. However, Dillon is going to take you to the wedding tomorrow. So you see Mama hasn't forgotten about you at all," she said, kissing the cute dog. He was a sweet dog who wanted every minute of her time. Yesterday she put blue bows on his ears and she spent $30,000.00 on hi one year birthday for a personalized diamond studded dog collar. The maid had furnished he guestroom for her changing every-thing from ivory to wintergreen and pink, as those were Ida Mae's favorite colors. Dana Ann called the maid into the living room and she gave her a bonus check of $10,000.00 and she told her to take the weekend off because she and Lance would be going to Brazil on their honeymoon tomorrow night after the wedding. After pouring Fifi some milk Dana Ann called the garage for her car. As she waited for the car, she tried to pretend that she was the happy bride, but it was not true. She did not love Lance. Her heart told her

Rovella Starr
The New Love-Starved Bitch
Author's Gold Edition

that, but he was a nice man who appreciated her for who she was. In addition to that, his family had given her a feeling of belonging like she had with Jon and Carol Morgan who did love Lance better than they ever liked Ray. She respected the Morgan's dearly for her great upbringing, but it was not the same as having the love of a mother and father who birthed you...Look at Ms. Rovella, who was willing to do anything for her children. Lance however was thoughtful and he had made all of the arrangements for the wedding. He ordered the flowers from France and had imported begonias from various parts of the country uniquely for this wedding. He hired the preacher and he even picked out the perfect pink color for her bridesmaid dresses. Because she had not the spirit to do it, Lance even picked out her wedding dress. When he saw the dress in a store window in New York City last year, he said he cried because he knew that Dana Ann would be a doll in the dress. Unfortunately, when she closed her eyes and pictured herself in the dress, Ray J.T. Starr was the man who was waiting for her at the end of the aisle. In an effort to move on in her life, Dana Ann wanted badly to feel something for Lance; however, the feelings were not evolving. His being smart and nice were going to have to be enough until time would allow her to love him. The heart does not lie and she knew his touches only made her long that much more for Ray. She had said she was going to get rid of the oil painting of her and Ray but she never had. All of her intelligence told her to let go of her thoughts of Ray and that she was not being fair to Lance, but this ideal of marriage was his idea and not hers He had intimated that he knew the risk of marrying a woman who did not love him, but he said he was willing to go through with it anyway because he loved her enough for the both of them. When Jim finally came with the car, he gave Dana Ann the keys and she took off speeding down the road for fear that she was going to be late getting to the airport to pick up Lance's mother.

At the same time Dana Ann was leaving the Oakland Hills, Ray J.T. Starr was too on his way to San Francisco against Rovella's wishes. She had told him that as of late, she was not feeling well. Her health had been ailing her for about eight months now and she wanted Ray to stay home because

CAROL D. MITCHELL

his brothers and their wives and kids were on the way over tonight, and she had planned for them to watch movies on her knew CD. Dressed to kill, in his signature black cap, his new white shirt, some blue jeans and his new style blue tennis shoes with the yellow stripes, Ray was going out to view the ocean. After that, he was going over to Tony Roma's on Ellis Street for some ribs. Later, he was set to hook up with Clay E and Lozetta Ann at a night club on Market Street, in San Francisco. Rushing out of the house he turned to kiss his mother goodbye. In her usual stubborn nature, the now tamed Rovella Starr, who finally appeared to be slowing down, smirked at her beloved son.

"Leave me alone boy!" she said, playfully. Then she smiled at Ray and told her son to have a good night.

As Dana Ann headed up the 580 Freeway going west towards San Francisco, she was surprised that the traffic was so heavy for a weekend night. Hoping to make it on time to the airport, she pressed down hard on the pedal. Unfortunately, her BMW did not have the speed that her Corvette of her Bentley had for that matter, so by the time she got to the 80 Freeway, she looked at her watch to find that she was late. Suddenly the traffic after the toll bridge was picking up. If Miss Ida could hold on a few minutes more she might make it to South San Francisco and to the San Francisco Airport no later than thirty-minutes. Now Dana Ann began to hop and skip from one lane to the other. Wanting to get a good start with her future mother-in-law, Dana Ann panicked that she would not make it to the airport on time. Suddenly, a 1985 Nissan Maxima jumped dead in front of her. When she braked, she could hear cars behind her come to a screeching halt. She had rarely pushed on the pedal before another car jumped in front of the Nissan.

"Oh, this is ridiculous," she thought. I will never get there. Next, Dana Ann saw a free lane and the traffic was finally moving freely again. But she was late and now she was going to have to step on it. Pretending that the traffic was not getting on her nerves, Dana Ann pressed all the way down on the accelerator to find that her speedometer was up to ninety-miles per hour.

"Sure doesn't seem like this car is going that fast," she thought.

Feeling that faster was better, Dana An pumped the pedal all the way down to the floor until she was going one-hundred miles per hour. She was safe now that she was approaching 101 south. She was sure that everybody was headed to downtown San Francisco, near the 5th Street of Fell Street exits or Fremont on the west side. That would provide her with a clearer path to 101 south where once she got there the lanes would be wider, providing her more space that would cut down on her having to maneuver the tight lane spaces. Looking in her rear view mirror, the last thing Dana

Rovella Starr
The New Love-Starved Bitch
Author's Gold Edition

Ann saw was a Green Jeep Cherokee on the tail of the car behind her. She took her eyes off of the road for a split second, the brown 1985 Nissan and the car between her BMW and the Green Jeep Cherokee slammed into the back of Dana Ann's automobile. A face of terror was written on the man in the Green Jeep Cherokee as the body in the red BMW that was Dana Ann went flying out of the windshield of her car.

As traffic came to a whistling stop, the woman whose body was slung on top of the windshield of her new BMW had blood running down her face and onto her hands. And at the exact moment her car stopped spinning, the woman who was holding onto her windshield wipers passed out. Minutes later, sirens brought with it police cars and ambulance and soon emergency officials were asking drivers that could talk what happened. Standing along the edge of the road, a petrified Ray, ran up to the BMW that was now on fire. Without thinking about his own life, he took off his new white shirt and he balled it up in his hands to pick Dana Ann's bloody body up off the hood of her burning car. As he tenderly paced Dana Ann's body on the other side of the single yellow line – he had flash backs of her and now he recognized the pictures that others had placed in his closets. As the world around him began transporting him into lost time, everything he had forgotten was coming back to him. This was the woman he loved. Ray brought his hands to his head. Something was happening to him and the words, "Don't you remember her man," from Clay E rang out in his head. Clay had asked, and those words play in his head like a symphony. As the siren grew louder, Ray pressed the side of his head for relief and in order to dim the growing sounds of the sirens. Six cars had been involved in this accident and now Ray watched in terror as four of those victims were already being placed and zipped up in blue body bags. In order to make sure that the lady was okay, Ray leaned down to give her CPR and he kept giving her CPR until her lifeless body began spitting out blood. Looking at her with great love and concern, he pleaded with her to hang on.

"Don't give up baby. Hang in there until we get you to the hospital!' he begged her.

CAROL D. MITCHELL

"Do you need another bag?" the EMT asked the rescuer.

"Not here," he said, looking at a sad Ray. "I think this gentleman may have saved her life. Let's lift her and get her to Highland Hospital's Trauma Center," the rescuer stated. As the rescue unit gently laid Dana Ann on the stretcher, Ray began crying and begging for Dana Ann to hang on and breath:

"Don't give up baby!" he hollered. "Please don't die on me!" Ray screamed. As they rushed her onto a gurney, his only concern was that she breathe, in order to maintain her precious life. After her body was strapped safely onto the gurney and was placed into the ambulance, Ray was directed by the police that if this woman was not a relative of his then he needed to step aside and he did.

On the 11:00 news a reporter told Lance and Beatrice as well as millions more that Dana Ann Arbor, a well-known award winning author had been in a serious car accident on the 101 Freeway in San Francisco. As beautiful photos of Dana Ann hit the television screens across the nation, shocked viewers around the world prayed for her recovery. However, from the house on Market Street in West Oakland, a somber mother and son prayed for Dana Ann's recovery, the most. At the hospital, doctors told Lance that Dana Ann had suffered internal injuries to her spleen and that she had nearly severed her right kidney. They said would be touch and go for a while because Dana Ann was in a coma and that she might not make it another day. Doctors on the newscast lauded the man who gave Dana Ann CPR and they praised whoever he was for having been the one that actually had save the Author's life. Lance refused to have Dana Ann taken out of Highland Hospital because he knew that the best trauma surgeons in the world were there and he did not want to risk moving her to a private hospital at this time. Having canceled the wedding, Lance called Dillon for a list of names of her relatives.

When Rovella Starr heard from her son what happened to Dana Ann, the aging beauty knew that her day of reckoning had finally come. Lately, doctors had warned Rovella that her high blood pressure was posing a serious threat to her life. She knew that her life was soon going to come to an end, and last month she reverted back to her mother Darnetta's religion, Catholicism. The change had initially come when she got the package in the mail a few months back. She had called her friend Peggy and told her that if anything happened to her that she wanted her to personally thank Dana Ann for giving Joe Bullet back his good name and his innocence. Joe Bullet meant everything to her and she was more than grateful to Dana Ann for what she had done in restoring her cousin's good name. This day as Rovella walked

–195–

Rovella Starr
The New Love-Starved Bitch
Author's Gold Edition

into Holy Names Church on pill hill, she asked the priest if she could conduct private sanctuary. He said yes. Feeble now and barely able to walk, Rovella dragged her frail body to the private sanctuary area of the church. There, she solemnly asked Saint Peter for forgiveness and especially for causing Zebbie to take his own life. She really had loved him, but had never told him so. She told Gold that she had donated the rest of Teresa's inheritance towards Make A Wish Foundation. The feeling of cleanliness revealed to Rovella how filthy her life had been. However, today a new woman presented herself before God.

"My gracious and precious Lord, I have not been a good soldier for you and forgive me if I am not saying the right words. Please forgive me for everything, especially what I did to Joe Bullet and for what I put my mother through. I want my son to fully awaken from his sleep to rekindle his love for Dana Ann Arbor. I had not known that a woman could really love the way this woman loves God because I have never seen love like hers before, God. I know that Dana Ann loves Ray and I trust you will bring her back to us. She is good people, my Lord. She is everything you ask people to be. I have never seen a person like her before; and, Master, only you know why I did all of these things in the first place. Heal my flesh for I know that your son died for my sins, Jesus. Give Dana Ann back to my Ray Lord in one piece. I will not be around to see his children, as I have seen for Shane and Eric. But, I want to leave this world knowing that my special child is loved. I have seen their love for one another, God and all I ask from you is that you sew this up and make them whole as a couple again. You know I have been fighting for Ray ever since the day he was born. His love was worth fighting for.

Thank you Lord. I could not have done it any other way than how gave him to me. Margaret's potion worked; but you're the one with the last word Lord. Thereafter, Ray is the way I wanted him to be. Now I want you to give my son what is best for him. My short days of the future will not allow me to take care of Ray much longer and Dana Ann would do the job with honors. Let it be your will Lord," she prayed

CAROL D. MITCHELL

Later that evening Rovella told a repressed Ray everything about the potion and his incubation period and she apologized for being so selfish in trying to shelter his love in such a foolish way. Together with that, her frustration over Joe Bullet's unexpected death left her not wanting to live this life without somebody's love. She had forgotten one day of the potion; so she knew the supposed ROL would never really have worked anyway. Ray then startled his mother, when he told her that what doctor's called his "self –imposed amnesia" had worn off when he saw his baby sprawled out on that freeway. He said it was a matter of time before he was going to tell other that his memory was coming back He told Rovella that the hardest part was watching the pain on Clay E's face, when he failed to job his lost memories of his relationship with Dana Ann.

There had indeed been good logic reasoning that the Oakland Police Department, the Courts and the US Government had over the year, repudiated Margaret ROL and COL claims. The long-time mentally ill woman's potion was nothing more than a clever mixture of anti-freeze, herbal ingredients including Magnesium, Sarsaparilla, Zinc, ephedrine and food coloring. Our mad scientist of East Oakland, Margaret Fisher was a diagnosed schizophrenic with a Yale College degree that she created on her home computer. Margaret Fisher was demented and deranged and had been diagnosed as such since 1962. The side effects of her well examined herbal formulas overall specifications, had been nothing more than people's allergic reactions. With good marketing and sold subjective opinions from user about her creations Margaret had for years gotten over; however, practiced and loquacious Margaret was, she had not been as successful, chattering with the Internal Revenue Service who was there to collect their share of Margaret's dough. On September 29, 2001, she checked herself into John George Psychiatric Pavilion. Three day later, the Internal Revenue Service was there to check her out. Margaret Fisher was arrested for tax evasion and would indeed face a long prison term for her crimes.

Ray, who was fully aware of his mother' need to protect him, had made the difficult and troublesome decision to let Dana Ann go for the sake of protecting both of the women he loved. The day his mother broke down over her cousin's death had been more than a sobering experience for Ray. He felt if he was to follow the course of his heart and may Dana Ann in September, that Rovella would hurt Dana Ann as she had hurt so many others in her life. Ray had desired to carry the incubus for his mother, and for Dana Ann. Ray had decided to weigh his options an because he loved both of these women, so he made the sacrifices that would be in the best interest of both his mother and the woman he loved

Part of his decision on September 15, 2000 was to pretend that he did not remember Ray also wanted to ensure that the love they had for one another was real and was real enough to stand the test of time. Avoiding her

Rovella Starr
The New Love-Starved Bitch
Author's Gold Edition

and not calling her had been the hardest thing in the world for him to do. When he learned, Dana Ann was marrying Lance, he was happy for her until he learned from Dillon that Dana Ann was not happy with Lance. With a burgeoning love in his heart for Dana Ann, he would wait and see if she still wanted to marry Lance before approaching her with the truth. That night Ray called Clay E to tell him the truth. Shocked, Clay E asked Ray what was he going to do and Ray told him that he and Dana Ann were going to get married because he could not hide his love for her anymore and he couldn't imagine living his life without her. Now that his mother was not a threat to the relationship and was mentally okay with them as a couple; neither would jeopardize his relationship with the woman that he loved.

    For each night that Dana Ann languished in Highland Hospital, Ray appeared at her bedside. When he saw Lance Dupree in the room with her squeezing her hand and crying, the strong man backed away to allow Lance to grieve for his fiancée. Dressed in a brilliant yellow Nike shirt with black Levi's, Ray committed himself to being there for Dana Ann until she woke up. Tonight after Lance left the room, Ray walked up to her bedside to do what he had been doing each night. First he kissed her on the forehead; then he told her that he loved her. She never moved. She never smiled, she never did anything but lie still looking like a sweet angel. Even with the many cuts that were on her face, to Ray she was strong and beautiful and he was glad that she was alive. He blamed himself for allowing all of this to happen to her. He was tired of Rovella's games and he was weary of all the naysayers who did not want them to be together. Now he knew that God had placed this Angel in his life to save his mother and to save him. Together, with her he was supposed to be here to bond with her as one. With a strong belief in this fate, Ray took out of his snapback a bottle of her favorite, orange Jovan lotion. He then gently picked up her limp right arm and he began rubbing the lotion on her skin until a clean glow sparkled before his eyes. He then looked at her with all of the love he felt for her and she looked so pretty and peaceful to him as she slept. The job God had given her was a difficult one. He was and had been 100% in love with Dana Ann and right now all he

CAROL D. MITCHELL

wanted was for her to wake up. As soon as she came back he would never leave her again if she wanted him. As he watched his baby, a warm smile came over his face. Together they had survived this and they had created love. She had taught his mother what true love was really all about. She was the first woman to come into his life that his mother trusted with her heart. Love to him meant caring enough about a person to let them find their way. Ray knew too that Lance loved Dana Ann and if she still wanted him – he would have nothing against him should Dana Ann decide to be with him. After he rubbed the second arm with the lotion, he leaned over the bed to kiss her again and she stirred. For the first time in three months, she stirred and Ray could not believe that she had actually moved. He wanted to be quiet and allow her the time to come out of the coma fully; and when the monitor told the ER staff that she was waking up, four nurses rushed into the room. All of them told Ray to leave. A soft voice reached out to the nurses and Dana Ann spoke her first words since the accident when in a weak voice she said, "No!" She didn't want Ray to leave her bedside.

As two of the nurses ran to get the attending emergency room doctor, the second pair of nurses worked diligently to keep Dana Ann awake. Ray held onto her hand tightly. She then opened her eyes and said it to him once again, "Ray, I love you." Ray then leaned down to kiss her on the cheek.

"I love you too baby," he said. "I always have loved you and I always will!" he said, excitedly.

"Don't leave me, Ray," she begged weakly.

"I won't leave you baby. If you want me to I will never leave you again," he said, ever so softly to her.

"It was a dream, huh? It was you who pulled me off of that flaming car hood. I remember it Ray," she said happily, she repeated it…"It was you," she said smiling.

He gave her his most beautiful smile. "You remember that?" he asked her.

They were like children discovering each other all over again, as if it was the first time.

"I never forgot it!" she said happily.

The medical staff had rushed into the room asking all visitors to leave while they worked on Dana Ann. Afterwards; a happy Ray walked out to the hallway, uncertain of what his next move should be. As he paced back and forth down the hollow hallways of the monstrous Highland Hospital, someone tapped him on the shoulder. He turned around to see that it was Lance Dupree.

Rovella Starr
The New Love-Starved Bitch
Author's Gold Edition

"Can I talk to you for a minute?" he asked Ray. Looking around, Ray asked him: "Where? You wanna go in the kitchen or wait here for the doctor? She's awake man," Ray said excitedly.

"Right here is okay, man. Thank God she is awake," he replied back nervously. Unable to contain his excitement that Dana Ann was doing better and had even recognized him on that horrible, eventful day, Ray had expected a different response from Lance – when he told him that Dana Ann was ok. Suddenly, the now subdued man, confirmed,

"I know man. I saw everything," he said, glumly.

He continued. "Look man, I am going to be frank with you. I know you have been coming here to see Dana Ann for months now. I know that Green Jeep Cherokee out there is yours. I have seen it dozens of times in Dana Ann's old picture books, back when she dated you. I am gonna make this quick man. She loves you and has never stopped loving you. Her biggest dream was to help your mother get to the truth about her cousin, Joe Bullet. That's all she ever really wanted me for. Her truest desires to please Rovella and you can't be topped. She succeeded in fulfilling your dreams. Now I want you to fulfill hers. You want her and you proved that to me by making the kind of sacrifices not any man could have made, man. She wants you Ray. Make sure you take care of that diamond, man. Take care of her," he advised. Lance shook Ray's hand and then hugged the bigger man tightly, showing real brotherly love.

"I love her too Ray," he swore looking into Ray's happy eyes, "but her feelings for me are not there and never have been. I wanted to marry her because she is a good person, a strong woman with abominable character and earthly beauty. I believed I could make her happy. I was wrong. All I want is for her to be happy and to tell you the truth man. I don't think her ultimate happiness will be with me," Lance ended.

A quiet man by nature, Ray smiled at Lance, before giving him one last hug. He could tell Lance loved Dana Ann and he could see the goodness of this man who he heard had suffered what no man should ever have to go through, when he lost his wife and his child in that house explosion. Right

CAROL D. MITCHELL

now, neither man said a word. This was a grim situation that calls on men to be men and rapaciousness to be thrown out of the window. Ray had first made the sacrifice that Lance was making now. Watching Lance with his hands in his pocket taking that slow walk down the huge hospital corridor was hard indeed for Ray to watch; and, more importantly though, he wanted to gear up and be strong for Dana Ann who needed his strength more than ever right now, he respected this to be the right transition for his love.

A few hours after her brain scan showed that Dana Ann was on her way to making a full recovery, John and Carol Morgan, Beatrice, Dillon, Brenda, Ray, Shane, Erica and their families, led by one Ms. Rovella Starr locked arms with each other as they surrounded a very happy Dana Ann with love, kisses and warm embraces.

Rovella Starr

The New Love-Starved Bitch

Author's Gold Edition

The Joyous Occasion

The special union that was born in December, 1999 inside the records sanctuary of a public domain; that blossomed out of one pair's extraordinary physical and emotional determination, was finally going to be fulfilled. Yes Lord! The joyous occasion took place one year following her accident, at *Evergreen Baptist Church, on MacArthur Boulevard, in Oakland, California.* Ray J.T. Starr and the stunning, Dana Ann Arbor had what the social pages called the wedding of the century. This special union was coordinated and put together by three wedding planning firms out of: *Oakland, Pleasant Hill and San Francisco, California.* Finally, on May 12, 2002, at 2:00 P.M., over a thousand people, including one *Ms. Rovella Jackson Starr, Peggy, Eric, Shane, Sam (yes, Sam); Paula, Lance Dupree, (yes, Lance Dupree); Beatrice, (her garbage man husband); Dillon, Pat, Brenda, Clay E, (recovered Maxine); Lozetta-Ann,* and many more attended the fabulous front page joining in wedlock of the **janitor and the author**. A week before the happy day, Dana Ann flew to Paris with Ray to pick out a diamond studded 1.5. million dollars Tiffany Tiara and what many called the most magnificent frosted/apricot wedding dress ever seen on the planet.

This day as she graced the aisle to meet her astounding future husband, who was statuesque and splendid in his black *Bob Mackie,* tuxedo, the emotionally happy bride was breathtaking in her stunning, 50's inspired *Vera Wang* gown. People could not take their wet eyes off of the beautiful bride. Viewers who did not get seats inside of the church watched the wedding form a satellite across the street at Moss wood Parks Recreation Center. Wearing the neck plunging, snug fitting, belted white garment that was cut form a gossamer fabric, many viewers cried helplessly as they watched Dana Ann march gracefully down the aisle to *Brian McKnight's "Love*

CAROL D. MITCHELL

of my Life" in her smoke-colored waist hugging full-skirt, strewn with patches of apricot lace, and winter white roses, all hand sewn around the hem of her gown by forty-five seamstress. When she met her future husband at the end of the aisle; the moment Ray lifted her veil to say his vows, he and all who were watching was taken aback by her amazing dark, precision beauty. Even movie stars commented how the surgeries on her face made her look younger than she had looked before the life-threatening accident. As a surprise and special wedding gift to her husband to be, Dana Ann, Lance, Brenda and Dillon had contacted the *State Bar Association* for a special lawyer. When they found Judge Carla Jeanette Scott at the Watt's Youth Center, in Los Angeles, California, Dana Ann asked her personally to preside over the wedding. When Ray looked up and saw Judge Carla Scott come from around the preacher's podium to officiate the wedding, a pleasantly surprised Ray thanked Dana Ann and looked back at his mother, who had a rather precocious smile on her face. Ray thanked the judge for doing the honors of performing their special nuptials. With tears in her eyes, the happy judge governed over the most beautiful wedding she said the world had ever seen.

Later, at the reception, which took place at Oakland's beautiful Parc Hotel, thirteen caterer's from Mexico to Greece, Pakistan and Africa put on a feast of national culture cuisine including over 150 foods from all around the world. Nine award-winning chefs, six of them from *San Francisco*, created carefully sculpted ice art portraying the bride and groom's names and award winning treats were served non-stop inside and outside the hotel for the many guests that were in attendance for the wedding. The luxurious wedding was said to have cost the couple a cool 3.5 million dollars and this time it appeared that everyone in Oakland, including Mayor *Jerry Brown* had a role in the spectacular nuptials. CNN filmed the wedding. Chuck Johnson's local black TV Network: Soulbeat sent reporters to cover the nuptials. Helicopters cruised above the festivities as twelve white stallions pulled the maple carriage that had seated the happy husband, wife and Fifi into their future.

The happy couple honey-mooned north of the Bay inside the Bridle Suite at *San Francisco's St. Francis Hotel.* Later for the newlyweds it was a night of love, passion and immense marital sex, as the newly potent Ray J.T. Starr could not get enough of his love as he made emotional, caring, penetrating love to her for the first time ever every hour of the night. Fully recovered from the accident that nearly took her life, the aroused Dana Ann Arbor thought she was dreaming as she assured her husband that his extraordinary love for her was fully and deeply appreciated! He told her he loved her too and she felt the same way too!

Rovella Starr
The New Love-Starved Bitch
Author's Gold Edition

The Epilogue

One month after witnessing the happy new beginning of her son's married life, Rovella Jackson Starr, my beloved mother-in-law died. The Catholic Priest whom issued her last rites gave God in her name, a long request for forgiveness. She left this world happy knowing the truth about Joe Bullet's innocence had been duly recorded on Tulsa, Oklahoma's Court Records and that my husband Ray, her prodigy child was married happily to a woman who loved him truly and dearly. On her last trip to Tulsa, sons, Eric and Shane had taken Rovella Jackson Starr back to where she and Joe Bullet met tragedy that turned into a darkly veiled secret that had shattered their lives, The anamnesis had turned kinder. She retrieved from a safe deposit box, the rest of her mother's estate with pictures of her and Joe Bullet enjoying life as small children with Teresa Peter, and the rest of her family at Christmastime. Shane Starr favored visiting the personable side of his mother's past, where she and her cousin had become timeless friends.

After taking white orchids to Teresa and Joe Bullet's resting spots, Rovella with her sons, took a trip to the south side of Tulsa to place Dandelions on Darnetta's and Emily Brookfield's' grave. There, Shane forgave his mother, while Eric stood quietly by his younger brother's side. The touching family moment of evolution and forgiveness left a son proud and a mother speechless. A face once breathtakingly beautiful glowed. This love without boundaries allowed Rovella to silently ask Mattie to forgive her for flushing her into a horrible end. Rovella no longer had to circle the ring fortifying the people she loved with the end so near. The resplendent green-eyed girl Zebbie Starr nicknamed **"The Pretty Girl"** found greater beauty within as she prepared to exit the ring of life a true and unforgettable winner!

With many of life's issued affirmed, Rovella Starr left Tulsa having worked out her issues with an amendment for her darkest family secret. One week later, Rovella Jackson Starr passed away peacefully in her beautiful home on Market Street, in West Oakland, California. Glad that their mother finally had peace in her heart, the family, Ray and I, newly pregnant – buried

CAROL D. MITCHELL

Rovella Jackson Starr at Forest Lawn next to the imposed grave of Zebbie J.T. Starr, the husband who loved her so dearly, and the man who was the father of all of her children. At the burial, Eric Starr kneeled down to kiss his mother goodbye. He placed a childhood photo of Rovella and her beloved, favorite cousin, the handsome, Joe Bullet right on top of her grave.

Here is thanking you for taking this journey with me and for sharing the fascinating life and secrets of one *Mrs. Rovella Jackson Starr*.

-----*THE END*----

Made in the USA
Charleston, SC
11 November 2013